TECHNIQUES FOR ELECTRONIC RESOURCE MANAGEMENT

TECHNIQUES FOR ELECTRONIC RESOURCE MANAGEMENT

TERMS and the Transition to Open

JILL EMERY
GRAHAM STONE
and PETER McCRACKEN

ALA Editions

CHICAGO   2020

2020 © Jill Emery, Graham Stone, and Peter McCracken

Creative Commons Attribution-Noncommercial 4.0 International (CC BY-NC 4.0):
https://creativecommons.org/licenses/by-nc/4.0.

Extensive effort has gone into ensuring the reliability of the information in this book;
however, the publisher makes no warranty, express or implied, with respect to the material
contained herein.

ISBN: 987-0-8389-1904-0 (paper)

Library of Congress Cataloging-in-Publication Data

Names: Emery, Jill, author. | Stone, Graham (Librarian), author. | McCracken, Peter,
author.
Title: Techniques for electronic resource management : TERMS and the transition to open
/ Jill Emery, Graham Stone, and Peter McCracken.
Description: Chicago : ALA Editions, 2020. | Includes bibliographical references and
index. | Summary: "Growing open access options, big-deal price pressure, fluid ebook
purchasing models. You need a framework for managing the many details of your online
material. TERMS – Techniques for Electronic Resource Management Systems – gave
you one. Now its creators, mining 5 years of notes and with input from many voices
in the field, have updated their influential life cycle model. In six sections you will
circle through selection, procurement and licensing, implementation, troubleshooting,
evaluation, and preservation and sustainability. The book's structure supports easy
reference whether a single team manages electronic resources or if responsibility is
spread across the library organization. Each section breaks into six categories which in
turn give guidance in three areas: Basic (80 percent of issues with electronic resources),
Complex, and the growing universe of Open Access resources"— Provided by publisher.
Identifiers: LCCN 2019024842 | ISBN 9780838919040 (paperback)
Subjects: LCSH: Libraries—Special collections—Electronic information resources. |
Electronic information resources—Management. | Open access publishing.
Classification: LCC Z692.C65 E47 2019 | DDC 025.2/84—dc23
LC record available at https://lccn.loc.gov/2019024842

Cover design by Kim Thornton.

Text design in the Chaparral, Gotham, and Bell Gothic typefaces.

♾ This paper meets the requirements of ANSI/NISO Z39.48-1992 (Permanence of Paper).

Printed in the United States of America

24 23 22 21 20   5 4 3 2 1

Contents

Illustrations

Acknowledgments

This version of the content grew out of conversations and interactions and from various professional events and is a crowdsourced effort. We are extremely grateful to those who we have engaged with on the project over the past ten years from its inception to publication of this volume.

We very much wanted the original project to be conceived by electronic resource librarians for electronic resource librarians everywhere. For this reason, as we developed each section, we posted it publicly and sought feedback from others to highlight best practices brought to our attention. Over the following two years, we traveled to various library events and outlined the project's framework for library workers. During this process we became aware of further concerns and attributes that should be incorporated into this framework. In our previous iteration, we convinced six eager colleagues to join us in the management of TERMs and gave each of them one of the six sections to edit and update as changes occurred in the electronic resources field. We are very grateful for the work undertaken by Eugenia Beh, Stephen Buck, Anna Franca, Nathan Hosburgh, Ann Kucera, and Anita Wilcox to keep TERMs relevant and timely during their duration as section editors.

Thanks to a generous grant supplied by the Portland State University Faculty Development Fund, this book is openly accessible.

1

What's New with TERMS

Techniques for Electronic Resource Management (TERMs) began in 2008 as a basic framework to help library workers become more familiar with a lifecycle of electronic resource management. Our initial vision expanded upon Pesch's electronic resources cycle and focused on the day to day activities of electronic resource management (see figure 1.1).

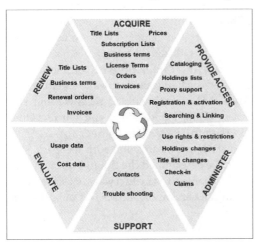

FIGURE 1.1
Pesch's Electronic
Resources Lifecycle[1]

The first iteration of TERMs (see figure 1.2) consisted of:

TERMs 1: Investigating New Content for Purchase/Addition

TERMs 2: Acquiring New Content

TERMs 3: Implementation

TERMs 4: Ongoing Evaluation and Access

TERMs 5: Annual Review

TERMs 6: Cancellation and Replacement Review[2]

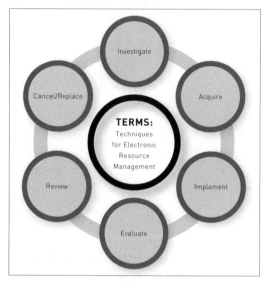

FIGURE 1.2
TERMs Version 1

We then moved on from TERMs and created a new framework around open access resource management in libraries, which we called Open Access Workflows for Academic Librarians (OAWAL).[3] We explored ways in which open access management could be folded into traditional library practices, and this was the subject of a presentation at a SPARC conference in 2014.[4] As OAWAL developed, we began to recognize overlaps between electronic resource management and open access workflows. Our work with Chris Awre and Paul Stainthorp on the HHuLOA project (Hull, Huddersfield and Lincoln Open Access) led to efforts to map OAWAL onto TERMs (see figure 1.3).[5]

From the collective continued work in this area and with feedback from others on the initial TERMs project, we determined the timing was right for a revised framework that reflected the changes to the lifecycle that have developed over the five years since the initial version of TERMs was published. In

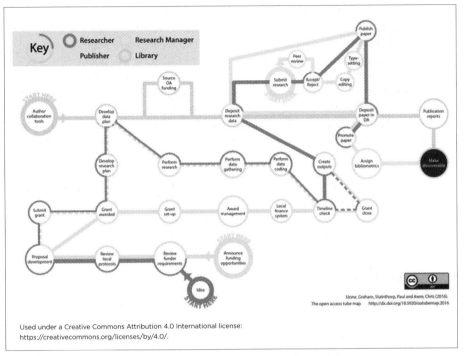

FIGURE 1.3
OA Tube Map[6]

order to help us achieve this goal, Peter McCracken joined the writing team. We decided to rebrand this version TERMs 2.0. As with the first version of TERMs, we are publishing a definitive version, this time as an open access monograph. However, the TERMs blog will live on and we very much welcome feedback from the community to keep the development of this project fresh.

Influence of TERMs

One of the most heartening things learned after the initial publication of TERMs was how it was incorporated into library and information science teaching and learning, particularly in the United States. There are two specific cases of note. TERMs has been used as a framework in classes on electronic resource management at the University of Wisconsin Library and Information Science (LIS) program as well as being utilized as a unit in the Master's of Library and Information Science program at the University of Illinois.[7,8]

In addition, the framework of TERMs has been incorporated into national electronic resource management conversations and software based on the TERMs framework has been developed.[9–11]

Three key publications produced in the past few years make direct reference to the work of TERMs: *Fundamentals of Electronic Resource Management, Reengineering the Library: Issues in Electronic Resource Management*, and *Electronic Resources Librarianship: A Practical Guide for Librarians*. The work of Verminski and Blanchat provides an excellent base of information on the management of electronic resources and highlights many of the issues that have arisen since the initial TERMs project began.[12] *Reengineering the Library: Issues in Electronic Resource Management* highlights major issues and concerns surrounding the area of electronic resource management occurring in libraries, from the management of knowledge bases and metadata to staffing for troubleshooting access issues to the management of openly available resources.[3] Talbott and Zmau's book refers to the initial iteration of TERMS as the "most definitive version of the e-resources life cycle," and provides a nice roadmap for the first three months of someone starting a new job as an electronic resources librarian.[14]

Intention

In an attempt to bring together TERMs and OAWAL, we acknowledge that the framework has to be more flexible than originally conceived. With the advent of OAWAL, we made an attempt to warn against siloing digital management work outside of the traditional technical services roles within organizations. We noted that much of the staffing and work of digital library management and electronic resources in particular is comparable, and we are not alone in this opinion.[15] Having a firm grasp of scholarly publishing models; licensing terms for access, utilization, and reuse; administrative and descriptive metadata management; knowing where to look to resolve problems and issues; and figuring out how to preserve and maintain content digitally are all issues that the two working groups in a given organization have in common. Putting half the group into another office or another building, and not creating shared policies and practices, results in a false dichotomy or separation of work within an organization (see the Audience section later in this chapter). We hope this expansion of TERMs allows for the recognition by more administrative bodies and personnel that this is shared work undertaken by these management areas. Ultimately, all of the work is scholarly output, whether published by a commercial provider or through a local repository.

Structural Updates

This version of TERMs adheres to our original matrix of six constituent parts:

- Investigating new content for purchase and addition
- Acquiring new content

- Implementation and troubleshooting
- Ongoing evaluation and access, and annual review
- Assessment
- Preservation and sustainability

These six topics are further broken down into at least six sections.

However, both the content and structure of each section underwent fundamental changes. The initial writing and publication of the TERMs project centered around the need to draw together disparate areas of library resource management into the electronic resources lifecycle. In 2008, we felt that electronic resource management as a specific area of library expertise was lacking in current practice, and relatively few libraries had implemented systems to manage this growing area of resources. The first iteration of TERMs focused on management of electronic journals and database subscriptions.

Around the time of our publication, e-book purchasing models were maturing; since then, the use of streaming media as a resource has grown, especially in North America.[16] Many colleagues noted that e-book management was not addressed in the initial iteration of TERMs. In the past five years the acquisition models for e-books have developed, changed, and become commonplace.[17] This version of TERMs considers the varying purchasing models currently available to libraries and this is a significant change in content. Day-to-day electronic resource management means working readily across these different types of purchasing models. Streaming media options present a similar issue. The new and different challenges that must be addressed with streaming media purchases are almost always based on licensing access as opposed to obtaining ownership of streamed content.

Another area that is more defined in this version of TERMs centers on the deal-breakers and negotiation techniques to use with licensing resources. Feedback from those initial communications with the library community and U.S. workshops informed us that this was a prime take-home from the content for many. The year after publication of the first version of TERMs, a key model license in North America was revised to include new issues and concerns developing around patron privacy, data-mining, and more robust user definitions.[18] For this version of TERMs, we spent considerable time reviewing notes from the past five years to develop a revised list of deal-breakers and to outline some of the techniques for pricing negotiation received as feedback from the community.

One area that was not anticipated in the conclusion to the first version of TERMs was the advent and growth of electronic resource troubleshooting as an area of expertise.[19] Although we recognized at the time there were going to be access issues and problems to resolve, the depth and extent to which this now takes up staff time and resources are quite significant. For this reason, we took troubleshooting and expanded it into its own chapter.

The framework stays agnostic on a specific tool but hopefully provides an overview that can help inform the tool adopted and used in a local environment.

The other major change to have occurred in electronic resource management is the growth and inclusion of open access content. There are now over 13,500 peer-reviewed OA journals listed in the Directory of Open Access Journals (DOAJ), 4,000 open access repositories listed in the Directory of Open Access Repositories (OpenDOAR) and approximately 19,000 open access books listed in the Directory of Open Access Books (DOAB).[20] In addition, there is more open content developing as the European Union pushes for greater openness with the scholarship these countries produce as part of the Open Science agenda. Bosman and Kramer define open science as content that is open for participation, open for (re)-use, and open to the world.[21] (See figure 1.4.) The most recent initiative around this is known as "Plan S," which was initiated and launched by the cOAlition S, a consortium involving more than a dozen national research funders in September 2018.[22] After consultation, revised implementation guidance followed in May 2019, which will fulfill its main principle:[23]

> With effect from 2021, all scholarly publications on the results from research funded by public or private grants provided by national, regional and international research councils and funding bodies, must be published in Open Access Journals, on Open Access Platforms, or made immediately available through Open Access Repositories without embargo.[24]

Even before the guidelines were released, the Wellcome Trust in the United Kingdom launched its new open access policy (already under review at the time of the Plan S announcement), which is the first Plan S compliant policy and will come into effect in 2021.[25] It should be noted that cOAlition S is not just a European initiative. The Wellcome Trust and the Bill and Melinda Gates Foundation announced their membership of cOAlition S in the same press release, noting that "the Gates Foundation will also update their Open Access policy—which is already broadly in line with the principles of Plan S—over the next 12 months."[26]

In what is a very fast-paced environment, an article by Johnson goes some way to explain the rhetoric that occurred in the two months after the initial announcement.[27] This will surely have a profound effect on electronic resources management.

Notwithstanding Plan S, to say there has been an explosion of open access content in the past five years is a bit of an understatement. Although developments around open access content streams were recognized at the onset of OAWAL in 2015, it is true to say that the impact that this content model would have on library workers and libraries was never fully grasped.

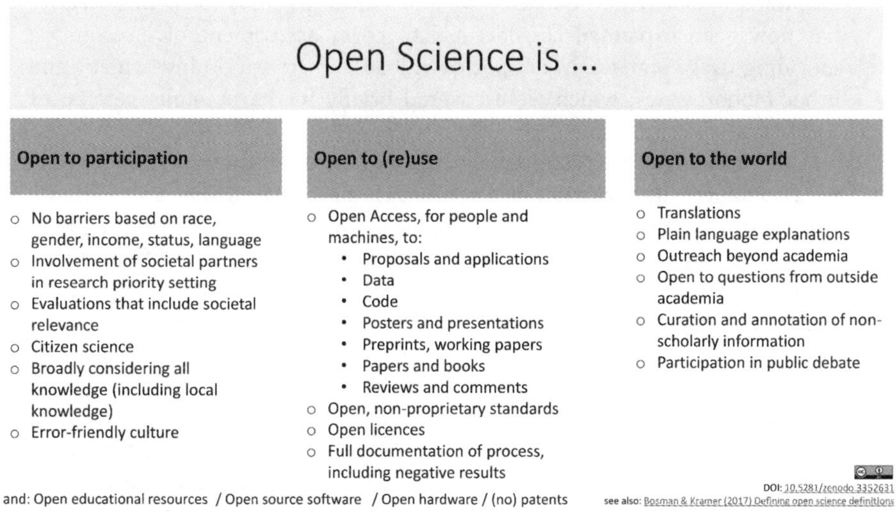

Open Science is ...

Open to participation	Open to (re)use	Open to the world
o No barriers based on race, gender, income, status, language o Involvement of societal partners in research priority setting o Evaluations that include societal relevance o Citizen science o Broadly considering all knowledge (including local knowledge) o Error-friendly culture	o Open Access, for people and machines, to: • Proposals and applications • Data • Code • Posters and presentations • Preprints, working papers • Papers and books • Reviews and comments o Open, non-proprietary standards o Open licences o Full documentation of process, including negative results	o Translations o Plain language explanations o Outreach beyond academia o Open to questions from outside academia o Curation and annotation of non-scholarly information o Participation in public debate

and: Open educational resources / Open source software / Open hardware / (no) patents

DOI: 10.5281/zenodo.3352631

see also: Bosman & Kramer (2017) Defining open science definitions

SOURCE: Jeroen Bosman & Bianca Kramer. 2019. http://doi.org/10.5281/zenodo.3352631

FIGURE 1.4
Open Science Is . . .

Open access has had profound effect on collection management and the negotiation of content licenses. If there are no strategies to address open materials, a growing tide of content from throughout the world would be ignored. While much of the current emphasis for a transition to open access journal content has come from Europe, the focus in North America has been on the development of open educational resources (OERs) and material used within classrooms as a way to defray student costs.[28-30] In addition, recognition must be given to acknowledge that the Global South started a decade earlier than Europe in their transitioning to open access content.[31] As these developments grow out of academic institutions, many academic folk are starting to realize that there are other avenues of openly available content to consider alongside OERs. In the United Kingdom, open textbooks offer an excellent example.[32,33] Within this book, we will not talk much if at all about OERs as those tend to develop and reside somewhat outside the framework we have created. However, there are a few places within the framework where we approach or talk about considerations that could be applicable to work with OERs.

A further change is the merging of two of the original sections of TERMs: Ongoing Evaluation and Access and Annual Review, into a single chapter. When converting the original version of TERMs into a series of workshops, these two sections were almost always combined in order to maintain the flow. In this iteration of TERMs, it seemed a natural progression to combine the two into a more coherent section. This allows further development of the chapter originally titled Cancellation and Replacement Review. This chapter has now been expanded considerably to cover assessment of e-resources, including usage statistics, cost per download and return on investment and other bibliometrics, which were covered briefly in the previous version of TERMs.

The merging of two chapters and the expansion of the assessment chapter also allows the inclusion of a completely new section that arose from a suggestion in a conversation with Liam Earney of Jisc in the United Kingdom. It was brought to our attention that a missing step in the workflow is that of preservation and continuing access after the cancellation review. However, this is only one aspect of preservation and sustainability and the new section also discusses the need to develop a preservation plan as part of the collection management and development policy. This includes choosing what to preserve, such as the weeding of e-books, the need for good metadata to aid the discovery of preserved material, preservation options for material that could otherwise be lost due to the "catastrophic failure" of a publisher or aggregator and the requirement to have an exit plan after cancellation review results in leaving the big deal.

As with the original published version of TERMs, the publication of TERMs 2.0 as a monograph will have the effect of fixing it at a given time. However, e-resource management will continue to evolve as new products, formats, and models come and go. For example, streaming media is still a relatively new concept and resource to manage. The transition from traditional legacy subscription models to an open access landscape in the medium (journals) to long term (monographs and textbooks) is still ongoing and naturally will have an impact on resource management workflows. In the short term, exit strategies for the big deal and using open access as a viable alternative are still required. At the time of writing, this is still a difficult process to fully automate. The introduction of COUNTER 5, and further developments of non-traditional bibliometrics will also have an influence on how electronic resources are assessed. Although covered in the following chapters, these areas are further discussed in the conclusion and will be developed as part of the TERMs blog, which remains an ongoing project.

Audience

We want this book to be available to everyone in a given organization. This is part of the reason for publishing the work open access.

Although some libraries or institutions have a single member of staff or team to manage the entire workflow, many organizations have one set of people who select resources, another set of people who acquire and license material, another set of people who implement resources, and yet a different set of people who analyze resources. Furthermore, there may be a completely different open access team and in some cases this team may not be based in the library at all.

Our hope is that this book can help each group understand each of these processes. We hope that an individual tasked with only one aspect of this work can recognize how to use the framework to their advantage to make that individual's own daily activities more efficient and find ways to evolve as new content streams emerge and are added to their processes. Not only does understanding the process in the broader context help to develop a greater appreciation of the work of each individual and what their contributions are to providing content to a given community, there is a genuine opportunity to make efficiencies in the various processes by working together more effectively. In addition, a greater understanding between subscriptions teams and open access teams may also help an organization save money by auditing publisher processes and making sure that discounts negotiated by one team are realized by others. This is especially important for the subscriptions team as we see a transition to open access publishing—the unchecked rise in article processing charges may be the next big negotiation point.

We have also written the book in a way that students in LIS programs can grasp the concepts provided and processes described in order to understand how the framework works overall.

Design

We designed the book to work on the Pareto Principle.[34] This is the idea that 80 percent of the work is invested in 20 percent of the content managed. The majority of the resources we subscribe, purchase, license, or provide access to are not problematic or difficult overall. Most electronic resources and digital assets take very little time and interaction to put into place, access, and promote for use. However, any given resource may become problematic at any stage of management. Given this, we have divided the six TERMs into six categories and within the six categories divided this further into three parts. The three parts within each given section are (see figure 1.5):

Basic resources, or standard resources, are those electronic resources that are relatively straightforward to administer and manage. These represent the 80 percent of the content where a librarian's time is used efficiently to manage the resource. We see no specific relationship between the cost of an electronic resources and the time taken to administer it. Very large aggregated databases may be fairly easy to set up and manage and still be costly, for example.

Complex resources are the difficult and detailed electronic resources that constitute the other 20 percent of content but take up the majority of a librarian's time to manage. These may be inexpensive resources.

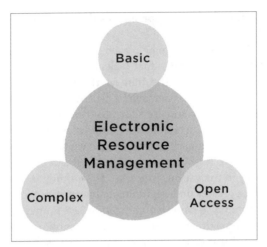

FIGURE 1.5
Subdivisions of TERMs Sections

For example, resources that are not primarily targeted at the educational market. However, time is also money, and therefore time spent on these resources can quickly lead to them being very expensive to administer. Complex resources also include large multifaceted resources, which include a number of different elements such as large offsetting or "read and publish" agreements.

Unfortunately, we seldom know if an electronic resource will be "basic" or "complex" at the beginning of the selection, negotiation, licensing, and acquisition process. Furthermore, a resource may be easy to negotiate and license, but may be very difficult to manage when you are trying to get usage statistics for it, for example. Through this work, we will try to identify ways of managing those complex resources and minimize the work that must be invested to make them work.

Open access workflows can often be seen as entirely separate workflows or a set of add-on processes. However, this view fails to recognize some important points. Firstly, open access content is a critical set of content, in the same way as paid-for content. As such, it should be exposed to the same level of scrutiny as any other part of the library's collection, management, and development policy. Secondly, open access resources also need to be implemented, embedded, monitored, and ultimately withdrawn just as would any set of resources. Finally, subscription and open access content is intrinsically linked in offsetting or read and publish agreements. These transformative agreements are increasingly becoming the norm as noted above regarding the launch of cOAlition S.[35]

TERMs 2.0 will present different ways OA content can be efficiently and effectively incorporated into the library electronic resources management workflow.

This book can be used in a number of ways. It can be read cover to cover to provide an overall picture of the framework. However, readers can also skip from section to section in order to find the information that is directly related to their work and process. This will be particularly helpful for those who have been asked to take on new responsibilities. For example, if someone who has worked on basic resources is being asked to take on more complex agreements, or if someone who looks after electronic resources is being asked to take on management of open access material, that individual can focus their reading on the relevant sub-section, i.e., complex or open access. In this way, we hope to have provided some ready paths for readers to follow to get more directly to the content they feel will be most helpful to them.

The lifecycle moves through the topic areas of: investigation of new content, procurement and licensing, implementation, troubleshooting, evaluation, and preservation and sustainability. Each section delves into each topic from the point of view of many voices and tries to present a cohesive sense of major themes within each subsection through the tracks of basic, complex, and open access realms.

We conclude by discussing what we see as significant developments and emerging initiatives. We think this is a successful framework when working with all online material within your library environment.

NOTES

1. Pesch, Oliver. (2008). Library standards and e-resource management: A survey of current initiatives and standards efforts. *Serials Librarian 55*(3): 481–486. http://dx.doi.org/10.1080/03615260802059965.

2. Emery, Jill, & Stone, Graham. (2013). TERMS. *Library Technology Reports 49*(2): 5–43. http://dx.doi.org/10.5860/ltr.49n2.

3. Emery, Jill, & Stone, Graham. (2015). OAWAL: Open access workflows for academic librarians. https://library.hud.ac.uk/blogs/oawal/.

4. Emery, Jill. (2014). Breaking silos: Staffing for the open access library. *Library Faculty Publications and Presentations 145*. https://pdxscholar.library.pdx.edu/ulib_fac/145.

5. Awre, Chris L., Stainthorp, Paul, & Stone, Graham. Supporting open access processes through library collaboration. *Collaborative Librarianship 8*(2): article 8. https://digitalcommons.du.edu/collaborativelibrarianship/vol8/iss2/8.

6. Stone, Graham, Awre, Chris, & Stainthorp, Paul. (2016). The open access tube map. http://dx.doi.org/10.5920/oatubemap.2016.

7. Chilton, Galadriel. (2013). LIS 755. Electronic resource management and licensing, University of Wisconsin—Madison, School of Library & Information Studies. https://wiseeducation.org/media/documents/2014/3/UWMad755Syllabus.pdf.

8. Oberg, Steve. (2018). E-resources management. https://docs.google.com/document/d/19IcMH3HCtSE7rs6jbrz3I5GSpJ5zE16RSn_xuPUKOOY/edit?usp=sharing.

9. Pesola, Ulla. (2013). TERMS: E-aineistot hallintaan yhteisön voimalla, *Signum* (5). https://journal.fi/signum/article/view/9393.

10. Jisc Collections. (2018). Collection management and development policy. https://www.jisc-collections.ac.uk/About-JISC-Collections/Collections-Management-Development-Policy/.

11. Open Access Directory. (2018). OA by the numbers. http://oad.simmons.edu/oadwiki/OA_by_the_numbers.

12. Verminski, Alana, & Blanchat, Kelly Marie. (2017). *Fundamentals of electronic resources management* (Chicago: American Library Association).

13. Stachokas, George. (2018). *Reengineering the library: Issues in electronic resource management* (Chicago: American Library Association).

14. Talbott, Holly, & Zmau, Ashley. (2018). *Electronic resources librarianship: A practical guide* (Lanham, MD: Rowman & Littlefield: .

15. Craig, Eleanor, & Webb, Helen. (2017). Bringing together the work of subscription and open access specialists: Challenges and changes at the University of Sussex. *Insights* 30(1): 31–37. http://doi.org/10.1629/uksg.337.

16. Hartnett, Eric. (2018). *Guide to streaming video acquisitions* (Chicago: American Library Association).

17. Ball, Joanna. (2016). Where are we now? Delivering content in academic libraries. *Insights* 29(2): 167–171. http://doi.org/10.1629/uksg.297.

18. LIBLICENSE. (2014). Licensing information: Model licenses. http://liblicense.crl.edu/licensing-information/model-license/.

19. Rathmel, Angela, Mobley, Lisa, Pennington, Buddy, & Chandler, Adam. (2015). Tools, techniques, and training: Results of an e-resources troubleshooting survey. *Journal of Electronic Resources Librarianship* 27(2): 88-107. https://doi.org/10.1080/1941126X.2015.1029398.

20. Open Access Directory. (2018). OA by the numbers. http://oad.simmons.edu/oadwiki/OA_by_the_numbers.

21. Bosman, Jeroen, & Kramer, Bianca. (2019, July). "Open science is ." [reusable slide with aspects of open science and scholarship]. Zenodo. http://doi.org/10.5281/zenodo.3352631.

22. European Commission. (2018). "Plan S" and "cOAlition S"—Accelerating the transition to full and immediate Open Access to scientific publications. https://www.coalition-s.org/.

23. cOAlition S. (2019). cOAlition S Releases revised implementation guidance on Plan S following public feedback exercise. https://www.coalition-s.org/revised-implementation-guidance/.

24. Plan S. (2019). Principles and implementation. https://www.coalition-s.org/principles-and-implementation/.

25. Wellcome Trust. (2019). Open access policy 2021. https://wellcome.ac.uk/sites/default/files/wellcome-open-access-policy-2021.pdf.

26. Wellcome Trust. (2018). Wellcome and the Bill & Melinda Gates Foundation join the Open Access Coalition. https://wellcome.ac.uk/press-release/wellcome-and-bill-melinda-gates-foundation-join-open-access-coalition.

27. Johnson, Rob. (2019). From coalition to commons: Plan S and the future of scholarly communication. *Insights 32*(1): 5. DOI: http://doi.org/10.1629/uksg.453.

28. Suber, Peter. (2018). Journal publishers and platforms outside USA, Europe and Australia. http://tagteam.harvard.edu/hub_feeds/119/feed_items/2421968/about.

29. Max Planck Digital Library. (2018). OA2020. https://oa2020.org/.

30. Diaz, Chris. (2017). *Affordable course materials: Electronic textbooks and open educational resources* (Chicago: American Library Association).

31. Babini, D., & Machin-Mastromatteo, J. D. (2015). Latin American science is meant to be open access: Initiatives and current challenges. *Information Development*, *31*(5), 477–481. https://doi.org/10.1177/0266666915601420.

32. Jisc. (2018). Institution as e-textbook publisher project. https://www.jisc.ac.uk/rd/projects/institution-as-e-textbook-publisher.

33. U.K. open textbook project. (2018). http://ukopentextbooks.org/.

34. Wikipedia, Pareto principle. (2018). https://en.wikipedia.org/wiki/Pareto_principle.

35. Science Europe, cOAlition S. (2018). https://www.scienceeurope.org/coalition-s/.

2
Investigating New Content for Purchase and Addition

Introduction

When working with electronic resources and open scholarship, the biggest learning curve in librarianship concerns the choices made with selection and procurement. These choices have impacts that can carry throughout the life of a given resource. So many of the most relevant decisions regarding electronic resource management and open access (OA) management occur at the point of choosing to include the resource into a given collection. How a resource is selected and purchased drives every other aspect of that resource's lifecycle. Some resources are purchased for short-term or temporary access whereas others are purchased in perpetuity. Accordingly, the level of description and implementation varies based on these decisions.

With electronic resources, the selection of content, as a process, is driven by use of the resources. In other cases, selection is determined by meeting community user needs, such as reading lists and core content. Over time, the trend of selecting content in libraries has shifted. Several decades ago libraries bought just a few online resources, but today libraries spend on average 70 percent of their materials budget on electronic resources.[1] For librarians working on acquisition and management of electronic resources, much of their time is spent vetting requests received rather than making selection directly. These requests lead to new, different, and challenging issues, such as licensing, ensuring accurate access, ongoing evaluation, and establishing preservation. New formats, such as streaming audio and video, data sets, GIS data, resources designed for text and data mining also present new challenges. In addition, electronic resources librarians must continue supporting community publishing and evaluating new paths to delivery, such as evidence-based acquisition and pay-per-view options.

Vetting demand driven requests is not just a check-box exercise but relies on a number of varying factors. The biggest factor being how well the choice of material fits into the current collection development plans and priorities followed by what the selection mechanism means in terms of long-term access to the content. In the case of supporting open access content development, the consultation of a campus or library open access policy is a consideration along with the need to support research outside of funder mandates for open access.[2]

This is then followed by analysis of how the purchase is made and whether the purchasing model fits within the financial arrangements allowed by the larger organizational financial practices. For many resources such as databases, historical archives, datasets, data visualization tools, alternative metric tools, and citation management tools, a trial may be necessary to ensure that the resource works as expected in the local environment. The initial negotiation with the provider over pricing and terms of service also begin at this stage. For many larger purchasing deals, the negotiation of an agreement is completed by regional or national consortia. The culmination of this stage of resource management results in purchasing, or not. For the uninitiated, the process seems daunting when first undertaken, but quickly becomes standard practice. There are always new challenges and considerations that occur with the investigation of electronic resource content and it helps to have a set process to fall back on when the purchasing strategy is not as routine as it first appears to be.[3]

1. Request

A request for a new resource often comes directly from academic faculty or staff via online forms, websites, reading list managers, ILL providers, and/or the academic liaison colleague serving various constituents.

Basic Resources

For basic resources such as standard archives, journal subscriptions, single e-book purchases, or databases, the goal in selecting and adding an electronic resource is straightforward. The electronic resources or acquisitions librarian contacts the appropriate vendor, provider, subscription agent, book supplier, or consortium contact to ask for price information, to review the license, and to implement the purchase. The delivery of these requests is through standard pathways within the library from community members via websites, web forms, or from liaison librarians that are working with particular faculty on course development and provision. If an institution's materials budget is static or shrinking, library staff and selectors may need to determine what subscriptions will be cancelled, to cover the cost of the new resource.

For monograph and serial content, one way of assessing a potential resource's value is to investigate the history of interlibrary loan (ILL) requests and associated costs. In cases where the library has already spent a fair bit of money on borrowing similar materials, acquiring that content may be a smart financial move; in any case, the community obviously values the content. For monograph content, a library might decide to automatically purchase a title after it has been requested via ILL a certain number of times, possibly within a set time period. For serial content, a subscription can generally expect to have 10 times the usage of an ILL. Some librarians monitor ILL activity as an early indicator of the predicted cost per download (CPD). For example, multiplying the ILL requests over a given year by 10 and then dividing the annual subscription costs by this figure. If the estimated CPD is more expensive than the price of an ILL this may indicate that the resource will not provide sufficient value for money from the library budget.

In the case of abstracts and indexes (A&Is), full-text databases, or other non-textual resources, the determination in purchasing decision often boils down to the platforms that host the given resource and what works best in the local environment. For example, most institutions designate platforms of preference, such as EBSCOhost, ProQuest, Ovid etc. Indeed, there may already be an agreement that offers a discount for future subscriptions via a particular platform. In addition, there may be an overlap with existing content. For example, business, health, psychology, and education full-text databases often have overlap so choosing the platform that hosts the majority of these resources becomes the choice to make.

It is important to set out the criteria to fulfill and map decisions made to the local collection management and development policy. Important questions need to be asked about the resource: Is the primary use for undergraduate teaching or postgraduate research? Are you purchasing within the existing budget or are additional funds available? How sustainable is this budget? Are multi-year deals a possibility or a practice allowed by your institution? If there are additional funds available, is there a contingency or pump-priming budget available for new courses or modules? Is there research funding available from faculty to cover or partly cover costs and for how long?

Recurrent funding is important because e-resources may need up to two years before they become vital additions in the curriculum. Very often, the first year of usage for a resource can be meaningless as the resource remains relatively unknown. Resources usually need a full academic year to appear on reading lists, research guides, within the research framework, etc., and only then will your usage statistics start to make sense. Whenever possible, do not make decisions about the success of a resource without at least two years' worth of data.

Collection management and development policies or collection priorities have various forms at multiple institutions. These documents often outline local institutional preferences and understanding them is a worthwhile goal. These preferences may focus on content types, business practices used to provide access to content, or criteria preferred for selection of content. These criteria can include a preference of print material over electronic material. This is often true for certain content types or subject areas, such as a preference for low thresholds of digital rights management for electronic access, and the preference for site-wide licensing over simultaneous usage. If an institution has a longstanding relationship with consortia, the consortia may also have its own policies to review and consider regarding the content or practices used to obtain resources. Examples of these collection management and development policy or priority documents are given in table 2.1.

TABLE 2.1

Examples of Institutional and Consortial Collection, Management, and Development Policies

UNIVERSITY	URL
Columbia University	http://library.columbia.edu/about/policies/collection-development.html
St. Thomas University	https://www.stthomas.edu/libraries/about/policies/collectiondev/
Colorado State University	http://lib.colostate.edu/cm/policies
University of Montana	www.lib.montana.edu/collections/cdpolicy.html

Consortia Policies

ORGANIZATION	URL
International Federation of Library Associations (IFLA)	https://www.ifla.org/files/assets/acquisition-collection-development/publications/gcdp-en.pdf
Jisc Collections (U.K.)	https://www.jisc-collections.ac.uk/About-JISC-Collections/Collections-Management-Development-Policy/
Orbis Cascade Alliance	https://www.orbiscascade.org/file_viewer.php?id=3411

Complex Resources

Complex resources are those that require greater effort, perhaps because of complicated purchase structures, particularly in patron driven acquisition systems. Limitations or complications with licensing, determination of access rights, and non-standard payment structures can all make the acquisition of a resource more difficult.

Streaming media requests are becoming increasingly prevalent in U.S. libraries. In the case of these requests, you may need to do quite a bit of work upfront to even determine if the content requested is available streaming or not.[4] This may take you as far as contacting the producer or director of the content. If it is learned that content is not readily available for institutional purchase, you will need to see if you are allowed permission to make secured electronic copies for teaching and learning. This can become rather complicated rather quickly. It is best to have determined the level of work that can be committed to discovering if streaming options are available along with a decision tree for what to do if streaming options are not available. You may find that guidance in your collection management and development policy. However, your policy may require a new section in order to cover this area.

There are growing demands from faculty to negotiate for online access to textbooks or "adopted texts," which are textbook equivalent resources and these negotiations are often cumbersome and complex. In the United Kingdom, the University of Manchester has done an intensive study to see how viable it is to supply students with needed textbooks.[5] The publisher knows this content is in high demand and that selling one copy to a library as opposed to selling multiple copies directly to students is not in their market interest. For libraries to purchase this content and make it available on reading lists, the librarians often must negotiate a "multiplier" price or price for multiple users of the content. In some cases, consortia can help with these negotiations, but not always.

Other e-books may seem to be relatively straightforward at first. However, they can also become very complicated very quickly. One issue is that faculty and even other colleagues are used to obtaining e-books through a very simple process with commercial vendors, such as downloading a monograph to a Kindle. For library purchases of e-books, it is almost never that simple. For example, your library or consortia may have a preferred supplier, usually a third-party distributor or book supplier—this may or may not be the same supplier as the print books supplier. A third-party distributor can indicate if titles are available online and what the user level may be for a given title. Unfortunately, different suppliers have different agreements with publishers around digital rights management (DRM) and concurrent users. You may have to check several different suppliers before you find what you are looking for. It may be worthwhile to explore purchasing directly from a publisher or provider as opposed to a third-party bookseller or platform depending on the DRM applied by a given supplier. However, many publishers do not sell individual copies, offering only bundled content.

Open Access

In the case of open access material, where the lack of upfront costs means that usage (or lack thereof) has little impact on the choice of whether or not to incorporate the resource into a collection. The choice to add openly available content into a collection falls to each individual library, but as there is growing interest in the wider availability of resources and content, adding open scholarship and open scholarship tools into the collection development policy or collection priorities is advantageous. The point of selection for open scholarship and what criteria used for addition falls to the collection development policy or priorities. Despite there being no cost for obtaining open resources upfront, there are costs of managing and maintaining open resources. At the point of adding an OA title, it is worth developing a retention and evaluation plan. Although there may be interest in adding an OA title today, would that title be kept if it went behind a paywall? Would a title still be of interest if it ceased after a single year of publication? There is clearly a cost in acquiring, selecting, and implementing these resources, even without invoicing. The staff costs associated with managing OA resources means that you should judiciously determine which resources justify staff attention. Examples for determining addition to your collection include:

- The number of accesses from faculty or learning management system web pages
- Inclusion in the Directory of Open Access Journals (DOAJ) or Directory of Open Access Books (DOAB),
- Institutional support for the ideals of the Open Access Scholarly Publishers Association (OASPA)
- Ease of use with accessibility software, discoverability through web-scale discovery systems
- Local focus on content selection, such as resources from specific countries

If the current collection development policy or collection priorities do not include open access content, it is worth the investment for the local organization to develop the criteria for this type of selection. There may be disciplines where a focus on open access is of particular interest for some members of the local community. In some disciplines, some may want to buy-in to open access memberships or support schemes, and others may just want to codify access to content.

Essentially, requests for open access material fall into two types:

1. Requests for open access resources. In this case, look for quality. Use the same selection criteria that you would use for all other content. Exercise caution, as it is very easy to fill your collection with free stuff, but that can quickly become unsustainable. Determine if journals are peer reviewed, if they use durable DOIs, if they are approved and listed in DOAJ, etc.

2. Requests to publish in open access journals. In this case, faculty/researchers notice the ability to publish their content as OA for a fee. The fee is usually an article processing charge (APC). Although it may not be the library's responsibility to pay the APC, there may be options open to the library to reduce the cost through supporter or membership schemes, which will then offer discounts to APCs. For example, membership of Biomed Central offers a discount to APCs, while membership of Open Library of Humanities supports publication with no fees involved. Therefore, it is the membership scheme that will need the assessment rather than the APC enquiry.

2. Developing Selection Criteria

In developing selection criteria, a number of different, often conflicting, variables need to be considered.

1. Selection criteria rely on the local collection development policy, collection development priorities, open access policy or local open access mandate, or collection development principles utilized by your organization.

2. Discovery, accessibility, and ease of access by anyone within your organization who may wish to use the content is part of the initial selection criteria. This includes research, teaching, and learning, on campus, remote access (including overseas) for most institutions. Other users who may request access include partner organizations, walk-in access, visiting faculty and students, and even small and medium sized enterprises (SMEs) or university start-up companies (these may be harder to include in licenses or require additional fees). Using the broadest terms for all local users such as anyone affiliated with your University allows for greatest access.

3. Budgets and financial support are also an extremely important factor that impact the selection of resources, as is the ability to demonstrate value for money after a resource has been acquired in order to maintain a subscription.

    4. Finally, content that meets the standards of accessibility and technical
       support set by your institutional values and goals.

In chapter 3, which addresses purchasing and licensing, we have listed a series of deal breakers. These can be adapted or refined to fit your local practices for most material or resources. These are an expanded version of an original list that appeared in the first iteration of TERMs.[6]

Basic Resources

For a single order, the criteria outlined will supplement your collection priorities/collection policy or the collection priorities/policy of your consortium. These criteria include the format choice, what platforms users prefer, meeting accessibility standards, and which resources are best in the local technological environment.

Complex Resources

For larger projects, the criteria become more involved. It is necessary to determine whether a big deal journal package will supply both heavily used content and esoteric content that is used more sparingly. Is the overall deal worth the funds to be committed? Another example is choosing an e-book platform or e-book provider; this requires defining what the desired content is and choosing the purchasing model you wish to employ. Consortia negotiations often determine these criteria. However, in the case of subscription agents and e-book vendors, there may be multiple suppliers available. You will need to justify to your local procurement office why a supplier was selected because this choice can advise the selection criteria. Furthermore, you may want to split subscription purchases between two suppliers (e.g., 70 percent with an existing supplier and 30 percent with the new kid on the block). In other cases, the bookstore contract has an impact on what e-books are available through the library. For larger deals not covered by consortia agreements, you may be required to issue a formal invitation to tender (ITT), a request for quote (RFQ), or request for proposal (RFP) as part of your institutional procurement regulations—often this will apply for multi-year deals where a certain price threshold is to be set. Make friends with your local procurement office and keep up the dialogue as part of the selection criteria.

    Another example of more complicated selection criteria occurs with streaming media collections. Do you wish to purchase single titles or are packages more appropriate for your institution's streaming media needs? Would a token-access purchasing system work best until you can evaluate demand of use? For streaming media, you should compile a list of criteria similar to other electronic resources, but you must also consider other things such as whether transcripts of the content are made available or if the content comes with closed captioning. You may find that there are specific browsers or platforms where the content may not be viewable. Does that mean that the media is not compatible with your institution's learning management systems? Is the content available for institutional purchase or only for individual access?

For e-books, your criteria should include the platform and DRM level preferred. You need to determine what level of simultaneous usage is acceptable. Can your institution accept paying more for content that has more flexibility regarding DRM? In some cases, if you cannot purchase the title you require, you may be able to digitize chapters locally and make them available on the local learning management systems (LMS) or virtual learning environment (VLE) by module or cohort.

Open Access

There has been much criticism of unscrupulous open access publishers or so-called predatory publishers over the years. However, predatory publishers are not purely an open access phenomenon. Quality checks should be a review criterion for all new content. The World Association of Medical Editors has made a document available that offers excellent and well-supported advice on identifying predatory or pseudo-journals.[7]

The following resources are good places to start when considering open access publications:

- DOAJ/ISSN ROAD—Inclusion in DOAJ is now peer reviewed and requires a number of review criteria made for each title. Titles receive the DOAJ seal of approval if they meet certain elements of best practice. ISSN ROAD lists DOAJ titles with ISSN.[8–10]
- DOAB and OAPEN perform a similar service for open access e-books.[11,12]
- OASPA and/or COPE membership is a further sign that a journal or publisher fulfills quality criteria.[13,14]
- Clear explanations on copyright licensing and a transparent pricing structure are signs of a reputable open access publisher.
- For universities, smaller foreign societies, and foreign governments that produce open access content that do not require payment for publishing, evaluating the copyright licensing offered as well as the reputation of the institution or organization that is producing the material is another way to discern quality.
- Other repositories can be tracked if a knowledge base containing details about them is part of a library discovery tool. Plans are underway so that CORE (Connecting Repositories from the United Kingdom) can also become discoverable in the future.[15]

Should authors contact you regarding publishing in OA journals, Rele, Kennedy, and Blas at Loyola Marymount University have developed a journal evaluation tool to assist authors "in making the best decisions for your work, and to avoid journals that may not be credible."[16] Another tool is the list created by Andy Nobes, a program coordinator at International Network for the Availability of Scientific Publications (INASP). It is a simple Google document outlining journal publishers and platforms outside of the United States, Europe, and Australia.[17] The list provides a good basis for identifying open content available from other countries.

If your library supports or has an APC budget available for faculty to use, you will need to set the criteria for what articles your institution will or will not fund. Some institutions refuse to support hybrid journals (subscription journals that also have APC fees for single article access). The practice wherein hybrid journals that are subscription-based but also charge APCs costs for individual articles is sometimes referred to as "double dipping." Others will have a selected list of publishers who are preferred for APC funding or even blacklists of publishers to which APCs will not be paid. Some institutions will not pay APCs if an author can seek or has grant funding available to pay for these charges.

3. Completing the Review Form

Many institutions and libraries have new resource order forms that outline specific purchasing criteria and their application. These may be Google Forms or a form created by library web developers that sends emails to a group in collection development or acquisitions. The forms can become the review mechanism for the subscription or purchase. Many libraries and institutions also have collection committees to review new requests; this is especially true of requests that may cost significant amounts of money. These review committees may be internal to the library or they may include discipline faculty from other areas on campus. Senior faculty often authorize or approve new resource orders when a review committee does not exist. This is particularly important if there is a one-in, one-out policy for subscriptions because it empowers faculty to make difficult decisions based on evidence, rather than purely a decision made solely by the library that may prove unpopular with those who stand to lose out by a cancellation. When funding is coming from foundational accounts or donor-supplied money, the review of the selection may also be more formal to insure meeting the conditions outlined by the donor.

It is worthwhile to develop a mechanism for review even if you are at a small institution so that the selection process is consistent. It may help to discard some requests at an early stage and therefore save administrative time. Include a section asking if an ILL will suit the needs of the academic or researcher; if it does, then an order is not a necessity.

Basic Resources

In the case of a single e-resource, this may just be as simple as maintaining an email file of requests that document the decision. Because requests for purchase or trials have a habit of coming back to haunt you, it is important to keep an audit trail. For some libraries, the information surrounding order selection is located within the notation fields provided in the procurement or resource management system.

Complex Resources

With larger scale databases and complex resources, the decision may require consultation with information technology infrastructure support personnel or even with university purchasing officers if the cost of the resource means that an ITT or RFP is required. In some cases, this would be an ad hoc group similar to the review committee mentioned and would consist of the

- e-resources manager
- subject team leader
- budget holder
- faculty

For other purchases, the selection will determine who needs to be consulted during the process. For complex purchases, consultations with procurement and fiscal management staff are necessary due to the complexity of the trans-actions. Once again, get to know your colleagues in procurement and learn about the processes in your institution. A purchase or subscription could be stopped at the final hurdle because local procurement rules were not followed correctly. Understandably, this could prove embarrassing to the library.

You should consider running update sessions for your liaison teams to discuss new e-subscriptions. This forum is useful for getting buy-in from liai-son colleagues. You should be as transparent and inclusive as possible about complex procurements and make sure no one is overlooked. The utilization of resources crosses many disciplines on a comprehensive college campus. Make sure to gather all possible input into a purchasing decision, which may mean reaching out to faculty who may not normally directly interact with one another. If your institution makes these decisions via a standing commit-tee, these committee members need to be directly involved in the selection process.

The University of California Libraries developed a workflow for a Trans-formative Scholarly Communication Initiatives Review Process. This outlines the processes to use when moving subscription services to vendors that may be more open or developing and implementing new mechanisms for support-ing open scholarship in their campus environments.[18] This workflow is used by the Scholarly Transformation Advice and Review (STAR) Team to make sure

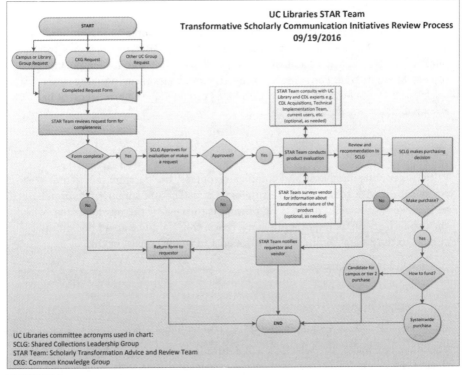

FIGURE 2.1
UC Libraries Star Team Transformative Scholarly Communications
Initiatives Review Process

all areas are evaluated upfront, and is reinforced by the use of a Master Evaluation Criteria Workbook that provides an in-depth outline of the transformation to take place (see figure 2.1).[19] Development of workflows and tools such as these are invaluable when mapping out how to move from standard subscription practices to new ways of providing content and services.

Open Access

For open access content, your institution or library may provide faculty and researchers with access to an APC fund to support the publication of their work as open access.[20] This could involve administering external funder budgets, such as block grants, or a dedicated library or faculty budget. If this is the case, you will need to make selection criteria publicly available when determining fund expenditures as noted above. Many publishers are now moving towards "read and publish" agreements where access is provided to all titles within an agreement and authors may publish open access at no additional charge to the cost of the agreement. In Europe, the ESAC (Efficiency and Standards for Article Charges) initiative maintains a registry of these transformative agreements by consortia.[21] There may be other criteria surrounding the quality of the OA publisher under consideration for funding support. Many institutions do not keep order records for open access materials and resources (although this is strongly advised, as many funders require this information); therefore, noting the selection details in another manner will be worthwhile for future retention decisions.

More and more, faculty are aware of the high costs brought to bear on students (particularly in North America) and are becoming more willing to use open access resources for course readings and open educational material. With open educational materials, faculty are direct partners in both the development of new resources and the choice of resources to be utilized.[22]

4. Analyzing and Reviewing

It is not unusual for academics to request resources that are available as part of another subscription or that are readily available. Academics new to an institution will often request a resource because they are unaware that alternatives are already available. Although acknowledging that "content is king," e-resource librarians have a fiscal responsibility to consider varying options before making a purchase.

Basic and Complex Resources

The first step in checking a new order is to see if current subscriptions can fulfill the needs of the academic. In times of austerity, we can no longer afford to subscribe to multiple resources that overlap. A quick review of the market and literature may be necessary if the request is for larger collections of electronic resource materials or when there is market competition for provision of a given resource. This tends to happen more with electronic A&I services, full-text databases, and e-book packages where reviews and trials of various versions may be critical to the selection of any one given resource. Increasingly, this is also happening with streaming media providers.

Before talking to suppliers, determine where there may be overlap within your current content array. Using commercial tools to check coverage and duplication of content between resources is recommended, especially for A&Is and full-text databases. These tools tend to come and go, but the more significant ones are:

- WorldShare Collection Evaluation[23]
- eDesiderata from Center for Research Libraries[24]

- DIY Title Overlap Analysis[25]
- 360 Core Overlap Analysis from Ex Libris[26]
- GoldRush Decision Support Tool[27]

Simple manipulation of A&I or full-text database title lists in Excel (title lists are available on most vendor websites) can also pay dividends, especially when looking at duplication of titles across a range of products. In addition, *The Charleston Advisor* is a great resource for finding product reviews and comparison studies of various content platforms as well as for discovering potential problems with given resources.[28]

Open Access

Duplication of an open access resource is less of an issue because it does not result in additional expenditure. However, it is worthwhile to assess full-text databases and e-book packages for their coverage of OA content. If there is a large amount of OA content in a full-text database, your review becomes more about the indexing provided than about the content. Many vendors will argue that they are bringing value to the OA resource by indexing it for you. However, if they are adding OA content just to hike up the number of journals and articles offered and not because the content provides a valuable perspective within the service, it becomes more problematic than helpful to your end user. If the OA resource is available in a free service such as DOAJ or DOAB, you may not need the content indexed in a full-text database. This is especially true if you are using a web-scale discovery mechanism that indexes DOAJ or DOAB—the metadata is already available to you in search results.

When reviewing a journal subscription, if you are investigating a hybrid journal, check the proportion of OA content available. If the OA content is increasing, you should expect a certain amount of offsetting; otherwise, you will be paying for content that has already been paid for through APC payments.

5. Establishing a Trial and Contacting Vendors

Almost all library electronic resource and electronic service providers allow trials of their material or products.[29] Many are willing to allow an extended trial of sixty to ninety days for evaluation. Sometimes having a resource available for a school term, semester, or high traffic time is helpful in determining the utility of the product for your environment. The major vendors and providers readily allow IP-based trials with remote access enabled. However, some smaller providers may require the use of usernames and passwords for trial reviews. The type of product often determines how much of a burden this may be. For example, a trial for a specialist resource that will only be used by a limited number of users could warrant username and password access, but a trial for a resource that is expected to be a major resource would be easier to trial via IP.

For a full evaluation of a product, it is recommended that you have a sandbox for your discovery tool. Turn on access through this mechanism to ensure that access will work as expected.

Basic Approach

Talking to providers will follow the desktop review of a trial setup. Be aware that some resources are available through different suppliers. In addition, there may be national or regional consortia agreements in place with preferential prices and licenses. Some suppliers may have exclusive deals in a given region or territory, meaning that your choice may be limited. Always make sure to let suppliers and vendors know when you are looking at more than one provider for a resource; this may result in your learning a bit more about the product as each tries to prove why its version would be an improvement over any others under consideration. Make sure that you fully understand all of the contract provisions and fees associated with a resource to avoid surprises at the point of acquisition.

Try to get a good representation of your team when talking to suppliers—preferably the same people will be present for each meeting—and have your specification document on hand to remain focused. If you encounter new information along the way, go back to previous suppliers to verify anything you've discovered. This may seem like a lot of preparatory work but remember some deals may be worth hundreds of thousands of dollars over the course of a three-year deal.

Next, use the specification to narrow the field. Look at trialing your short list. It is very important to get the timing of your trial correct—it can be very frustrating when faculty get in touch on the last day of a trial! Use your faculty contacts to confirm the best time of year to conduct a trial and publicize it on your blog, wiki, social media instances, or web pages. Make sure you get usage statistics for the trial. Put a comment sheet together to solicit feedback. The length of the trial is also very important. Some suppliers will negotiate a sponsored trial where, for a small administration fee, the trial can be extended for up to six months. This allows you to get a real feel for the potential demand and is particularly useful for larger subscriptions. Use the budget cuts to your advantage. Suppliers may be prepared to negotiate the price down—remember, there is no such thing as a list price.

When you disseminate information about the trial, make sure that you have feedback mechanisms in place and that you record any comments and feedback you get and from whom. This will allow you to justify any decisions and to collate feedback for the suppliers or vendors.

Complex Resources

Many esoteric scientific, business, or data resources have more limited trial periods and setups. Try to negotiate for the broadest access possible for as long as you can in order to insure the product will work optimally in your computing environment. Many times, remote access is not allowed for more complex trials and this lack of access complicates testing and evaluation. Try to arrange at least one day of remote access to fully investigate the product. Streaming media providers are often unwilling to provide extensive trials for longer trial periods. In these cases, it may be advantageous to negotiate a lower-cost trial period during which you can pilot a resource to see if it is of value to your community. E-book providers also are generally willing to work with you to pilot-test new purchasing options or content provision. Evidence-based purchasing models allow you to obtain a large swath of content for a limited time frame, generally either six months or a year, and then make purchasing decisions based on the usage up to a pre-specified amount. However, you must be willing to commit to the predetermined amount at the end of the evidence-based timeframe.

Open Access

Open access material is readily available to your library or institution. However, you may want to perform a citation review of faculty publishing to see if there are specific publishers or providers in which they regularly publish. If this is the case, you may consider subsidizing APCs of hybrid journals from a given publisher or provider, or even fully support all campus publishing with a given publisher or provider through additional payments with your big deal packages or through memberships in their open access programs.

You may also be interested in supporting various patron driven open access models where you pay a pre-planned cost to ensure that content is produced open access. These are models like the Open Library of Humanities, Knowledge Unlatched, or Reveal Digital collections.[30–32]

6. Making a Decision

When making the decision to purchase content from a provider, the next step is to determine the purchasing model to employ. Will the attempt to purchase content be outright, that is, in a one-time expenditure with a nominal hosting fee? Will the selection result in an evidence-based plan where a certain amount of money is set aside, and the provision begins with a larger content base then determined by usage? Will it entail an annual subscription cost?

When going into negotiation with a vendor, keep the ideal expenditure amount in mind and be forthright and forceful in your negotiations. Almost all providers prefer some money over none, so look for creative ways to insure your finances go a bit further.

After this review (which may take only a few hours given a single resource or a few months if purchasing a large collection of content), it is essential to document the ordering process and any relevant points that went into the purchase decision in a resource management system (a spreadsheet will do). These details could be as simple as subscribing to other journals on the same platform or noting that the platform functionality works well with other library resources or includes any relevant comparison information gathered. It is as crucial to document decisions *not* to purchase content as it is to record the documentation for purchased resources. Material not purchased is likely to be requested again and knowing the reasoning used initially will become important in reviewing a second time.

Basic Resources

For basic resources, there may be very little negotiation involved. Costs are known upfront and the initial contact indicates the desire to purchase. Generally, this decision is made readily and takes a short amount of time. The biggest decision point may be the choice of whether to pay a provider directly or through a third-party vendor or supplier.

Complex Resources

These resources tend to require more time during upfront evaluation as well as for purchase negotiations. This is where a checklist is extremely useful and provides the insurance that all the needs expressed by your community are being met by making the purchase. As noted above, this may require a formal tender or RFP process in order to arrive at a decision to purchase.

If this is the case, there may be a cooling off period after the decision. For a deal where a formal procedure is used, the decision to select a provider will need to be well-documented—this is where documentation is essential for the business office or administrative team.

Open Access

Because people can add OA material readily to the collection at any time, the biggest considerations will concern the longevity of the publication platform and tracking for sustainability. There may also be future reasons to stop maintaining or preserving access to OA content that is no longer of interest to local end users. However, for some hybrid packages or APC funding accounts, a deposit account may need to be set up. First, make sure the local budget can cover these costs within a twenty-four-month time span because there is often a delay in publishing articles. This means ensuring that any unspent money in deposit accounts rolls over into the next fiscal year's deposit account or is returned to the local institution as a credit. Otherwise, the publisher may choose to provide credit on subscriptions that are not desirable.

NOTES

1. Publishers Communication Group. (2017). Library budget predictions for 2017. www.pcgplus.com/wp-content/uploads/2017/05/Library-Budget-Predictions-for -2017-public.pdf.

2. SPARC. (2018). Coalition of Open Access Policy Institutions (COAPI). http:// sparcopen.org/coapi/.

3. Machovec, George. (2015). Consortial e-resource licensing: Current trends and issues. *Journal of Library Administration 55*(1): 69–78. https://doi.org/10.1080/019 30826.2014.985900.

4. Morris, Sara E., & Currie, Lea H. (2016). To stream or not to stream? *New Library World 117*(7/8): 485–498. https://doi.org/10.1108/NLW-03-2016-0021.

5. Broadhurst, Dominic. (2017). The direct library supply of individual textbooks to students: Examining the value proposition. *Information and learning science 118*(11/12): 629–641. https://doi.org/10.1108/ILS-07-2017-0072.

6. Stone, Graham. (2009). Resource discovery. In *Digital information: Order or anarchy?* (London: Facet), 133–164. http://eprints.hud.ac.uk/5882/.

7. Laine, Christine, & Winker, Margaret A. (2017). Identifying predatory or pseudo-journals. www.wame.org/identifying-predatory-or-pseudo-journals.

8. DOAJ. (2018). About DOAJ (Directory of Open Access Journals). https://doaj.org/ about.

9. DOAJ. (2015). DOAJ Seal is now live on the site. https://blog.doaj.org/2015/06/ 11/doaj-seal-is-now-live-on-the-site/.

10. ISSN. (2018). Directory of open access scholarly resources. http://road.issn.org/.

11. DOAB. (n.d.). Directory of open access books. https://www.doabooks.org/.

12. OAPEN. (n.d.). Welcome to OAPEN. www.oapen.org/home.

13. OASPA. (2018). Open Access Scholarly Publishers Association. http://oaspa.org/.

14. COPE. (2018). Committee on Publication Ethics. http://publicationethics.org/.

15. Jisc/Open University. About CORE. https://core.ac.uk/about.

16. Rele, Shilpa, Kennedy, Marie, & Blas, Nataly. (2017). Journal evaluation tool. *LMU Librarian Publications & Presentations 40*. http://digitalcommons.lmu.edu/ librarian_pubs/40.

17. Nobes, Andy. (2018). Journal publishers and platforms outside USA, Europe and Australia. https://docs.google.com/document/d/1ilW5ggwq4G5po_uCMFa Bt3exFnrI5oDvf-5UGuHhXGg/edit#.

18. University of California Libraries. (2016). UC Libraries STAR Team Transformative Scholarly Communication Initiatives Review Process. https://libraries.universityof california.edu/groups/files/sclg/star/docs/STAR%20Team%20review%20process %20flow%20chart.pdf.

19. University of California Libraries. (2018). Master Evaluation Criteria Workbook. https://libraries.universityofcalifornia.edu/groups/files/sclg/star/docs/STAR _EvaluationCriteriaWorkbook_20161121_Blank.pdf.

20. Horava, Tony, & Ward, Monica. (2016). Library consortia and article processing charges: An international survey. *Serials Review 42*(4): 280–292. https://doi.org/10 .1080/00987913.2016.1237928.

21. ESAC. (2019). Transformative agreements. https://esac-initiative.org/about/ transformative-agreements/.

22. England, Lenore, Foge, Melissa, Harding, Julie, & Miller, Stephen. (2017). ERM ideas & innovations. *Journal of Electronic Resources Librarianship 29*(2): 110–116. https://doi.org/10.1080/1941126X.2017.1304767.

23. OCLC. (n.d.). WorldShare collection evaluation. https://www.oclc.org/collection -evaluation.en.html.

24. Center for Research Libraries. (2018). EDesiderata. https://edesiderata.crl.edu/.

25. Belvadi, Melissa. (2015). Do-it-yourself title overlap comparisons, Proceedings of the Charleston Library Conference. (2015). http://dx.doi.org/10.5703/ 1288284316261.

26. Ex-Libris. (2018). Working with overlap and collection analysis. https://knowledge .exlibrisgroup.com/Alma/Product_Documentation/010Alma_Online_Help_ (English)/040Resource_Management/070Advanced_Tools/010Overlap_Analysis.

27. Colorado Alliance of Research Libraries. (n.d.). GoldRush. https://www.coalliance .org/software/gold-rush.

28. *The Charleston Advisor.* (2018). www.charlestonco.com/.

29. Bhatt, Anjana H. (2015). E-trials in academic libraries: 101 and beyond. *Journal of Electronic Resources Librarianship 27*(2): 121–127. https://doi.org/10.1080/19411 26X.2015.1029424.

30. Open Library of Humanities. (n.d.). https://www.openlibhums.org/.

31. Knowledge Unlatched. (n.d.). www.knowledgeunlatched.org/.

32. Reveal Digital. www.revealdigital.com/.

3

Purchasing and Licensing

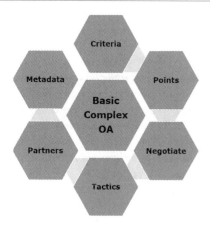

Introduction

This chapter builds on the previous chapter and highlights practices for the procurement and licensing of content. After selection is made, the license negotiation and procurement process for new resources begins in earnest. If the added material is open access (OA), it may be important to establish the relationship between the OA resource and related purchased material. For OA resources added to local collections and repositories, noting the Creative Commons license, which designates the use and reuse of the material, is a significant factor to consider in order to allow seamless implementation and use. Another important aspect that occurs at this stage is the recording of purchasing and licensing decisions that may impact the implementation and use of the content. This section identifies common contract negotiation points and offers suggestions on how these licensing terms can be negotiated with providers to provide favorable outcomes to librarians.

During the selection process, the checklist or criteria created help to provide structure for the acquisitions process. For instance, if in the selection process the decision is made to buy an e-book collection using an evidence-based plan, as opposed to an outright purchase or demand driven purchase, this selection criteria dictates how the acquisition process proceeds. For basic resources, the purchasing plan tends to be a straightforward endeavor of working with a third-party agent or vendor or directly with a known or established publisher. In some cases, the purchase will be for perpetual access to a historical collection, a single data set, or online journal backfiles. In other cases, when payments end, access to the content that was created or released during the time you paid (and sometimes prior content as well) will still be accessible, but new content may not be. Access to this content is referred to as post-cancellation access (PCA) or post-cancellation entitlements.[1] The impact of PCA will be discussed further in chapter 7. In other cases, after paying a one-time fee you will have continuous access to the resource, which is referred to as perpetual access—but often only for as long as you are paying annual maintenance fees.

Electronic resource licenses have two main sections. The first section outlines the access and content provision the provider makes available to the licensee and the second outlines the business terms for purchasing the access.[2] There may be a third section or addenda portions that outline the details of the content licensed and further service provision. In most cases, providers are willing to negotiate parts of the terms they provide regarding levels of access and use. There are also clauses in licenses regarding the amount of access to content that can be changed, removed, or added in a given licensing period and this section of the agreement needs close attention. Other concerns that may arise are the access limits imposed with a given institution. These limits can be restrictive in regard to who may access content or from where the access may occur. The general rule of thumb is to try to obtain the broadest reach of access to the broadest constituency. The business terms given can also be general in nature or may be very specific about how the payment process occurs. The licensing business terms may or may not be in agreement with local accounting and purchasing practices. Determining this may require review by members of your organization outside of the library.

According to Geschuhn and Stone, "Many new big deal agreements between research institutions and scientific publishers are now being negotiated as 'offset agreements.' Besides access rights to the publisher's content, these agreements entitle authors (usually corresponding) affiliated with the research institution to make their articles available as an open access (OA) publication. Offset agreements attempt to link article publishing charges (APCs) with subscription charges, looking to increase one while the other reduces. Some such agreements reduce the APC charge, some allow unlimited OA publishing for a capped amount and others provide a refund or publishing credit."[3]

The purchase of content that includes open access provision or credits is often complex. Micropayment processing schemes help with OA support. Memberships or annual support drives can generate some of the support for open access provision, but not all of it. In an environment where each payment for content must be justified to the larger academic or library structure, determining the mechanisms through which open access purchasing occurs is vital. Finally, in some cases you may need to purchase locally created course content in order to maintain content from faculty who are moving to another institution. You may have to negotiate agreements about how locally created content may continue to be used locally from faculty no longer employed at that institution.

1. Establishing Negotiation Criteria

The best place to begin is with the selection criteria which determines the reasons for a request as well as how well content fits into current content platforms in use. These criteria include aspects of the local collection development policies or principles. When considering a purchase, the first step will be to compare the selection criteria against both the content desired and the business terms presented by the content provider to determine compatibility. Although content may be of value and great interest to local users, if the business terms are not in line with your institutional business protocols, the purchase of content can become harder or impossible to achieve.

It is important to be clear about what the "red lines" or deal breakers are and what can be negotiated to a greater or lesser extent. The best practice is to establish these terms locally prior to beginning the negotiation practice. It is also helpful to look at licensing agreements in a more discrete and granular level to fully understand what is being agreed to and where you can be more or less flexible depending on the needs of your local environment.[4]

There are numerous examples of model licenses available to consider or adopt to a local educational environment. Taylor and Beh undertook a valuable evaluation of model license agreements in 2014 that described some of the better-known model licenses at the time.[5] The article notes there are current scholarly information concerns that may not be fully represented in current agreements. Other notable licenses are:

- California Digital Library[6]
- Canadian Research Knowledge Network/Reseau canadien de documentation pour la reserche[7]
- Center for Research Libraries[8]
- International Coalition of Library Consortia EKUAL (National Academic License for Electronic Resources)[9]
- IFLA Licensing Principles[10]
- Jisc Model Licences[11]
- Northeastern Research Libraries[12]

In some circumstances, institutions may want to make their deal breakers or their model licenses public in order for content providers to readily customize the agreement. The University of North Texas Libraries provide a good example of a public document to share with vendors of library collections.[13] More recently, the University of Washington Libraries took their Licensing Principles and Expectations for Vendors to the faculty senate for full faculty approval before enacting.[14, 15]

Lastly, the University of California's Scholarly Communications Office has published a negotiations toolkit for North American libraries to help with transforming standard subscription deal agreements to more open purchasing models.[16] Toolkits such as these are invaluable in reaching greater transparency on subscription deals and to change publishing models to be more in line with the current demands of academia. The toolkit provides an overview of transformative agreements and also provides negotiation points that can be used to restructure current agreements as well as transform them into read and publish deals.

Basic Resources

Not all electronic resources require a license for the content, so the negotiation will focus primarily on the purchasing terms. It may be necessary to create some sort of order for your purchase in your Integrated Library System (ILS) or purchasing management system in addition to posting the invoice details for payment. If no contract for content is presented, the first step is to ask if the provider will accept the Shared Electronic Resource Understanding (SERU) guidelines in place of a license agreement.[17] The SERU guidelines spell out how the purchase takes place; however, you will need to edit it to reflect the common business practices of your institution. Some institutions prefer a dual-signed document and the SERU format can be adapted to meet this requirement to create a very basic license.[18]

When you negotiate a contract with a provider for content or service, it is best to create a model record or checklist of acceptable terms to use as a starting point. In its most simple form, the checklist would include the following:

1. Parties involved with the payment transaction
2. The term of the payment for access and content (e.g., a year, two years, in perpetuity)
3. The amount of the purchase
4. Any required business terms by your institution's accounting office
5. Dual signatures and date of signatures

Complex Resources

In complex agreements, such as large purchase on-demand acquisitions (PDA)/demand driven acquisition (DDA) or evidence-based purchasing or acquisition (EBP/EBA) programs, complete annual e-book collections, multiple resources from the same provider, big deals for journals, resource discovery systems, streaming media, or scholarly portals, your institution may have an existing structure for procurement. Internal procurement guidelines may be available and procurement services or centralized fiscal services will lead the process. Generally, these guidelines provide the roadmap through the procedure on a step-by-step basis.

With agreements over a certain threshold, such as those over the lifetime of the deal (e.g., the total subscription costs over a given number years), you may be required to follow specific procurement laws. For example, in the European Union you would be required to issue a tender or RFP (request for purchase) in the United States for public institutions.[19] For private and smaller institutions, your financial offices may have a set dollar amount over which a tender or RFP is needed.

In addition, your state, regional, or national library consortia may have already agreed to a license for a resource you wish to acquire. You may find the license already covers the negotiation criteria agreed to at the consortia level. If this is the case, check whether you can join an agreement part way through the contract. Even if this is not permitted, it may be possible to adopt the same clauses and contract and opt in at the next available date. For example, at the next renegotiation of the deal by the consortia.

Open Access

OA material is supported in a couple of ways through licensing criteria. For OA content, there are two licensing models to consider. The first is an agreement with a commercial scholarly content provider regarding APCs and the incorporation of these models either as a cost-break or overall price structure with a subscription purchasing model. The second consideration is the model author/publisher agreement for digital scholarship and how to work with faculty on their publishing agreements.

When working on an offsetting negotiation there should be a transition to full open access. The agreement should reduce or do away with the cost paid for APCs in regard to the subscriptions held by an institution or subscription costs should decrease by the amount to be paid in APCs over a given time period. This becomes incredibly complex in that content published by a given content provider lags a year behind what is paid upfront as a subscription cost. In many cases, hybrid APCs for articles published in one year are offset against institutions' expenditures on subscription and license fees in the following year.[20] However, some publishers prefer to give the cost break on the APC charge by having faculty use a specialized code when they submit their articles for publication. In other cases, a voucher, token, or APC credit provision occurs based on the overall subscription spend by an institution. These offsetting agreements may be set at a consortia level or negotiated at the local level.

When adding OA content to local collections or repositories, assigning a copyright statement allows authors to determine the level of access to their content. Most academic institutions use Creative Commons licenses.[21] These copyright statements designate the owner of the content and dictate attribution rights but can also restrict the reuse of the content by others.

2. Common Points of Negotiation in License Agreements

This section lists our top negotiation points or deal breakers for libraries when licensing electronic resources. For any given library, these may or may not be applicable, so best practice would be to create a local version of these points to use in negotiation. These deal breakers illustrate topic areas that many librarians consider when developing a local model license or checklist. Table 3.1 gives a summary of the deal breakers.

Cost (Relative to Other Options, Available Budget, etc.)

When working out payment terms, the primary negotiation point is the price to be paid. If you will be doing a large volume of business with a vendor or have done so previously, do not be afraid to ask for discounts. If your expenditure will be in the ballpark of a five to six figure sum, then a discount is likely to be available. Always try to negotiate a 5 to 10 percent cost break at the very least. Always remember that there is no such thing as list price!

Determination of cost is often linked to potential usage. Find out if the initial purchase option can be based on the number of users or seats or if a site license is the only purchase option. Because a resource can sometimes take up to two years to become embedded in the institution, start with a lower user base prior and upgrade to a site license as demand or use indicates. Make sure you include the possible step-up in cost in future budget forecasts. You do not want a nasty surprise when the subscription costs go up a few years down the line when you move to a larger usage level or unlimited users. If you are starting at a lower use level but expect to step up to higher simultaneous usage or site licensing, find out if you can step back down to lower usage levels if use

TABLE 3.1

Negotiation Deal Breakers

	DEAL BREAKERS		
Negotiation Point	**Extremely important**	**Somewhat Important**	**Not Important**
Cost	X		
Technical Access	X		
Site Definition	X		
User Definition	X		
Accessibility Requirements	X		
Usage Measurement		X	
Interaction with Discovery System			X
Indemnification Clauses	X		
Privacy Clauses	X		
Exigency Clauses	X		
Venue of Agreement	X		
Perpetual Access Rights/ Preservation	X		
Text and Data Mining			X

drops off. Sometimes, providers only allow for increasing user levels and do not allow the reverse to happen. You may find that a lower user base is sufficient to supply the access needed. If purchasing an archive or annual e-book collections, ask for a waiver or prepayment option for ongoing access fees with the initial purchase.

Cost is dependent upon the purchasing model used. Will this order be a subscription or an outright purchase of content such as an archive, data set, or set of e-books with or without maintenance fees? Are you testing the viability of the content via a DDA/EBP model of content, or are you choosing a multi-year contract for content? All of these factors determine the final price.

It is worthwhile to evaluate and understand the subject or overlap with existing available content. Using the decision tools noted in the previous chapter will assist in identifying the overlap between resources. This can lead to a negotiation point by using overlap analysis to discover if content is readily available. For full-text database agreements there is a fair amount of overlap between products with similar content bases from the same vendor or provider. If there is a 30 percent overlap, ask for a 30 percent discount to avoid paying for the same content twice.

If the content or service is intended for a niche or small group of people, then negotiate for the lowest level of end users possible or base pricing on the intended user base from a dedicated department or area. For example, a specialist chemistry resource should align with the use anticipated from that user community. The same is true for many art-related resources. It is unlikely that large swaths of a given campus will be utilizing specialized resources and, as stated above, it is always best to start at the lowest level and build up from there through usage tracking. Determining the demand of a resource up front helps to define the user-level requirements. For example, graduate students and post-degree students use more complex and niche resources. Although some resources cross over to higher-level undergraduate programs, there are many others that do not.

Price Cap Allowances for Ongoing Purchases

The general rule of thumb is to negotiate for annual price increases of no more than half of the current inflation rate. EBSCO produces an annual set of price predictions that is a useful guide to the market.[22] For example, in September 2018, EBSCO predicted that publishers' prices could increase 5 to 6 percent with additional increases depending on the currency of the institution and the publisher. Most big deal subscription packages are negotiated down to 2 to 5 percent of the subscription cost, especially if the negotiation is for a multi-year agreement. Often a provider or vendor will use a lower price cap as a negotiation technique to entice librarians to purchase multi-year deals. When agreeing to a multi-year subscription, be sure to include an exit clause in case the institution experiences financial hardship. An example would be a 1+1+1 agreement instead of a three-year agreement.

Technical Access

In today's academic institutions, students and faculty may or may not be located within a single site or even on a particular campus (or even in a particular country). With the dramatic growth in online learning, many students and faculty are now both learning and teaching far from the parent or main degree-granting institution. At many institutions in the United States and Europe, the standard access protocol used for off-campus access to resources are proxies. Proxies can be set up via Shibboleth or EZProxy.[23,24] There is currently a movement underway in the publishing and vendor community to switch access authentication to Rights Access 21 (Rights Access for the 21st Century), known as RA21.[25] This protocol would work through a registration process similar to the way circulation management currently works via an ILS platform. It is likely that providers will begin to license for RA21 in the near future. You will need to determine if your institution will be willing to utilize this protocol for access. For some niche or specialized resources, access provision is via username and password, so you will need to develop a way to handle access to these resources. Finally, for some extremely esoteric proprietary content platforms, a dedicated terminal will be necessary. When signing an agreement for access to content, make sure the access method employed will work in the way the end users expect. This is discussed further in chapter 4.

Site

The license definition of "site" can result in technical access issues if that definition does not meet local need. When negotiating for a site license it is imperative to ensure that the local site is defined accurately. With the development of online learning courses and programs, students and faculty are not always limited to a specific geographical area. Students and faculty can literally be all around the globe but will still require access to the content purchased locally. Collaborations with campus information technology (IT) offices help to insure content can be utilized in virtual learning environments (VLEs) and learning management systems (LMSs). It may be useful to have representatives from campus IT review agreements for compatibility with campus-level definitions of "site."

Authorized User Definition

The definition of who is an authorized user of licensed resources is also critical. It is best to define authorized users as any persons "affiliated" with the local institution. This language will generally cover adjunct faculty members, students who may be taking classes at multiple campuses within a geographic region, visiting faculty members, cooperative education programs, and researchers hired to work on specific local research initiatives. It is always better to be more expansive with the user definition when possible.

Authorized user definitions should also include on-site visitors and users of the site. Typical language used in agreements refers to "walk-in users" or "walk-in usage" rights. This allows visitors to your site to have local access rights to the same content as students, faculty, and staff. There are communities that are adjacent to your parent institution such as joint-appointment faculty, dual-enrollment students, and research start-ups. Publishers and providers consider these communities as auxiliary to current students, faculty, and staff. When reviewing the authorized user community, be sure to identify or include language that will cover research affiliates. This can get a bit problematic if your institution is collaborating directly with private industries on research projects.

Students who are jointly enrolled in multiple campuses can prove challenging in relationship to the user definition. Another category of patron that can cause problems are visiting scholars of faculty from other institutions. Again, using the term "affiliated" generally will cover these users but you may find you have to pay more for students in joint-enrollment programs to have access to needed resources.

Accessibility for Those with Disabilities

Access to resources is a human right and at institutions of higher education this is often governed by law. Resources licensed by libraries should be compatible with the Web Content Accessibility Guidelines 2.0.[26] In the United States, the Voluntary Product Accessibility Template (VPAT) provides a vendor-created overview of how its site supports compliance with federal accessibility guidelines. The VPAT Repository contains a collection of VPATs generated by library vendors.[27] These are not legal documents and they do not guarantee the level of accessibility that a vendor will provide. However, they offer a useful view into the level of attention a vendor has paid to accessibility issues. Willis and O'Reilly offer a useful overview of VPATs and their value among library vendors.[28] Local governments, state governments, and even individual campuses may also have pre-determined VPATs they expect resources to meet. In the United Kingdom, Jisc provides a guide to getting started with accessibility and inclusion, which is a useful starting point.[29] Try to use the adopted guidelines but also be specific to your institution.

Your institution will most likely have an accessibility officer or campus center. Get to know them and include them in your licensing discussions in order to write a clause into your license with the expectation of the accessibility level. If there is not a current clause in the license agreement covering mobile access, you may consider adding one to cover this type of use by your end users.

Usage Measurement

All purchased resources undergo evaluation for use. COUNTER compliant usage data is the standard for obtaining and recording regularly usage of electronic resources. COUNTER is discussed in chapter 6. However, an important point to note is that a new version, COUNTER Release 5, was set to become standard from January 2019 with content providers fully compliant by January 2020.[30]

In cases where COUNTER statistics are not available, then the ability to measure use through web or system analytics is recommended. If the agreement is silent on providing any sort of evaluation mechanism, again, this is an area to develop local specifications.

It is also important to see what the license agreement says in regard to collecting and using data from your end users. You will want to make sure that data collected from your end users does not violate their privacy rights. This is another place where campus information technology (IT) offices may be good collaborators in both defining what the end-user rights are and what can and cannot be agreed to in a license. One way to develop this language is to utilize the campus policy on end user privacy and noting any national or state laws to that affect.

Interaction with Discovery Layers

Prior to the advent of discovery systems and layers, some producers created MARC record sets that were sold separately or alongside content platforms. Many of the license agreements for MARC records restricted the use to single catalog systems or to a single institution. These agreements may need to be revisited and renegotiated especially if an institution or organization partici-pates in a consortia catalog with a discovery tool. For future resource records, especially those that may be in XML format, the ability to use this metadata in the broadest way possible is the preference. If you can obtain a commitment from the provider in the agreement to supply KBART files, then you will be able to manage your content entitlements more readily.

Resources that cannot be added to federated or harvested search mech-anisms are effectively invisible to today's user, who expects a just-in-time approach to resource discovery. This ability to provide access and connectivity to other resources using a third-party link resolver at the article level, chapter level, or dataset level, and not just at the title level is tantamount to obtaining optimal usage of resources. Try to work in language that allows for the great-est share-ability of descriptive metadata for all resources.

Indemnification Clauses

Indemnification should be mutual to both parties and not favor one or the other. In addition, the indemnification should extend not just to the insti-tution or organization but all to of the authorized users. There should be no other clause in the agreement that overrides the mutual indemnification clause.

Privacy Clauses

It is worth including a privacy clause stating that any information gathered by individual account creation from authorized users will not be sold, offered to third parties, or otherwise reused without explicit agreement by the autho-rized user. Asking for a provider to share how they plan to use information gathered from individual accounts, especially in the contract, is worthwhile. Understanding what risks end users are taking with creating individual accounts on commercial platforms is an increasing area of concern for librarians and having this in a formal written document allows you to best understand what risks are at stake.

Exigency Clauses

The incorporation of a loss of funding clause is important for all institutions in the twenty-first century. Funding for higher education is reliant upon many factors outside of a given institution and the need to cancel resources due to loss of supportive funding is a very real possibility. This clause is significantly important with multi-year agreements and consortia agreements. If multiple institutions are subscribing to resources together, a clause stating the other institutions will not be liable for picking up costs from the cancellation by a single institution should be included but rather the overall cost of the package will be renegotiated at this point.

Venue of the Agreement

When looking at the contract details check to see which country's law the contract uses for governing law (e.g., U.S. law or U.K. law). Always negotiate to get this altered to your own country's law and if needed in North America, to province or state venue law. Most state institutions are required to change contract language to meet state or location requirements. Vendors that will not agree to change language to another state or location may agree to strike the location information completely.

Confidentiality, or Nondisclosure of Agreement, Information

Many providers, especially those more accustomed to the corporate market, will initially demand that pricing information not be shared with others. Restrictive disclosure clauses regarding price and details of the agreement are items many librarians try to strike or re-write in order to meet open record laws of a greater body such as a state, province, or nation. More than ever, there is a greater call for transparency with business practices of commercial scholarly publishers. It is important for everyone to argue for the right to share both cost information and licensing details. Some providers in the library market are more comfortable with customers having the right to share this information if they so choose. If your library has a policy that forbids signing nondisclosure agreements (e.g., Cornell University Library's policy; see also the University of Alberta's modification and implementation of this policy), the majority of vendors will agree to strike these sections).[31,32]

Perpetual Access and Preservation

The ability to maintain perpetual access to content can be tricky because journal content shifts so readily from one provider to another that perpetual access is sometimes not honored by the content purchaser. In regard to e-books, perpetual access is still being worked out by most providers, especially as many book suppliers do not own the perpetual rights to the content. This clause may be omitted if the demand for content outweighs the desire to maintain access in perpetuity. Ask the provider to participate in an archiving scheme such as LOCKSS, CLOCKSS, or Portico (see chapter 7). Because local authors should be able to load articles into your digital repository as a way to maintain a scholarly record of local content creation, use the SHERPA RoMEO service to check publisher copyright policies and self-archiving.[33] In addition, local authors should retain the right to reuse any content as designated in their copyright agreements with the same content provider. The open access license pioneered by Harvard University enables Harvard faculty and staff to do just this.[34] Harvard also provides model policy language that others can adopt. This has also been championed in the United Kingdom by the U.K. Scholarly Communications Licence and Model Policy (UK-SCL).[35]

Text and Data Mining (TDM)

Research institutions should request the ability for authorized users to perform TDM of content for both research and teaching and learning purposes. When negotiating this access, it is best practice to define these uses within the educational context. Provision of text and data mining should not require additional payment or fees by an institution.

In the United Kingdom, the text and data mining copyright exception applies, which "permits any published and unpublished in-copyright works to be copied for the purpose of text mining for non-commercial research. This includes sound, film and video, artistic works, tables, and databases, as well as data and text, as long as the researcher has lawful access."[36] Often this clause will have to be negotiated with publishers in order to prevent the publisher from blocking use (see chapter 5).

3. License Review and Signature

Each institution has a different mechanism for license review. In some cases, the review occurs within the library by librarians trained in contract review or by administrative librarians. Either can be the signatory or signing authority for the agreement. Numerous academic librarians hold law degrees and participate in reviewing resource agreements and leading copyright work on behalf

FIGURE 3.1
Example License Agreement Signature Relationship

of the library. In other institutions, contracts may need review by the business or contracts office and the signatory authority resides within these offices. For some US academic libraries, resource contracts are reviewed also by the Offices of Information Technology (IT). In general, the technology office's interest is in reviewing resource agreements for security and privacy risks. In order to fully understand a local campus review of resource contracts, it is helpful to create a checklist and/or workflow document outlining who must see an agreement and sign off on it (see figure 3.1).

Basic Resources

Negotiation for basic resources tends to move rapidly. The review and signature of these agreements should also go quickly. In cases where the license is an addendum to a contract already on file, include a copy of the main agreement when the workflow for review and signature begins. Another way to improve the efficiency of this process is to create a cover sheet or profile for the purchase that lists other resources provided by the same platform or provider. When it is a new platform and/or provider for the purchase, ensure that the contract offices or purchasing offices have fully vetted and approved the provider prior to the agreement showing up. This may require the provider to fill out additional forms for your purchasing or contracts office.

Complex Resources

With complex resources, especially when an RFP or tender is used, there will be a significant amount of paperwork included with the agreement. Again, it is helpful to create a cover sheet or summary page outlining the steps involved with the purchase or license agreement. An example can be seen in figure 3.2. For complex purchases and those with significant costs, the contracts office or purchasing office is likely to require extensive documentation and to thoroughly evaluate both the license and the purchasing terms. The review may

Documentation Checklist		Document Included	Document Needed	lIncludes
1	Evaluation of Providers	✕		• Overall provider scorecard • Individual proposals received • Criteria for evaluation
2	Full Product Description		✓	• Description of Needed Resource(s) • End users served by product • Feedback received from end users
3	License Agreement	✕		• Full contract • Addendums • Negotiation Emails

FIGURE 3.2
Checklist for Tender or RFP

require multiple members of your campus financial group to sign off or agree to the signature of the agreement. For this reason, the review will take longer as it requires more involvement by other members of campus.

Open Access

With the exception of offsetting or read and publish contracts, most OA contracts are between the author and a publisher. In many cases, library staff do not see these agreements and the signing authority is the author of the work. For librarians in Europe, it may be necessary to check the agreements against funder requirements to insure no embargoes are added when a funder designates immediate OA publication or if an embargo period extends beyond what a funder designates. In many countries including the United States, most APC support occurs with fully open access journals (as opposed to hybrid journals) and provided when grant funds are not available or cannot be used to cover the publication costs. Therefore, checking author agreements against fund mandates is not generally part of a librarian's role. In the United States, the best practice is to hold workshops and short clinics for faculty on how best to make their works open and most available for reuse by others.[37]

4. Negotiating and Renegotiating Contracts

At the point of receiving a license agreement for content, the first step is to focus on the local deal breakers or guidelines. Checking the content definition given in the agreement against the order placed is the next step. It is best to keep negotiation matter-of-fact and straightforward by designating a main negotiator at the local institution. This person should be trusted to incorporate all of the main points the local team or library have agreed upon regarding purchasing. The negotiation or renegotiation takes on different aspects depending on the type of resource purchased.

Basic Resources

For basic resources, the negotiation will take a few hours to a few days at most. In many cases, there are multiple agreements with the same provider, and the criteria check just insures that the contract terms are the same as any other agreement with the same provider on hand. There may be a bit of back and forth over the pricing and an attempt to negotiate a preferential annual price increase. Basic resources can be single titles or single platforms of content or can be subject collections or multiple resources from the same provider under the same agreement. In some cases, a content provider may have a signed agreement on file from the local institution and only ask for an addendum to that agreement for a new collection or new product. This negotiation is likely to take place via email and concluded fairly quickly between you and the salesperson or license coordinator for the content provider.

Complex Resources

Negotiation always takes longer with more complex deals. The complexity may arise due to the purchasing model, the need to set up an evidence-based purchasing plan or demand driven purchasing model, and the orchestration details for this purchasing model. If these are incorporated into the agreement, they can be outlined in the business terms section or in appendices and will require scrutiny. The negotiation may be complex because a decision has been made to increase, or more than likely decrease, the amount of content purchased. Technical access is also a point upon which there can be quite a bit of back and forth in reaching the level of access that works best for the local environment. For more complex resources, the negotiation is likely to take between one to three months to reach full agreement by both parties. Consortia negotiations for big deals can sometimes even go into the next calendar year, which means that a one-year extension to the existing agreement is agreed upon as an interim while negotiations continue.

One major complex issue is content changes within package deals either in scope of content provided or with content shifting from one provider to another. Many librarians find it is useful to add a couple of statements during contract negotiation regarding content transfer between publishers/providers. These clauses almost always include what is considered a reasonable time frame for notification regarding content transfer as well as referencing the standards used when content does transfer from one resource to another such as journal packages. However, sometimes a significant shift in content happens with an e-book or streaming media provider. A reasonable time frame for content transfer notifications would be within sixty days of transfer. If significant content is lost in any given year or quarter, then the purchasing institution should have the right to cancel or receive a discounted price upon this notification.

Referring to the Transfer Code of Practice for instances when content moves from one provider to another is encouraged.[38] In particular, backfile content should reside either with the original provider or move to the new publisher or provider. With the transfer of content, access to back volumes or issues can be lost and may be hard to restore due to the new publisher's or provider's lack of payment information.

Data sets are often the most complex resources to license and purchase. With data sets, there may be requirements concerning secure server space in order for the data to be used and analyzed by a limited number of authorized users. Many providers of economic data and financial data purge content from time to time, so paying close attention to the preservation capabilities of this information is important. There is not a consistent business model for academic purchasing of data, so this procurement will require creative approaches to meet the needs of a local environment.[39]

Open Access

As noted above, offsetting is often negotiated in conjunction with a subscription package deal. Determining how to negotiate an offsetting contract depends on whether an institution is negotiating on its own or through a consortium. When multiple libraries are involved, the overall cost breaks are likely to be more significant.

Offsetting agreements are important as one of the consequences of the transition to open access has been the rise of the hybrid journal. Hybrid journals mix traditional subscription with the option for an author to select open access via a fee known as an Article Publishing Charge (APC). The possibility of publishers charging both subscription fees and APCs for the same content was referred to as "double dipping." Publishers were accused of earning revenue from institutional subscriptions and APCs—an accusation that was hotly denied by many publishers at the time. This is where offsetting comes in. First introduced by the Institute of Physics Publishing in 2014, Lawson defines offsetting as "recognizing the total spend that an institution makes . . . the 'total cost of ownership.'"[40,41] This can either be at the local or global level.

Put very simply, offsetting is where the total cost of ownership stays the same as the journal transitions to OA. Therefore, as more OA articles are published via APCs, the subscription costs decrease. This is global offsetting.

Some of the newer agreements allow unlimited OA publishing for a capped amount while others provide a refund or publishing credit. An example of one of the newer forms of offsetting agreement is the Springer Compact, which was piloted between 2016 and 2018 by four national consortia—the Netherlands, Austria, the United Kingdom, and Sweden as well as the Max Planck Digital Library. A number of blog posts are starting to report on the analysis of the first years of these agreements.[42–44]

In his paper on offsetting, Earney lists the offset agreements in place in the United Kingdom with major publishers during 2018: American Chemical Society, Cambridge University Press, De Gruyter, Georg Thieme Verlag, Institute of Physics, Oxford University Press, Royal Society of Chemistry, SAGE Publishing, Springer Nature, Taylor & Francis, and Wiley.[45]

This may seem like progress. However, there is a serious flaw in hybrid journal offsetting schemes that is beginning to be highlighted by both funders and institutions and their consortia, most notably Plan S.[46] Many funders contribute to APC costs for articles where the lead author is publishing the results of funded research. This is to encourage the transition to OA of all research outputs. In many cases, it has been suggested that this transition is not happening fast enough (and if it is happening at all) and that the hybrid journal is just another legacy of the big deal. In his discussion about the challenges and opportunities for offsetting, Earney argues that although there is evidence to say that offsetting agreements are reducing the cost of ownership, the case for offsetting is "clearly far from proven" and that they "have far too easily come to be regarded as business as usual" and even contradictory to the objective of open access.[47-51]

Schimmer, Geschuhn, and Vogler see the hybrid model as an evolutionary step in the transition from a subscription model to a fully OA business model.[52] The next step in the evolution from a pay to read to a pay to publish model is the read and publish model, which Geschuhn and Stone describe as converting "former subscription charges of institutions into a publishing fee, often also supplemented by a reading fee." They go on to urge libraries "to use this transformational phase in order to actively shape the new model according to their needs and to the benefits of researchers" in order to avoid Earney's "business as usual" concern.[53]

In order to address this, the Efficiencies and Standards for Article Charges (ESAC) initiative, hosted by the Max Planck Digital Library, has held a number of workshops that have attracted interest from Europe, North America, and Japan. In 2016, the Joint Understanding of Offsetting was agreed, this introduces the pay as you publish model as a strategic goal.[54] This was followed in 2017 by a workshop that aimed to provide an opportunity for institutions and publishers present to exchange ideas on three topics. After discussion, these became the three principles of the ESAC Recommendations for article workflows and services for offsetting and open access transformation agreements:[55]

1. Author and article identification and verification

2. Funding acknowledgement and metadata

3. Invoicing and reporting

Since their release there has been coordination between ESAC and library consortia in promoting the recommendations. For example, in 2018, Jisc Collections released the first draft of its Requirements for Transformative Open Access (OA) Agreements with the intention of evaluating hybrid agreements against these requirements and making the results publicly available.[56] There is also a very useful case study by the University of Vienna.[57]

It is suggested that libraries and consortia wishing to enter into read and publish agreements use these principles and requirements, which call for greater automation and efficiencies in the workflow. For example, in negotiation with publishers, use them as an addendum to the deal breakers outlined above. Many publishers may not have the processes and workflows in place to meet your recommendations from the outset of an agreement. Therefore, it is also recommended that these principles are revisited at the assessment stage (see chapter 6) along with evidence of the transition to open access.

This part of negotiation will be taken to a new level after the announcement of Plan S (as mentioned in chapter 1). ESAC has developed an OA market watch feature on its website in order to monitor progress and an agreement registry as part of its work on transformative agreements.[58] The agree agreement registry lists the major criteria of consortia agreements from a host of countries and consortia in Europe and the United States.[59]

Libraries may wish to follow suit and consider their commitment to APC spend with publishers that do not support a genuine transition to OA via offsetting or read and publish agreements model (see chapter 6).

On a separate note regarding open access, if faculty members create content locally and own that intellectual property (IP) per the campus IP policy, they can refuse to allow the local campus or its environment to continue to use their work for courses after they leave that campus. A department or campus administration may wish to license or purchase the content from them prior to their departure in order to maintain certain courses. In these cases, you can adapt the SERU agreement to spell out the understanding between the faculty member and the local institution.[60] These agreements consist of:

1. The parties involved (in this case an individual and an institution)
2. The amount of the purchase
3. The timeframe for the purchase to be valid (this is often in perpetuity)
4. The ability for the institution to make needed edits or upgrades to the content to insure its timeliness and that the content can be kept accessible within its learning management system (LMS) or virtual learning environment (VLE)
5. Dual signatory line with dates

Another development with long-form digital scholarship and digital humanities projects has arisen from librarians and scholarly publishers working together to develop a model publishing contract for digital scholarship.[61] The model is primarily for OA books and other long-form digital scholarship. It is adaptable for new forms of scholarship that are emerging from the academy. As Open Educational Resources (OERs) grow in prominence along with other faculty resources used in teaching and learning, this model provides a mechanism to be used when capturing this digital scholarship in a library collection or repository.

5. Working with Other Departments and Areas on Resource Contracts

There are multiple areas both within and beyond a given organization which may need to be consulted about procurement and licenses. At the local institution, the main work will be accomplished with procurement and contract offices. Other times, it will be necessary to work directly with other departments on campus and even some outside of the local environment such as consortia or other libraries in the geographical area. Any time you work with partners outside your institution, the amount of times required to finalize selection and negotiate the contract will increase. For a new contract, it is best to start discussions with the parties involved and allow up to a year for contract negotiation. When working with contract renewals, this time frame can be shortened by three to four months but will still entail extra time to allow for obtaining consensus by everyone involved.

Basic Resources

Basic resources such as stand-alone databases and small journal or e-book packages can be readily ordered and licensed through consortia. Most consortia have a model license agreement they use that encompasses the needs of their members. The buying power of multiple institutions can make the cost of a resource much more affordable by negotiating a lower annual inflation rate for everyone. In many cases, an individual library does not have to sign or agree to a contract at the local level and payment details are orchestrated through the consortia personnel. Renewal information is usually sent out ninety days in advance to allow for renegotiation as member libraries cancel or add on to the purchase.

In some situations, a department on campus can choose to license a resource for a limited group of users. Many times, these requests come from specific laboratories or business departments. For example, resources such as taxation databases are of limited interest to the majority of resource users on campus but will be heavily used by the department teaching taxation. In these cases, library personnel may help with the purchase and negotiation of the products but not necessarily promote or manage the usage of them directly.

The work will be orchestrated among one or two faculty members and the departmental office staff to insure the financial reporting structure is in place and that billing occurs consistently.

Complex Resources

For large journal packages and collections of databases, consortia play a helpful role in negotiating the best cost and access models. The initial orders and renewals will take longer when multiple parties are involved but it is worth the length of time spent to achieve the lower cost structures and the greater access models. Title sharing agreements get very complex in determining what is part of local title entitlements and what access comes from the other members participating in the agreement. Part of the negotiation process occurs internally with the consortia concerning what the title list will be comprised of as well as the negotiation with producer of the content.

With campus departments, complex resources and tools often require specific software compatibility, which must be negotiated and orchestrated through university technology offices. In addition, the technology office often has concerns about the use of certain software or resources with overall technical site security and privacy. It is worthwhile to collaborate with a main contact in your local institution's technology office to help address the office's concerns and issues. Instructional design groups on campus will also need to work directly with library personnel on embedding resources in courseware and providing stable links to content from within courseware platforms. When using IP authentication to access content, developing proxied links for use in courseware is a chore beyond the capability of most faculty and teaching assistants. Communicating how access is made available to these departments and other areas on campus is important and will be discussed further in chapter 4.

Open Access

For libraries supporting APCs, the funding sources can be individual departments, research and sponsored program offices, or other faculty administrative bodies on campus. In these cases, the administration and management of the APC fund must be coordinated among all the parties involved.

With the deposit of electronic theses and dissertations and undergraduate programs producing content that gets into library repositories, librarians will likely work with offices of graduate studies and designated undergraduate program directors. This may require the utilization of a memorandum of understanding between the student authors or a form on which the student signs off on to allow the deposit of material into the repository. These documents are a collaborative effort among all the participating groups. It is worthwhile to have students note their expectations for the preservation and continuation of the hosting of content.

Finally, when working with faculty depositing content into a local repository, whether pre-print resources or other open access content, it is valuable to have a memorandum of understanding outlining the intent for preservation and maintenance of the content. There have been instances where faculty members moving from one institution to another ask to take their deposited scholarship with them. It is helpful to work with faculty either through their departments or through various faculty groups to develop a local practice or agreement that is consistent for all deposited content.

6. Recording Administrative Metadata

The final part of this chapter discusses the recording of all administrative metadata so that it can be readily retrieved for future reference and use. Librarians record this information through various mechanisms. Some librarians choose to create licensing databases, internal web portals, or shared network drives that run outside of current library information systems. For smaller institutions, the information can be recorded in financial management systems. Some larger library information systems allow for the upload and description of the major terms of license agreements. The terms can remain within the staff portal or be displayed publicly to allow end users to fully understand any limitations that exist with a given resource. In the case of repository content, the administrative metadata will include the use of a specific Creative Commons license or internal coding, which indicates the memorandum of understanding agreed to with the deposit of the material.

Regardless of where the metadata is stored for retrieval, it is important to try to be consistent with the administrative metadata captured. Use one of the checklists created for the licensing and procurement process to determine

Purchase Terms	Access Terms	Content Information
• Who to Pay • What to Pay • Term of Payment (Sub/One-Time) • Inflation rate • Evidence based terms	• Who can use resource • Where resource can be used (library/remote/course ware/ILL) • Simultaneous usage • Any access restrictions	• Content description (bib record) • Package title lists • Associated resources • Perpetual access rights

FIGURE 3.3
Administrative Metadata to Capture

which criteria are most likely to be needed in the future. This can include the conditions that align to the deal breakers, the different offices or parties who signed off on an agreement, or all documentation from the license agreement and procurement process. It is also possible to create an administrative metadata template to outline the information to record (see figure 3.3).

Finally, it is essential to communicate where data is stored through an outline or workflow document. Questions will arise about purchase decisions and licenses signed. Making it easy for other library personnel and campus parties to find this information works to everyone's advantage.

Basic Resources

In the case of basic resources, the administrative metadata is likely to be quite simple. It can potentially be recorded readily in the ILS or campus accounting system by recording the resource purchased, the party that paid for the resource, and the amount paid, along with a note as to the license agreement used. Although it is not likely to be substantial information accompanying the purchase of basic resources it is worth recording contact information for troubleshooting access issues, contact information for resolving order or payment problems, and any specific platform or hosting body information. For resources purchased and licensed through a consortium, indicating how to access documentation held by the consortium becomes important.

Complex Resources

With complex resources, the amount of administrative metadata grows. For package purchases, it is important to make note of where title lists of the content are found and any expected changes to the content base whenever possible. When using an evidence-based purchasing plan, recording the final amount spend and the anticipated purchased title base volume. If an agreement is a multi-year license and gives the anticipated inflation rate for each following year, capturing this information in the local accounting system is wise as it helps to project what costs may be from one year to the next. For resources that required a tender or RFP, capture or scan all the pertinent documentation outlining comparison to other the products and resources considered. If there were particular deal breakers that ended up being unsuccessfully negotiated, it is good to note why the choices were made to make exceptions and purchase anyway.

If the purchase of a resource occurs in partnership with other areas of your institution, indicate if there is information held by those departments and who to contact to obtain necessary documentation. Record all information that appears relevant to establishing access and for future management of the content. It is important to recognize that not all future information needs can be anticipated. Therefore, capturing as much information as possible about the purchase decision and the license agreement for the purchase becomes key.

Open Access

Where offsetting agreements are in place, noting what the terms of the offset agreement for the reduction of APCs or the reduction of subscriptions should be easily found within the ILS or campus financial system. The promotion of these terms also occurs through the library website or in direct communications to those who can take advantage of these funds.

For material added to the local institutional repository, noting the type of Creative Commons license used is essential. In addition, any other terms regarding the deposit of materials to the repository should be made clear. When utilizing a memorandum of understanding about deposits, some of this information may be kept on the staff side of the repository and not made public. This includes arranged embargo periods, notation of content that cannot be shared readily, or any withdrawal or "take down" policy in place.

NOTES

1. Jisc Collections. (2016). Post Cancellation Access Co-Design Project. https://www.jisc-collections.ac.uk/KnowledgeBasePlus/Related-Services-and-Projects/jisc-co-design-programme/Post-cancellation-access-co-design-project/.

2. Lipinski, Tomas A. (2013). *Librarian's legal companion for licensing information resources and services* (Chicago: American Library Association).

3. Geschuhn, Kai, & Stone, Graham. (2017). It's the workflows, stupid! What is required to make "offsetting" work for the open access transition. *Insights* 30(3): 103–114. http://doi.org/10.1629/uksg.391.

4. Dygert, Claire, & Van Rennes, Robert. (2015). Building your licensing and negotiation skills toolkit. *Serials Librarian* 68(1–4): 17–25. https://doi.org/10.1080/0361526X.2015.1013384.

5. Taylor, Liane, & Beh, Eugenia. (2014). Model licenses and license templates: Present and future. *Serials Librarian* 66(1–4): 92–95. https://doi.org/10.1080/0361526X.2014.879027.

6. California Digital Library. (2017). CDL model license revised. https://www.cdlib.org/cdlinfo/2017/01/25/cdl-model-license-revised/.

7. Canadian Research Knowledge Network. (2018). Model license. www.crkn-rcdr.ca/en/model-license.

8. Center for Research Libraries. (2018). Model license. http://liblicense.crl.edu/licensing-information/model-license/.

9. International Coalition of Library Consortia, EKUAL (National Academic License for Electronic Resources). http://icolc.net/consortia/251.

10. IFLA. (2001). IFLA licensing principles. https://www.ifla.org/publications/ifla-licensing-principles-2001.

11. Jisc. (2017). Jisc model licences. https://www.jisc-collections.ac.uk/Help-and-information/How-Model-Licences-work/.

12. Northeastern Research Libraries. (2018). NERL model license. http://nerl.org/nerl-documents/nerl-model-license.

13. University of North Texas. (2018). University of North Texas manifesto: Expectations for vendors of library collections. https://digital.library.unt.edu/ark:/67531/metadc1114882/.

14. University of Washington Libraries. (2019) Licensing principles and expectations for vendors. https://www.lib.washington.edu/cas/licensing-principles-and-expectations-for-vendors.

15. University of Washington Libraries. (2019). UW Faculty Senate votes to support UW Libraries bargaining and licensing priorities in scholarly journal subscription negotiations. https://www.lib.washington.edu/about/news/announcements/uw-faculty-senate-votes-to-support-uw-libraries-bargaining-and-licensing-priorities-in-scholarly-journal-subscription-negotiations.

16. University of California, Office of Scholarly Communication. (2019). Negotiating with scholarly publishers: A toolkit from the University of California. https://osc.universityofcalifornia.edu/open-access-at-uc/publisher-negotiations/negotiating-with-scholarly-journal-publishers-a-toolkit/.

17. National Information Standards Organization. (2012). Shared E-Resource Understanding (SERU). https://www.niso.org/standards-committees/seru.

18. Chesler, Adam, & McKee, Anne. (2014). The Shared Electronic Resource Understanding (SERU): Six years and still going strong. *Information Standards Quarterly 26*(4): 20–23. http://dx.doi.org/10.3789/isqv26no4.2014.05.

19. European Union. (2018). Tendering rules and procedures. https://europa.eu/youreurope/business/selling-in-eu/public-contracts/rules-procedures/index_en.htm.

20. Earney, Liam. (2017). Offsetting and its discontents: Challenges and opportunities of open access offsetting agreements. *Insights 30*(1): 11–24. https://doi.org/10.1629/uksg.345.

21. Creative Commons. (2018). https://creativecommons.org/.

22. EBSCO. (n.d.). Serials price projections: 2018. https://www.ebscohost.com/promoMaterials/EBSCO_2018_Serials_Price_Projections.pdf?ga =2.160537469.1759684831.1542711296-677018613.1542711296.

23. Shibboleth. (n.d.). https://www.shibboleth.net/.

24. OCLC. (2018). EZproxy. https://www.oclc.org/en/ezproxy.htm.

25. RA21. (n.d.). https://ra21.org.

26. Web Accessibility Initiatives. (2018). How to meet WCAG 2 (quick reference): A customizable quick reference to Web Content Accessibility Guidelines (WCAG) 2 requirements (success criteria) and techniques. https://www.w3.org/WAI/WCAG20/quickref/.

27. VPAT Repository. (n.d.). https://vpats.wordpress.com/.

28. Willis, Samuel Kent, & O'Reilly, Faye. (2018). Enhancing visibility of vendor accessibility documentation. *Information Technology and Libraries 37*(3). https://doi.org/10.6017/ital.v37i3.10240].

29. Jisc. (2018). Getting started with accessibility and inclusion. https://www.jisc.ac.uk/guides/getting-started-with-accessibility-and-inclusion.

30. COUNTER. (2018). The COUNTER Code of Practice for Release 5. https://www.projectcounter.org/code-of-practice-five-sections/abstract/.

31. Cornell University Library. (2018). Nondisclosure policy. https://www.library.cornell.edu/about/policies/nondisclosure.

32. University of Alberta. (2014). University of Alberta Libraries statement of principle on non-disclosure clauses in licenses. https://www.library.ualberta.ca/about-us/collection/disclosure.

33. Jisc. SHERPA RoMEO. www.sherpa.ac.uk/romeo/index.php.

34. Harvard University. (2018). Open access policy. https://osc.hul.harvard.edu/policies/.

35. U.K. scholarly communications licence and model policy. http://ukscl.ac.uk/.

36. Jisc. (2016). The text and data mining copyright exception: Benefits and implications for U.K. higher education. https://www.jisc.ac.uk/guides/text-and-data-mining-copyright-exception.

37. ACRL. (2018). Scholarly communication toolkit: Take action: Ways librarians can engage in scholarly communication. https://acrl.libguides.com/scholcomm/toolkit/engagementideas.

38. NISO. (2018). Transfer. https://www.niso.org/standards-committees/transfer.

39. Center for Research Libraries. (2017). eDesiderata forum: Licensing big data summary report. https://www.crl.edu/sites/default/files/event_materials/eDesiderata_Forum_Summary_Report_Jan_10_2017.pdf.

40. Geschuhn, Kai, & Stone, Graham. (2017). It's the workflows, stupid! What is required to make "offsetting" work for the open access transition. *Insights 30*(3): 103–114. http://doi.org/10.1629/uksg.391.

41. Lawson, Stuart. (2015). "Total cost of ownership" of scholarly communication: Managing subscription and APC payments together. *Learned Publishing 28*(1): 9–3. https://doi.org/10.1087/20150103.

42. Marques, Mafalda. (2017). Springer Compact agreement: First year evaluation. https://scholarlycommunications.jiscinvolve.org/wp/2017/03/06/compact-agreement-first-year-evaluation/.

43. Kronman, Ulf. (2018). Evaluation of offset agreements—Report 3: Springer Compact. https://www.kb.se/download/18.2705879d169b8ba882a5560/ 1556566760356/Evaluation_of_offset_agreements_SC_Report_3.pdf.

44. Olsson, Lisa. (2018). Evaluation of offset agreements—Report 4: Springer Compact. https://www.kb.se/download/18.2705879d169b8ba882a5561/ 1556566760424/Evaluation_of_offset_agreements_SC_Report_4-20181008.pdf

45. Earney, Liam. (2018). National licence negotiations advancing the open access transition: A view from the U.K. *Insights 31*(11). http://doi.org/10.1629/uksg.412.

46. European Commission. (2018). "Plan S" and "cOAlition S"—Accelerating the transition to full and immediate open access to scientific publications. https:// ec.europa.eu/commission/commissioners/2014-2019/moedas/announcements/ plan-s-and-coalition-s-accelerating-transition-full-and-immediate-open-access -scientific_en.

47. Earney, Liam. (2017). Offsetting and its discontents: Challenges and opportunities of open access offsetting agreements. *Insights 30*(1): 11–24. https://doi.org/ 10.1629/uksg.345.

48. Lawson, Stuart. (2016). *Report on offset agreements: Evaluating current Jisc Collections deals. Year 1—Evaluating 2015 deals* (London: Jisc). https://doi.org/ 10.6084/m9.figshare.3985353.v1.

49. Lawson, Stuart. (2017). *Report on offset agreements: Evaluating current Jisc Collections deals. Year 2—Evaluating 2016 deals* (London: Jisc). https://doi.org/ 10.6084/m9.figshare.5383861.v1.

50. Lawson, Stuart. (2018). *Report on offset agreements: Evaluating current Jisc Collections deals. Year 3—Evaluating 2017 deals* (London: Jisc). http://doi.org/ 10.5281/zenodo.1473588.

51. Lawson, Stuart. (2019). *Evaluating U.K. offset agreements (2015–17)*. (London: Jisc). https://doi.org/10.5281/zenodo.3256642.

52. Schimmer, Ralph, Geschuhn, Kai, & Vogler, Andreas. (2015). *Disrupting the subscription journals' business model for the necessary large-scale transformation to open access* (München: MPDL). https://doi.org/10.17617/1.3.

53. Geschuhn, Kai, & Stone, Graham. (2017). It's the workflows, stupid! What is required to make "offsetting" work for the open access transition. *Insights 30* (3): 103–114. http://doi.org/10.1629/uksg.391.

54. ESAC. (2016). Joint understanding of offsetting. http://esac-initiative.org/wp -content/uploads/2016/05/esac_offsetting_joint_understanding_offsetting.pdf.

55. ESAC. (2017). Customer recommendations for article workflows and services for offsetting/open access transformation agreements [first draft]. http://esac- initiative.org/wp-content/uploads/2017/04/ESAC_workflow _recommendations_1st_draft20march2017.pdf.

56. Jisc. (2018). Requirements for transformative open access agreements: Accelerating the transition to immediate and worldwide open access. https://www. jisc-collections.ac.uk/Transformative-OA-Reqs/.

57. Pinhasi, Rita, Guido Blechl, Brigitte Kromp, and Bernhard Schubert. (2018). The weakest link—Workflows in open access agreements: The experience of the Vienna University Library and recommendations for future negotiations. *Insights 31*(27). http://doi.org/10.1629/uksg.419.

58. ESAC. (2018). OA market watch. http://esac-initiative.org/.

59. ESAC. (2019). Transformative agreements. https://esac-initiative.org/about/transformative-agreements/.

60. National Information Standards Organization. (2012). Shared E-Resource Understanding (SERU). https://www.niso.org/standards-committees/seru.

61. Model publishing contract for digital scholarship. https://www.modelpublishingcontract.org/.

4

Implementation

Introduction

Once the acquisition and licensing of content is completed, implementing access to resources is the next step. The implementation of a given resource requires multiple processes to occur: the administrative configuration for access is set up along with determining the access points utilized, and then the branding and promotion of content occurs. Figuring out how to establish access that works best in a given environment is often a trial-and-error process. Some resources are very easy to add, such as a standard subject database or a single ejournal, a single streaming video file, or e-book title. In many cases for these resources, the administrative configurations are already in place and it is simply the addition of one more resource to the structure in place. However, the challenges faced with complex resources can be quite troublesome and time-consuming.

An important point to note is that there is sometimes no correlation between the acquisition process and the implementation process. What was easy to negotiate and pay for might be nigh on impossible to make accessible. In other cases, sometimes the difficulties in licensing and paying for a product are greater than establishing access to a resource. This could be true with the complex negotiation of offsetting agreements, for example. Although open access (OA) content appears not to be an issue for implementation, there are considerations to be made as to the levels of access provided with open access materials. For instance, if you put all of your electronic theses and dissertations into your local institutional repository, do you also catalog these titles for access through your integrated library system (ILS) or discovery tool? Ultimately, for all resources, the level of implementation or access provided must be determined.

Many resources are available consistently from the same providers on the same platforms. Therefore, implementing new packages or adding content to these platforms or from these providers becomes routine and simple to accomplish, especially after the administrative setup is agreed upon. The amount of time required for this is relatively short and the work is routine. There are also fewer considerations to be made with these implementations because there is usually a set protocol in place for how access to content occurs. The focus of the implementation is only expanding the content availability. The main work with these implementations tends to be around description, promotion, and marketing so that end users realize they now have expanded or enhanced access to content on a particular platform.

The other point to note about implementation is that this work is often an iterative process year after year for both licensed material and open access content. The iteration occurs for a number of reasons. Electronic resources and open access content are not static entities. In the print world, there were only a few changes that occurred with content: title changes, publisher changes, and cessation or discontinuation. In the online environment, there are many more variations. Content moves from one hosting platform to another, vendors redesign their platforms, subscription content becomes open access, open access content becomes subscription-based, security protocols change the uniform resource locator from http to https, and so on. Usually, these changes happen on an annual basis but sometimes the change happens out of a scheduled timing sequence and often there may be little notice or overlap between two platforms. Understanding how the initial implementation took place is important to fully understand future steps. This will be covered in greater detail in chapter 5.

There is also the issue of temporal access to electronic resource content. Again, this is a very different process to print. Print materials are generally seen as resources that will be around for a significant amount of time to be utilized over decades. With electronic resources, use is often more time-dependent, and the content is not always expected to be available in perpetuity. If the terms of access to content on offer to a given organization or institution revolve around pay-per-view or demand driven acquisitions models then the access period of the content may be provided on a limited basis.[1,2] Part of what occurs with implementation is the use of metadata descriptions that allow for the quick removal of content from catalogs and discovery systems when the pay-per-view or demand driven plan ends. The other important part of this implementation is publicizing the temporal nature of the content offered. Otherwise, end users may expect to continually use content made available in this manner only to discover that it is no longer available to them. This issue will also be examined in the context of exiting an agreement in chapters 6 and 7.

The launching of new content and the marketing of electronic resources and open access content is a vital part of implementation.[3] Launching new products and services may require staff training and introduction to both new content and new service models in the overall library environment. The highlighting of significant content additions and removal through library websites is a standard practice for many librarians, but it is important to develop and adhere to an ongoing marketing plan for all resources through many different communication mechanisms.

Electronic resources are not the only thing to change in a library environment. It is important to remember that end users are constantly changing and may not be aware of services and content purchased in previous years. In this way, the marketing of electronic resources becomes a part of the iterative process as well.

In this chapter, we will focus on ways of implementing electronic resources and open access materials. Part of the chapter will serve as an introduction to the technologies and tools used in this process. When looking at how to manage challenging implementations, this exploration covers a variety of strategies for managing the process and minimizing problems. Documenting how a product or service is implemented is important in order to train and allow others to become familiar with the work needed to support access to the content. The chapter will also focus on how to launch and market content both internally to other library workers as well as to the end users of the products.

1. Access

Seamless access is key to the success of any given resource. One of the main jobs of a library worker is to arrange access to content. Making access work can be a major challenge. However, in many cases basic resources are easy to access. The library provides the content provider with a list of an institution's internet protocol (IP) addresses, or a library worker goes to an administration site for the product and adds the IP ranges to its administrative toolkit. Patrons within the IP range are then able to use the resource licensed; this is known as IP authentication. Utilizing a proxy system, along with the completion of the configuration of URLs in this system, allows patrons from both on- and off-campus to access a resource. As long as the correct IP ranges are provided, everything works fine.

Alas, this is not always the case. Some content providers with little or no experience working with libraries may be uncomfortable providing broad access based on IP addresses, or ask for limitations regarding usage through limitations of IP ranges or sites. Sometimes this means that the only offer for access is through the use of Shibboleth or another form of single sign-on mechanism, a username and password, or a set single terminal or desktop.

Basic Resources

In this section, we will review a variety of methods of providing access. Some of these can be described as basic resources, while others are increasingly complex. However, the reader will quickly become aware that elements that might appear basic can become complex very quickly.

On-Campus Access

The most common method for providing access to electronic resources is through IP authentication, but even this relatively simple technology offers challenges. Although IP addresses do not change too often, and most institutions have simple setups, addresses can change and notifying all vendors about these changes can be a Sisyphean task. As an example, it is quite likely that at least some providers still have the IP address for the Arecibo satellite dish installation in Puerto Rico among Cornell University's IP addresses, even though administrative control of Arecibo transferred from Cornell to the University of Central Florida (UCF) in 2011.[4] This is likely not a major problem; UCF probably subscribes to many of the same electronic resources as Cornell, and the passage of time will eventually resolve the remaining discrepancies. But institutions with multiple campuses, or significantly different schools (e.g., medical or dental schools)—particularly in different physical locations from the central campus—may find they have long, complex sets of IP addresses, and require different sets of IPs for different resources, such as when a resource is licensed only for the main campus or only for the medical campus.

Two situations where IP authentication is seen as highly suspect by content providers are:

1. Business incubators in an academic setting that are intended to develop a business or business-oriented service

2. Cooperative student programs where students are spending part of their educational time working directly at for-profit institutions

Tools like RedLink Network and IP Registry offer potential solutions for managing complex IP address setups. These tools highlight different approaches to managing IPs.[5,6]

Requiring users to log in to access resources, even when they are physically present in the library, can lay the groundwork for better access management, better intellectual property control of library-subscribed content, and foster better understanding of usage, but this type of access entails a loss of patron anonymity. Having said that, it does offer a uniform experience to all users.

When used in conjunction with IP authentication, but not necessarily through a proxy server as well, Shibboleth can allow local users to access resources without logging in. The utilization of Shibboleth to manage access to *all* library electronic resources usage offers benefits such as much better usage data.[7] However, this is at the cost of preventing walk-in users from accessing these resources. This would not be acceptable at many public institutions, which are obligated to provide access to local communities. The importance of this issue is very much a local decision. Using a single sign-on (SSO) authentication method such as Shibboleth can be a helpful way of limiting problems associated with unauthorized downloads from pirate sites and by implementing two-factor authentication for all users. However, institutions that aim to provide access to walk-in users must ensure that they will still be able to offer access content to all community users. SSO generally requires that every individual log in to the system, and if walk-in users do not normally have login credentials, they may not be able to access resources. That said, local security protocols may require that all users to be traceable in order to prevent misuse. In the end, authentication of resources is often a fine line between insuring patron privacy and providing the greatest level of access possible.

Some publishers feel that IP authentication is too insecure to access their resources. Instead, the publisher requires the creation of accounts based on the email domain of the institution. This poses several problems. First, it does not allow for walk-in users who do not have email addresses within the email domain. Next, because the provider does not have access to the institution's email database; they cannot confirm the accuracy of an email address, anyone can create a made-up email address that will grant access to the resource. (So, in fact, as long as the provider does not require some form of account confirmation through a link provided by email, walk-in users can create accounts to access resources.) In addition, accounts will remain active after students graduate because the provider cannot determine the status of the individual associated with the email address.[8]

Off-Campus/Remote Access

To support community usage, online learning initiatives, and distance and part-time student use, libraries offer remote access to as many resources as possible. In most cases, this requires two components: contractual access and technological access. We address contractual access issues in chapter 3. However, some providers will simply not allow off-campus access. If this is not a red line for the institution, then that must be respected as part of the signed contract. When registering IPs with these providers, the proxy IP must be removed from the ranges provided.

When off-campus access is allowed, EZProxy is a very common and relatively cost-efficient tool for providing off-campus access.[9] EZProxy changes an off-campus user's IP address to one within the library's IP range in a manner that is allowed and acceptable to publishers. An important activity to consider with EZProxy is a semi-annual or annual review of the resource configurations. Resources move platforms and change their domain and URL structure. An annual or semi-annual evaluation of your EZProxy logs may uncover resource entries that are no longer needed due to cancellation or platform changes or that may be out of date. Through the review process, you may be able to correct access problems before they become widespread.

SINGLE SIGN-ON (SSO)

Although Shibboleth provides a widely known method for establishing single sign-on (SSO) access to resources that has some significant benefits, it also must be handled with care. It generally requires more technical skill to manage than does EZProxy, although EZProxy can become complicated quickly. Hosted solutions for implementing Shibboleth through OpenAthens do simplify the experience for library administrators at a cost to the budget.[10] In 2011, NISO released Suggested Practices Regarding Single Sign-On (ESPreSSO), which outlines recommendations for content providers and libraries on the best ways to support this authentication method.[11]

LibLynx offers an alternative to EZProxy, in the form of its own hosted proxy server service.[12] It also offers access through SSO, and so can provide whichever path seems most useful for a particular resource at a given institution. It provides several other services, such as user management, patron authentication, publisher authentication, and a library portal; each may be useful for libraries that seek more extensive customizations in those areas.

RA21 is a solution that comes from the commercial sector.[13] RA21 aims to establish a minimal, baseline amount of information to determine the association an individual has with a particular institution, and thereby provide appropriate and legal access. RA21's advantage over EZProxy is its ability to maintain access more seamlessly when going from one resource to another. Many librarians have expressed concerns about the information that publishers might try to collect about individuals when using RA21, so it is important that librarians remain aware of this and ensure that they are comfortable with the amount of information that is being shared. In addition, there are concerns about this authentication method restricting walk-in user access because a login is required to use this method successfully. Research on a corporate pilot project has been published that may be worth reviewing to understand how this authentication method could work in libraries, especially those in non-academic settings.[14]

USERNAME AND PASSWORD ACCESS

The use of usernames and passwords is one of the most difficult authentication setups in most library environments. It is difficult to understand why electronic resources vendors cling to the use of usernames and passwords in an institutional environment.[15] Whether they provide one username-password combination or ten, any institution that provides access will be required to share those passwords with patrons, which will immediately negate the security of the username and password. Depending on the website structure, it might be possible for library workers to store the username and password in a URL that is passed to access the site automatically. This might seem more secure than simply giving the information out on a piece of paper at the reference desk, but of course it isn't. Ultimately, the username and password are hiding in plain sight and it only takes a moment for an individual who is viewing the URL from any place to find and obtain the access information. Furthermore, if the vendor does not change its usernames and passwords on an annual basis, all alumni, or academic staff leaving the institution, maintain access indefinitely.

Other sites try to mitigate the problem by having multiple usernames and passwords, with the expectation that only those who need access will receive passwords. Of course, this system also fails in a library setting. Despite these problems, some alternatives do exist: if there is a webpage that is only accessible to those with an institutional username and password, then a page storing the separate usernames and passwords might be a solution, but even then, all the credentials are available for anyone with access to copy and share. Some institutions might share credentials using a password manager, which would provide access while preventing the recipient from seeing the password, but this adds a layer of complexity that is not, in fact, the responsibility of the subscribing institution. Library workers can only do as much as the vendor provides, and it is absolutely the responsibility of the electronic resources vendor to make available an effective access solution to access.

VIRTUAL PRIVATE NETWORKS

Some institutions offer access through a Virtual Private Network (VPN) as an alternative to, or replacement for, a proxy server. Using the VPN requires that users download a VPN program to their machines, then set up and establish correct settings. The VPN will then assign a campus-based IP number to the machine, even when it is not on campus—but only when the system is properly installed. Because the machine itself is viewed as being within the institution's IP range, access to all online resources should work. It isn't necessary to access resources through EZProxy, and as a result there is no need to worry about the challenges associated with maintaining EZProxy stanzas. But users must ensure they regularly update the VPN software, if it is required to address security concerns, and the setup on the patron side can be challenging, since a VPN is basically a "tunnel" into a campus network, there can also be problems with latency where response time of access to resources is slowed down.

Complex Resources

Even basic resources may become complex very quickly depending on vendor and institutional requirements for access. However, the access methods below are more specialized or complex from the start.

Limited IP Range Access

In some cases, a vendor may limit access to a range of computers, usually in a set physical location. This may mean that only those machines in a particular building can access the resources. If the WiFi network is a campus-wide network, computers that are connected to the WiFi network will not be able to access the resources because they are not within the building's IP range, and so do not have access. This is a common practice with some legal resource vendors, for example.

Although this is not ideal, and in many cases a deal breaker, it may be the only option for a particularly expensive and essential resource. Each institution will need to consider its options and preferences, and in some cases this path might be preferable to shared username and password access. In this case it would be seen as a marked improvement to access.

An additional problem occurs for institutions that do not allocate IP addresses to physical buildings. Many universities randomly allocate an IP address within a given range to each unique login and therefore cannot provide that IP address information to the vendor. In these cases, a case-by-case approach must be taken to decide if the results of a change to access is an acceptable tradeoff.

IP Versioning

Any time a new version of IP is released, access to electronic resources can become problematic. In some cases, certain areas of campus or a site may upgrade to a new IP version before others. This will result in some of the campus using a higher or more advanced version of IP access than others, which can inhibit using resources in those buildings only. It may take time for an information provider to optimize their products for newer versions of IP access. For providers offering an array of products some may become optimized before others. Maintaining a close connection with the site or campus information technology office helps in understanding of the IP versions in use.

In addition, sharing information on which resources are optimized for which IP version is good to know when trying to troubleshoot access problems.

Dedicated Terminal Access

The most limiting tool to control access to electronic resources is probably the dedicated terminal. Nowadays limited almost is used solely for very expensive business-related databases like Bloomberg, Capital IQ, or Thomson Datastream. Dedicated terminals ensure that not only do users have to be physically on campus, but they must be at a particular terminal to be given access to the resource. Individuals must almost always create their own accounts, which may require confirmation or authentication from the vendor before access is granted. Given that this will be the only way an institution can offer access to such a resource—if the publisher is even willing to provide such access—there is not much that can be done to mitigate these concerns unless an alternative product can be found.

An example of this is the Digital Library of the National Assembly Library of Korea, which limits its access to workstations on which resource-specific access software has been.[16] Unlike IP-limited access, this resource is specifically restricted to a small collection of particular workstations.

Bookmarklets and Browser Extensions

When using a proxy service, an off-campus user accesses library resources most easily through the library's interface. However, end users do not always think to begin at the library's website.

Bookmarklets and browser extensions provide a solution to this problem. Although not perfect, they are an improvement over the existing setup and so can be useful in many instances. Bookmarklets and browser extensions are features of specific web browsers, so it is necessary to use the browser on which they have been installed. This is not an impossible task to manage, but it is worth noting that education will be needed to encourage patrons to download, install, and use these products.

Bookmarklets and browser extensions have different pros and cons. Bookmarklets will slow down a browser less than an extension, because the extension is always running in the background but the bookmarklet is only activated when the user clicks on it. In addition, a bookmarklet can be used in any browser, while extensions are browser-specific.

However, there are drawbacks to bookmarklets. Once set, bookmarklets cannot be updated automatically. Therefore, in order to update, an institution must attempt to contact all users to tell them to install a new bookmarklet, which is clearly an almost impossible task in most institutions.

Passkey

Use Passkey to access library resources, wherever you are.

When you're off-campus, connect to databases and journals that would otherwise be restricted or hidden behind paywalls through Passkey. Just drag the Passkey icon (below) to the top of your browser. Next time you hit a restricted website, click the Passkey icon. If the Library has a subscription to the resource you're trying to access, you'll then be prompted for your NetID.

Installation

In Firefox, drag the icon to your bookmarks toolbar.

In Chrome, drag the icon to the bookmark toolbar (the bookmarks toolbar needs to be visible, you can try ctrl-shift-b to enable it).

In Internet Explorer, right-click the icon, add to Favorites.

For the iPad: In Settings/Safari, select Always Show Bookmarks Bar. Bookmark any page and add it to the Bookmarks Bar. Now edit the bookmark. Name it whatever you want, and then paste in the following (including the semicolon at the end):

```
javascript:void(location.href="http://encompass.library.cornell.edu/cgi-
bin/checkIP.cgi?access=gateway_standard%25&url="+location.href);
```

Or add the direct link to your bookmarks or favorites on your favorite browser:

```
javascript:void(location.href=%22http://encompass.library.cornell.edu/cgi-
bin/checkIP.cgi?access=gateway_standard%%25url=%22+location.href);
```

FIGURE 4.1
PassKey from Cornell University[17]

A locally built bookmarklet can provide similar functionality, although it will still have a significant learning curve for users. Off-campus patrons need to know that they have access to a particular resource and that they must click on the bookmarklet, which will then add the proxy string to the URL in order to log in with their appropriate credentials. Cornell University created one such bookmarklet, called "PassKey" (see figure 4.1). But as noted above, it cannot be updated—the URL used there is no longer current, but redirects allow it to continue to work effectively.

Open Access

Accessing OA resources should be simple. The whole point of OA, after all, is to remove the paywall to published content. However, OA access can be complex, and in many cases can be far more difficult than accessing subscribed content.

When a resource meets the evaluation criteria and can be added to central indexing of OA content, such as the Directory of Open Access Books (DOAB) or Journals (DOAJ), it is relatively easy to add those collections to your link resolver or discovery layer and let that third party manage the issues associated with linking to content.[18,19]

However, this approach only works for journals that are fully open access. Hybrid OA journals create problems. If an author in a given institution publishes an article on open access in a hybrid journal to which the library does not subscribe, it effectively becomes invisible to the institution via the discovery layer. Most link resolvers work at the journal level, not the article level. In this situation, a link resolver, which makes links based on page numbers, issue numbers and publication date, does not know which articles are OA. Therefore, the whole hybrid journal could be marked as being outside the library's collection, even though OA articles might be accessible.

One solution to this is a metadata string known as oaDOI.[20] This DOI structure helps to redirect users to freely available content instead of hitting a paywall. Using an application programming interface (API) or browser extension, it is possible to search to find open versions of titles that would otherwise only be available through subscription.

Many full-text abstracting and indexing databases include OA content, which allows for retrieval within a subject-oriented context. In these cases, it may be less important to a library to add that content to their catalogs or discovery tools because discovery will take place within a subject-based context. Many library workers see this access point as the primary one for OA content and a reason not to add or worry about other access points to OA titles.

There are also a number of open source tools available to aid the discovery of OA content. These tools include OA Button, Unpaywall, and OASIS.[21-23] OA Button and Unpaywall are two services that are readily available and utilized by many libraries. Both are freely available for use by anyone who wishes to find OA content. OA Button was launched in 2013 as a mechanism to cross-search numerous open access content platforms and repositories. Unpaywall, launched in 2016, is a browser extension created to search across the digital object identifiers (DOIs) made available in the Crossref directory and other known OA sites such as the Directory of Open Access Journals, commercial journal platforms, fully open institutional repositories and CORE (an aggregation of open access research outputs from repositories and journals worldwide), and disciplinary repositories such as arXiv and bioRxiv.[24-26] Both mechanisms search reliable and vetted websites for scholarly content as opposed to the entire open web or commercial social networking websites such as ResearchGate or Academia.edu, which often hold content that has been added without the correct permissions and licenses and is subject to loss of content due to publisher take down notices.[27,28]

There are multiple ways to use both OA Button and Unpaywall. Library workers often have either OA Button or Unpaywall as a browser extension in Chrome or Firefox. For some academic libraries, this browser extension is made available on public access terminals used daily by students and community users. Another way to use OA Button is by loading an entire comma separated value data set (as a CSV file) up to the OA Button site or through the use of an open API. Unpaywall works in much the same way, except that instead of being able to upload a CSV file, you can download its database and run queries against it to find features. In addition, a for-fee service has been developed that allows for the establishment of a specific data feed from the database.

To date, OA Button can be embedded into ILL and discovery systems. Both tools have their strengths and weaknesses and many librarians choose to provide both options to end users to help find freely available content.

There is certainly potential for these tools to bypass the problem of access to non-subscribed content issue in library discovery systems and should feature in any exit plan from the big deal. This will be discussed further in chapters 7 and 8.

Openly Available Sources Integrated Search (OASIS) is a new tool developed by SUNY Geneseo to help end users readily find open educational material.[29] Although there are compilations of open textbooks, such as the Open Textbook Library, these sites are rarely comprehensive and tend to focus most on resources that resemble an actual textbook.[30] With OASIS, the search includes videos, interactive simulations, and modules that can also be reused by other faculty members. What is particularly useful about the OASIS extension is that it can be embedded into courseware platforms to help faculty who are designing courses to find free or open resources to use.

2. Descriptive Metadata Management

Content that is purchased or leased but is not cataloged or made discoverable is warehoused content. Therefore, discovery is absolutely essential to ensure that end users know that a resource has been acquired. This is not, however, a new problem; for a century, libraries have been describing 600-page books with just three dozen words, or less—and many of those words are used to describe only the physical features of the book, not its contents. With e-resources, this should be much easier, because so much more data can be searched from within a library's catalog. But this can also cause problems, as the addition of the full text of that 600-page book can add too much noise. Multiplied by hundreds of thousands, or millions, of titles, the problem becomes much worse, and easy searching may become untenable.

Basic Resources

One aspect of the selection process discussed in chapter 1 is determining what level of descriptive metadata is needed for each type of resource acquired. It may be enough to add a resource to the A–Z listing of offerings, for example, with abstracting and indexing tools or other tools that provide an indeterminate coverage of given resources within the platform.

Many full-text databases also fall into this area. They may not hold complete runs of a journal title, for example. In addition, this content moves in and out of the database on a fairly regular basis. This makes fully cataloging the contents something of a fool's errand that takes up too much time to accomplish the end goal of greater understanding of the content provided.

E-book collections are more discoverable and more successful when the individual books are added to a library catalog. Indeed, many provide free MARC records to achieve exactly this. When using an evidence-based purchasing plan for streaming media, use will increase if catalog records are loaded into a library catalog or discovery system. It may be more cost-effective to leave these resources accessible or described at the collection level. Outlining the level of description needed at the point of selection helps to provide the guidance needed at the point of implementation.

Complex Resources

Although using an A–Z list is simple and straightforward, in most scenarios, the complex option is preferable because it will ensure that descriptive information about electronic resources is searchable but will not overwhelm the user with too much data.

Link resolvers connect a citation in one resource (a "source") to the full text of that citation in a different resource (the "target") using software and a knowledge base. The linking method is standardized through the OpenURL format (ANSI/NISO Z39.88-2004).[31] The knowledge base tracks which full-text resources a specific library can access electronically, and where they are located. A link resolver is only as good as the knowledge base behind it; if information about the contents in a newly subscribed electronic resource is not added to the knowledge base, then it will never be able to lead to a citation to the full-text content a user seeks. So, for e-monographs and e-journals, it is vitally important to add holdings information about e-resources to an institution's link-resolving knowledge base. Although the constant flux of titles in large full-text databases does not make them 100 percent accurate, it is still a huge step up from trying to keep up with these resources by hand. However, the quality of the metadata in some full-text database metadata files can leave a lot to be desired, and often fixes have to be put in place to try to find the content. For example, an article or even a title search query may be needed if a target cannot be located automatically.

Link resolvers are fantastic tools to use within subject-oriented abstracting and indexing databases because many researchers and students begin their search for content in these platforms outside of the main library catalog or discovery tool. The link resolver within a database is usually designated with a "Find-It @ [given institution]" or "Get Resource" button or access point (e.g., an icon for a given library) that allows end users to query their library's holdings.

Link resolvers are most effective for e-monographs and e-journals. Although they can, in theory, be used for other resources, these tools work less well with more discrete objects. This is particularly true for digitized collections of archives or manuscripts or for any collections that do not offer accurate holdings metadata. Although link resolvers are becoming more fine-tuned for the discovery of article level and book chapter data, they often fail with data sets and visual collections even though these objects may be assigned a DOI.

Bibliographic descriptive records are another critical tool for helping users identify and locate resources that are available. Many link resolver providers offer bibliographic records that can be added to a library's online catalog. This discovery mechanism is a similar-but-different way of searching for a resource. Both paths are equally important, in different ways: a link resolver helps a user who is starting in a database that does not have full text of the article or resource readily available, while MARC records help a user who begins in the library's online catalog or discovery layer. This can be particularly useful for e-books, where a user may be starting a search in the library catalog, which is historically print-based. A MARC record for an e-book offers an alternative solution. Most e-book publishers and vendors offer MARC downloads at no extra cost to the library.

MARC records or catalog records differ from link resolver data because they provide the addition of a controlled vocabulary for subject-relevant paths to discovery. This type of descriptive metadata encourages discovery at the title level, rather than at the article level, as the link resolver does. MARC records often provide greater detail about the contents of a given resource. For journals this can include previous or subsequent titles; for books, table of contents information is often included.

One challenge of MARC records is that standard cataloging practice states that each format for a resource, be it print, microfilm, or electronic, should be on a separate record, as the bibliographic record has just a single character to represent the format of the item being described. Many bibliographic records for online resources are from third-party solutions that they can be easily updated programmatically on a set schedule.

Discovery layers help to present MARC data in more usable ways than in traditional integrated library systems (ILS). Most discovery layers provide facet searching approaches so that an end user can search titles by formats, by years of publication, or by location of the content. In this way, end users do not have to be confronted by myriad formats for any given title but can narrow down or scope their searches to specific formats such as e-journals, streaming media, or e-books as opposed to print journals, DVDs, or print books.

In addition, discovery layers are set up to draw on knowledge bases that expand beyond the local library holdings to include consortia holdings and content that can be borrowed from other institutions in the area either through borrowing agreements, interlibrary loan (ILL), or document delivery mechanism. For articles and e-journal access, this makes obtaining content more seamless and easily available from a single interface as opposed to having to toggle or tab between multiple websites or web pages to obtain all the services needed. However, as we mention in chapter 7, there is a significant drop off between accessing e-resources and requesting an ILL.

Given the ubiquity of discovery layers, many publishers choose to make their resources discoverable through these resources. However, many others do not, often for business reasons. For example, in 2018, the Modern Language Association's new full-text version of its standard MLA Bibliography was made available exclusively via EBSCO's discovery layer. For any library worker, the exclusive agreement between a publisher or vendor and discovery system is a disturbing policy because it reserves content exclusively, which will often incur the wrath of the community.[32] Libraries are unlikely to switch discovery layers based on a small number of exclusive deals. Therefore, the publisher risks its database or service being sidelined when its content is not discoverable.

Once the decision to share data with discovery layers has been made, the cost of providing that content is not especially high. But the way a particular discovery layer vendor manages the data can become an issue of some contention. If a discovery layer vendor is slow to import data and update the database metadata, then new content will not be discoverable. For some e-journal issues, this can become a real problem. Users will expect to find content in the discovery layer on publication, and if that content has not been loaded in a timely fashion, users quickly become disillusioned with the discovery service.

Conflicts can also arise between MARC records where resources have been fully cataloged and then also turned on in a discovery knowledge base as a target. These conflicts are most common with e-book collections and streaming media collections. If the choice of a library is to fully catalog these holdings, it is often better to leave them off the central indexing within the discovery layer to ensure that content is as accessible as possible. When setting up resources in a discovery layer, it is best to test the access to make sure content works the way intended.

The importance of data accuracy in a knowledge base cannot be overstated. Content providers rarely provide accurate holdings data about a library's resources. As discussed above, it is an absolute requirement that electronic resources content providers deliver timely and accurate information about the holdings to which a library has access through an approved format, such as Knowledge Bases and Related Tools (KBART) files. Unfortunately, this often-complex situation can often run into difficulty.

KBART provides definitions for how such data should be provided to help ensure that library users can access all of the entitlements to which they have access, and to ensure publishers have the opportunity to expose as much of their content to students and faculty as possible in order to increase usage.[33] As we mention in chapter 6, increased usage may encourage renewals because it lowers the cost per download of a resource. Publishers have a significant incentive for wanting library patrons to access their products readily through library systems.

If a knowledge base provider does not provide accurate and timely data, then library users will be led to links that fail to deliver full-text content, or worse, will *not* be provided with links that *should* get them to such content. In these cases, the content provider creates a poor user experience (due to the failed link) or loses out on usage that could drive renewals.

Open Access

Open access material does not differ greatly from other material in respect to metadata management. To this end, the same issues around the quality of metadata apply. Many OA journals lack DOIs at article level, for example, which creates a problem in a discovery system. Users may find themselves at the journal title level and will have to search for the article all over again.

Many OA presses are very small operations with only one or two staff, meaning that specialist knowledge may be lacking in some areas. A U.K. landscape study of new university presses and academic-led publishing suggested that best practices in metadata were drawn up as the quality of metadata created by these initiatives were at various levels of maturity.[34] This view was confirmed at a European level by a report on the visibility of metadata, which stated that metadata was "inconsistent and variable in quality" and that collecting and aggregating that data "was a challenge due to inconsistency in bibliographic metadata processes and formats."[35]

There is a further issue for the OA monograph. Whereas discovery of metadata via a resource such as DOAB is relatively straightforward providing a library selects DOAB as a target, print is still important to monograph users and it is important for OA monograph publishers to make their publications available via the library supply chain. However, the supply chain is very much set up around print and there is often no option for a zero-priced product in a book vendor's catalogue. In 2018, a stakeholder forum in the United Kingdom recommended that "there is a need to agree to a minimum metadata requirement, which could then be used in all metadata in the library supply chain, such as ONIX, MARC, KBART etc. This would go some way to allow all parties to understand what they each mean by the term metadata and what it is describing. The minimum level of metadata must include ISBN, chapter level identifiers and abstracts. There is potential to scale this model internationally."[36]

3. Administrative Portals and Metadata

Almost all library platform and resource providers have constructed administrative sites for their content. When implementing resources for the first time on a new platform or from a new provider, the decision is made where to house the administrative login information. Library workers may approach the management of these logins differently. In some cases, the information is added into the ILS along with the purchasing data. In other cases, the login credentials for administration and usage retrieval is housed on a shared drive or within a shared document that is limited to those working with these resources or with a direct need for the administration information.

Administration portals help to set up resources in ways that any given institution prefers. This may mean preferring advanced search over a basic search mechanism for the end user display, which plug-ins or APIs that may take an end user to guides, chat features, or further information on a library website. It is within this framework that library workers would include the IP ranges being used, the configuration for the local link resolver, and the branding mechanisms of their own libraries. When setting up resources for the first time, it is important to have established guidelines that are agreed to by the library community at large prior to setup. These decisions points include:

- Use of basic or advanced search
- How the name of the library is displayed in branding
- Which library logo is used
- What the link resolver configuration looks like (e.g., a button or text)
- When linking to chat occurs
- When linking to web guides occurs
- Whether there are certain features to disable
- Whether there are certain features to always use

By having these guidelines in place, the administrative setup can function somewhat seamlessly without having to be reviewed or checked by multiple members within a library environment. The other decisions to be made are if any of these criteria also need to be added to the ILS or procurement system.

This may be something as simple as a statement indicating that access followed established guidelines, or it may require spelling out specific aspects of the access established (e.g., IP authentication) or explaining the use of one searching mechanism over another.

4. Subject Portals, Reading Lists Management Systems, Courseware, and Local Digital Collections Discovery

There are other access points that many libraries employ to help with the discovery of resources.

Basic Resources

Subject portal access or class-oriented access to content is usually provided using a service known as LibGuides.[37] The strength of LibGuides is the unified way in which subject, topic, and class access to content is provided. This is especially true of web pages dedicated to specific courses because LibGuides help to contextualize resources in ways that appeal to specific audiences such as the faculty teaching those courses and the students enrolled in them. Using the tab creation feature in this portal library highlights different content formats such as databases, ejournals, e-books, or online reference works. In addition, these portal pages provide the opportunity to highlight tips and tricks for utilizing the content effectively (see figure 4.2).

Within the platforms that support subject guides, there are often options to create a single A–Z listing. The A–Z listing is usually used to draw attention to databases and large packages of information or to freely available content from government websites or other areas of interest within your local community. The A–Z listing can be used as a base resource for the content that populates the subject pages so that links to material do not need to be replicated multiple times, but rather just pointed to in a single place. In many cases, it is helpful to have an A–Z listing as these forms of content get lost in the details of large library catalogs and discovery systems. The particular use described here, within subject guides, is much better practice than adopting one very long A–Z list across the whole set of resources. Indeed, some of the very specialist resources noted above, which require either limited IP access or usernames and passwords can be inserted in a subject guide list. This provides the opportunity to explain the complexities of access to a particular discipline, such as a law or business faculty.

Local digital collections may exist as standalone web pages or within the local institutional repository within a library's web presence. Although this

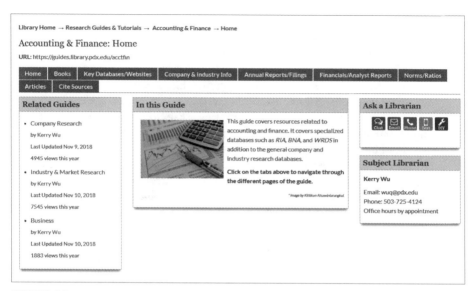

FIGURE 4.2
Portland State University Library Accounting and Finance LibGuide[38]

setup allows for easy promotion using social media or library blogs, access can become lost in the larger scales of the world wide web. For this reason, it is recommended that local digital collections be assigned DOIs and follow digital metadata standards to allow for greater indexing and retrievability from large scales indexes like Google. Furthermore, when a library self-publishes local digital content, it is also good practice to assign an appropriate Creative Commons license to let individuals know what reuse rights of the content are or are not available.[39]

Complex Resources

Another way to provide contextual access to content in academic institutions is through the use of reading list management systems (RLMS). Reading list management systems allow for greater flexibility and functionality as more content has moved online. The implementation of reading lists can be laborious and requires a number of considerations upfront regarding interoperability with other systems, management by various stakeholders, and the scope of the system.[40] In cases where the library populates the resources on the reading lists, the department in the library assigned this work should be well staffed. In cases where faculty or faculty departments are populating the resources to be used, it is helpful to have a mechanism to check to see if the library holds the resources or to be able to request access to content from the library if not readily available. Having resource requests funnel through the library helps library workers identify the resources that can provided openly. Recent studies have shown that students find reading lists to be quite helpful and are generally aware if a library has them available for use.[41]

There is a crossover between the RLMS and the learning management system (LMS) or virtual learning environment (VLE). Although the RLMS may be a separate piece of software, it is often accessible directly through the LMS.

For this reason, many academic libraries in the United States offer limited online course reserves at this point but try to find ways to more easily provide discoverability of library resources within the various courseware products. One way to do this is through the use of a contextual widget that can query the library catalog or subject guides within the courseware. At Portland State University, this type of widget is embedded into the local courseware system D2L (Desire2Learn) (see figure 4.3) and allows ready access to the library's resources on any given page the faculty or student sees.[42] Many commercial content providers are beginning to develop similar widgets and making them available in courseware systems to drive use to their content platforms.

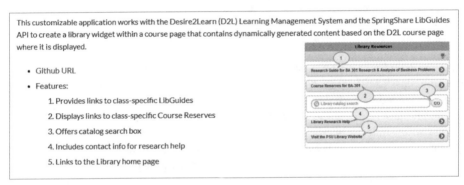

This customizable application works with the Desire2Learn (D2L) Learning Management System and the SpringShare LibGuides API to create a library widget within a course page that contains dynamically generated content based on the D2L course page where it is displayed.

- Github URL
- Features:
    1. Provides links to class-specific LibGuides
    2. Displays links to class-specific Course Reserves
    3. Offers catalog search box
    4. Includes contact info for research help
    5. Links to the Library home page

FIGURE 4.3
Contextually Aware Library Widget for D2L (Desire2Learn) at Portland State University

Open Access

For OA content, subject guides serve as a mechanism for calling attention to resources alumni and community users can access readily. For instance, at Portland State University Library, a LibGuide for social workers provides access to openly available resources to help with their evidence-based practices after they graduate from the university.[43] Other libraries, such as the Queen Mary University Library in the United Kingdom, embed OA content within their subject guides to highlight what is readily available to students.[44] As with specialist resources, some of the best things that can be promoted using the A–Z listing within a subject guide are pre-print services and tools that search across repository platforms like CORE to provide access to all OA content within these platforms.[45]

Regarding the OA materials in the LMS, many scholarly led publishers feel that OA is often treated in a far less formal way than purchased material and that this helps to fuel the perception that OA is of lower quality, even if the resources are fully peer reviewed.[46]

5. Testing Access

Establishing access and description is not enough. It is necessary to test and confirm that access works from the various access points provided.

Basic Resources

At its most basic level, part of the workflow process must include some type of testing process both on-campus and off-campus access. It is not enough to confirm that users can access the site in question, but also that they can access the full content and print it as well. If time allows, the investigation of any sort of account creation process is worth exploring to see what functionality works there. It is also worthwhile to test how resources work through discovery layers, courseware systems, or LibGuides if these mechanisms are being used for access.

Complex Resources

Testing off-campus access is extremely important. For IP authenticated access, there are a range of tools to test off-campus access, for example, through smartphones on the cellular network. Although this also provides an opportunity to see how the site operates on a smaller and more mobile screen, a more reliable and effective tool is a VPN application that creates an environment in which the user is accessing resources from outside the institution's range. It is useful to establish an outdated laptop with a subscription to a private internet provider running it, the VPN-checker. This laptop can be used just to check off-campus access to electronic resources as questions arise. This can be particularly useful for troubleshooting (see chapter 5).

In chapter 6, we explore how the evaluation and assessment of usage reports may indicate there is an implementation problem with a given resource. If a resource is added due to high demand by end users, but then shows that it is seldom—or never—used, this often indicates that something went awry in the implementation process or that the current access model may not allow the retrieval of the content. An error may have occurred with registering IP ranges, for example, or there may be a problem with the EZProxy setup.

Finally, it is also valuable to announce new resources, whether purchased or made freely available to the local collection committee, group of liaison libraries, and/or database team prior to making a broad announcement of availability. These groups can also help with testing access. They also are good for recognizing if a resource is appearing in all the modes needed to garner the greatest use and recognition. These groups are often more attuned to testing the use with LibGuides and other subject portals.

6. Branding and Marketing

For many libraries, branding is a critical part of establishing electronic resources.[47] This is understandable; many patrons do not realize that the resources they use are paid for by the library, and it makes sense to ensure that there is at least some portion of the resource that indicates who is providing access. Columbia University Libraries has compiled an extensive set of documents that describe exactly what they expect to see from vendors regarding their branding.[48] Indeed, the Columbia Libraries contend that "library branding is more important than the vendor's or publisher's corporate brands." Although not all electronic resources vendors can provide the level of branding that Columbia would like to see—and for various reasons, some cannot provide any at all—the goals that Columbia have outlined are clear and admirable. For the library community, insisting on the ability to highlight library branding and co-branding within proprietary systems is good practice.

For the companies that do offer library branding or co-branding, this is a function in the administrative portal. In most cases it simply requires loading a small .gif or .png image of the library logo. For more sophisticated platforms, you may be able to add a redirecting link back to your library website. Another way to brand or co-brand could be just as simple as a text string stating that the resource is provided by your library. It is also good to ask the provider for the redirect back to the library website where possible in order to allow end users to move between resource platforms and the library website.

Once a resource has been fully implemented and publicized to library workers, the next step is to let your local community know about the new resource. It is best practice to develop a marketing and outreach plan to use for resource advertising. It is also advisable to annually review and determine which resources to promote and feature. For new resources, the focus is the development of recognition and utility to your community. With resources that the library has had for a while, promotion should emphasize increasing usage and may need to be tied to current educational practices or new programs in the community. When it comes to OA, the focus is on the content as well as the services that allow local faculty and researchers to make their content freely available.

Basic Resources

In the cases of single e-journal titles or e-books, promotion is as simple as letting requestors know the content is now available for them to use. At most, with this level of content access, you are communicating to a small group of people or a subset of the community. This would be true for one-off OA titles as well. Subject and liaison library workers can easily incorporate this into their work and general communication plans with their constituents.

Complex Resources

For more complex resources or larger collections of material, the investment to purchase the content and make it accessible may be significant. In these cases, it is worthwhile to provide more extensive marketing.[49,50] Writing blog posts and including promotion in quarterly bulletins that are shared more broadly in your community is one approach. The encouragement of broader communication channels to promote the material, such as the university communication office or your instructional designer community, is another path to informing users. If the library or broader community environment supports digital signage, considering running advertisements for resources on these platforms. Most libraries maintain a social media presence; use this avenue to highlight new content and to promote content whose usage has dropped off. If there is an event occurring on campus, such as a lecture or performance, where the resource may be of use or of significance to those attending the event, tie the promotion of the resource to the event by having flyers or posters posted at the venue.

Open Access

As noted above, with OA material the marketing focus is split between the actual content and the services offered to make content readily available. Although creating websites and guides spelling out the OA services are important, more is needed to spread the word regarding what provisions the library makes for OA support. Marketing directly to deans of schools and colleges is a good idea, especially when there are significant news stories being circulated about open access content. One of the best times to market the services a library offers regarding OA provision is during international Open Access Week, which occurs in October each year.[51] However, this work cannot be limited to once a year. Consider holding a workshop series for graduate students and early career faculty on the benefits of publishing OA.[52] Another option is on focused outreach to research and graduate studies offices to highlight what journal offset deals are in place, where cost breaks for APCs are given, and what the benefits for making various content deposits into institutional repositories are. Again, subject and departmental liaison librarians are instrumental in helping to spread the word and encourage uptake.

It is hoped that the marketing of OA resources has an influence of the perception of some researchers to open access, particularly around the professionalism and quality of some open access content.[53] For the most part, the lack of quality and prestige of OA is a completely false assumption. If the selection criteria have been followed, then at this stage the OA resources being implemented will have passed through all the quality checks that any other resource will have been expected to meet.[54] The more high-quality, peer-reviewed OA resources that academics encounter, the greater the chance they will choose to publish in this way.

In conclusion, given that implementation entails many different aspects, it is helpful to create a checklist of the marketing processes needed for each resource. Using tools such as checklists benefit library workers by insuring that no part of the implementation process is skipped or overlooked. Recording the necessary implementation steps will also help with troubleshooting problems when they arise. Troubleshooting will be covered in the next chapter.

NOTES

1. Hosburgh, Nathan. (2012). Getting the most out of Pay-Per-View: A feasibility study and discussion of mediated and unmediated options. *Journal of Electronic Resources Librarianship* 24(3): 204–211. https://doi.org/10.1080/1941126X.2012.706112.

2. Fisher, Erin S., Kurt, Lisa, & Gardner, Sarah. (2012). Exploring patron-driven access models for e-journals and e-books. *Serials Librarian* 62(1–4): 164–168. https://doi.org/10.1080/0361526X.2012.652913.

3. Kennedy, Marie R., & LaGuardia, Cheryl. (2018). *Marketing your library's electronic resources: A how-to-do-it manual for librarians*, 2nd edition (Chicago: ALA).

4. Bhattacharjee, Yudhijit. (2011). New consortium to run Arecibo Observatory. www.sciencemag.org/news/2011/05/new-consortium-run-arecibo-observatory.

5. Redlink. https://redlink.com/.

6. IP Registry. (n.d.). https://theipregistry.org/.

7. Shibboleth. (n.d.). https://www.shibboleth.net/.

8. Janyk, Roen. (2010). Customize host error message. https://ezproxy.ls.suny.narkive.com/y0BHEnKq/customize-host-error-message.

9. OCLC. (2018). EZproxy. https://www.oclc.org/en/ezproxy.html.

10. Eduserv. (2018). OpenAthens. https://openathens.org/.

11. NISO. (2018). ESPReSSO: Establishing suggested practices regarding single sign-on. https://www.niso.org/standards-committees/espresso.

12. LibLynx. (2016). www.liblynx.com/.

13. RA21. (n.d.). https://ra21.org.

14. RA21. (2018). Resource Access for the 21st Century (RA21) Corporate Pilot Report. https://ra21.org/index.php/results/ra21-corporate-pilot-final-report -september-2018/.

15. McMullen, Anthony. (2016). Transient technologies: The end of the username and password? *The Bottom Line 29*(4): 230–232. https://doi.org/10.1108/BL-02 -2016-0005.

16. Digital Library of the National Assembly Library of Korea. https://www.nanet .go.kr/.

17. Cornell University Library. (2018). PassKey. https://www.library.cornell.edu/ services/apps/passkey.

18. DOAJ. (2018). About DOAJ (Directory of Open Access Journals). https://doaj.org/ about.

19. DOAB. (n.d.). Directory of Open Access Books. https://www.doabooks.org/.

20. Impact Story. (2016). Introducing oaDOI: Resolve a DOI straight to OA. http:// blog.impactstory.org/introducting-oadoi/.

21. Open Access Button. (n.d.). About. https://openaccessbutton.org/about.

22. Unpaywall. (n.d.). https://unpaywall.org/products/extension.

23. SUNY. OASIS. (n.d.). https://oasis.geneseo.edu/.

24. Jisc/Open University. (n.d.). CORE. https://core.ac.uk/.

25. Cornell University Library. (1991). ArXiv. https://arxiv.org/.

26. Cold Spring Harbor Laboratory. (2018). bioRxiv. https://www.biorxiv.org/.

27. ResearchGate. (2018). https://www.researchgate.net/.

28. Academia.edu. (2018). https://www.academia.edu/.

29. State University of New York-Geneseo. (2018). Openly available sources integrated search. https://oasis.geneseo.edu/.

30. Centre for Open Education. (n.d.). Open textbook library. https://open.umn.edu/ opentextbooks/.

31. NISO. (2018). ANSI/NISO Z39.88-2004 (R2010) The OpenURL framework for context-sensitive services. https://www.niso.org/publications/z3988-2004-r2010.

32. ICOLC. (2018). Consortial letter of opposition to MLA's exclusive relationship with EBSCO. http://icolc.net/statement/consortial-letter-opposition-mlas -exclusive-relationship-ebsco.

33. NISO. (2018). Knowledge base and related tools (KBART). https://www.niso.org/ standards-committees/kbart.

34. Adema, Janneke, & Stone, Graham. (2017). *Changing publishing ecologies: A landscape study of new university presses and academic-led publishing* (Bristol: Jisc). http://repository.jisc.ac.uk/6666/.

35. Neylon, Cameron, Montgomery, Lucy, Ozaygen, Alkim, Saunders, Neil, & Pinter, Frances. (2018). The visibility of open access monographs in a European context: Full report. http://doi.org/10.5281/zenodo.1230342.

36. Stone, Graham. (2018). OA monographs discovery in the library supply chain: Draft report and recommendations. https://scholarlycommunications.jiscinvolve .org/wp/2018/10/25/oa-monographs-discovery-in-the-library-supply-chain-draft -report-and-recommendations/.

37. springshare. (2018). LibGuides. https://www.springshare.com/libguides/.

38. Portland State University. (2018). Accounting and finance: Home. https://guides .library.pdx.edu/acctfin.

39. Creative Commons. (n.d.). https://creativecommons.org/.

40. Brewerton, Gary. Implementing a resource or reading list management system. *Ariadne 71*. www.ariadne.ac.uk/issue71/brewerton.

41. McGuinn, Kate, Stone, Graham, Sharman, Alison, & Davison, Emily. Student reading lists: Evaluating the student experience at the University of Huddersfield. *The Electronic Library 35*(2): 322–332. http://dx.doi.org/10.1108/ EL-12-2015-0252.

42. Portland State University. (2017). pdx-contextually-aware-library-widget. https:// github.com/pdxlibrary/pdx-contextually-aware-library-widget.

43. Portland State University. (2018). Open access social work: Home. http://guides .library.pdx.edu/opensocialwork.

44. Queen Mary University of London. (n.d.). Educational and professional development. https://www.library.qmul.ac.uk/subject-guides/educational-and -professional-development/.

45. Jisc/Open University. (n.d.). About CORE. https://core.ac.uk/about.

46. Stone, Graham. (2018). OA monographs discovery in the library supply chain: Draft report and recommendations. https://scholarlycommunications.jiscinvolve .org/wp/2018/10/25/oa-monographs-discovery-in-the-library-supply-chain-draft -report-and-recommendations/.

47. Frumkin, Jeremy, & Reese, Terry. (2011). Provision recognition: Increasing awareness of the library's value in delivering electronic information resources. *Journal of Library Administration 51*(7–8): 810–819. https://doi.org/10.1080/0193 0826.2011.601277.

48. Columbia University. (n.d.). E-resource branding. https://library.columbia.edu/bts/ cerm/e-resource-branding.html.

49. Germano, Michael A. (2010). Narrative-based library marketing: Selling your library's value during tough economic times. *The Bottom Line 23*: 5–7. http://dx.doi .org/10.1108/08880451011049641.

50. Brewerton, Antony. (2003). Inspired! Award-winning library marketing. *New Library World 104*(7/8): 267–277. https://doi.org/10.1108/03074800310488040.

51. SPARC. (2018). International Open Access Week. www.openaccessweek.org/.

52. Oregon Health & Science University. (2018). Workshops: Research communication and impact. https://www.ohsu.edu/library/workshops.

53. British Academy. (2018). Open access and monographs: Where are we now? https://www.britac.ac.uk/publications/open-access-monographs-where-are -we-now.

54. Deville, Joe, Sondervan, Joroen, Stone, Graham, & Wenstrom, Sofie. (2019). Rebels with a cause? Supporting new library and scholar-led open access publishing, *LIBER Quarterly*. https://www.liberquarterly.eu/articles/10277.

5

Troubleshooting

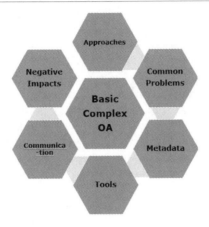

Introduction

In the first version of TERMs, troubleshooting appeared in a subsection under Evaluation and Ongoing Access. Unfortunately, links fail, platforms change, content moves from one provider to another, new security measures are implemented, subscription models change, and strange problems crop up that simply defy explanation. Therefore, with the increasing use of electronic resources in library services and the expansion of content made available online, this topic now requires a section unto itself. This is another area where the Pareto principle comes into play.[1] With troubleshooting, a single problem or issue can take days or weeks to resolve whereas multiple other problems are readily understood and resolved quickly. In this chapter, the aim is to establish and share some guidelines about how to determine where the problem lies, and how best to solve it, when access does fail.

Since 2014, there have been over twenty-five articles published on handling problems and issues with electronic resources. Library workers identify multiple platforms and systems to use when troubleshooting problems to find in-house solutions, often by repurposing other information system tools to function as customer relationship management tools (CRMs).[2] Determining how to troubleshoot problems is a complex and confusing process in its own right and requires ongoing investigation and analysis to establish a local framework or approach. Most libraries develop a triage methodology in order to try to identify more problematic issues in a structured way.[3] Although it might seem that troubleshooting problems applies only to subscription-based resources, there are also problems that arise with open access (OA) content.

Choosing a systematic approach to use with troubleshooting problems is only the first step. In *Reengineering the Library: Issues in Electronic Resources Management,* Carter and Traill note that library workers must understand the basic concepts of e-resource access and provision before they can assist with troubleshooting problems.[4] Staff training is key to identifying and quickly resolving problems that arise. Training is not a single activity—it requires ongoing refinement of the practices employed and identification of new issues and concerns. Library workers who may be best at resolving problems and access issues are usually not the same people working directly at a public service desk with the end users. Part of the training provided should cover best practices for responding to problems and issues reported and developing templates for common or known issues. Library workers at public services counters may not always have the depth of knowledge required to fully diagnosis why problems are occurring. Knowing when and how to hand over problems between front-line library workers and back-room library workers becomes part of the overall necessary training.

Human error can be the cause of many issues. For example, with metadata entry and around the renewal of resources. Many libraries purchase and activate resources upon request as opposed to having a set time period when new resources are activated. This results in varying renewal periods for many online items. If a renewal period is missed, either by the provider or the library workers, access may be temporarily terminated. Again, these problems can be rectified fairly quickly, and access restored. This is the opposite of an issue described in chapter 6, where a resource is acquired by the library, but the publisher forgets to replace the trial with a subscription and access is terminated.

More challenging problems occur when resources have been fully renewed and activated but access problems persist. There could be server issues, a problem with the version of IP authentication being used, or a malware problem occurring at the provider end that will require confirming problems with the provider. In many cases, this means there is not a problem with the web site overall but rather a single aspect within the provider's platform, such as subject searching not occurring as anticipated, the loss of the facets, or discrete searching mechanisms that should be available. This requires working through a problem with technicians at the provider's site.

If material is freely available, then does it follow that there will be no access problems? Regrettably not. Problems with open access materials are as numerous as with paid resources. Some publishers like to provide free, open access to content when first launching new titles, which is known as bronze open access, but then move these titles to paywall access after interest proves market viability. This will result in loss of access. For embargoed titles, the annual or semi-annual changes in content availability means having to update coverage descriptions regularly in order to provide end users with the required availability of OA titles. For hybrid journals, where a subscription is paid for access, but single articles or single issues may be offered OA, the goal becomes helping users understand this landscape of access. In some cases, library workers may activate subscription-based resources in their discovery tools to allow discovery of OA content but may not hold subscriptions to all the titles. This requires letting end users know that access content through the discovery tool may be limited. This issue is discussed further in chapter 7.

Troubleshooting resource problems has become a familiar and regular part of online resource management in the twenty-first century. The following sections will outline ways to approach troubleshooting to help your users obtain access to the content your institution provides.

1. A Systematic Approach to Troubleshooting

The best approach to all troubleshooting requires an open mind. For all e-resources and OA resources, money and time are spent to select and activate resources for the user community. When these resources are not available, the loss is felt by everyone, even those who do not report problems.

Problem reports come from many areas within and outside the library. Other library workers may report problems using resources in their instructional sessions with end users, there may be a help form or CRM system enabled on the library website or within the library catalog that end users and other library workers use to report problems, or direct emails may be sent in from other library workers or regular end users to a centralized email list or specific individual. It is also worth noting that many problems go completely unreported as users simply move on to the next resource.

Along with providing users a choice in the ways they can report issues, it is better to have a systematic approach. For example, it is helpful to set up an email list either for problem reporting or for responding to issues. In addition, establishing service time frames for staffing is important for there to be more timely responses to problems.

When using a team approach to address troubleshooting, setting up a timetable or time slots for key responders is a good idea. Having overlap with at least one person or group allows for responses when a single individual may be out of the office.[5] An out-of-office reply when trying to report an urgent issue is often the last straw for the user and can quickly escalate into a complaint. A troubleshooting team should not just be a group to report problems to, but also a team that directly communicates problems back out to the library as a whole so that everyone is made aware of significant or ongoing issues.

The best way to be efficient when troubleshooting is to aim to answer two questions:

1. Where is the problem?
2. What causes the problem?

Basic Ways to Troubleshoot

Developing and using a consistent mechanism for reporting problems and issues helps to determine where these problems occur in order to better identify them and develop solutions. If using a web-based form, keep the reporting fields simple and ask for contact information from the person reporting the issue so you can circle back to them as needed (see figure 5.1).

In many cases, particularly within smaller institutions and libraries, using a group email suffices for problem reporting. This also allows for immediate response back to the person reporting the problem if there is a need for follow-up. This can be manageable in an environment where only one or two individuals do the troubleshooting, and its greatest benefit is that it is essentially cost-free. An email address is created, and library workers assigned

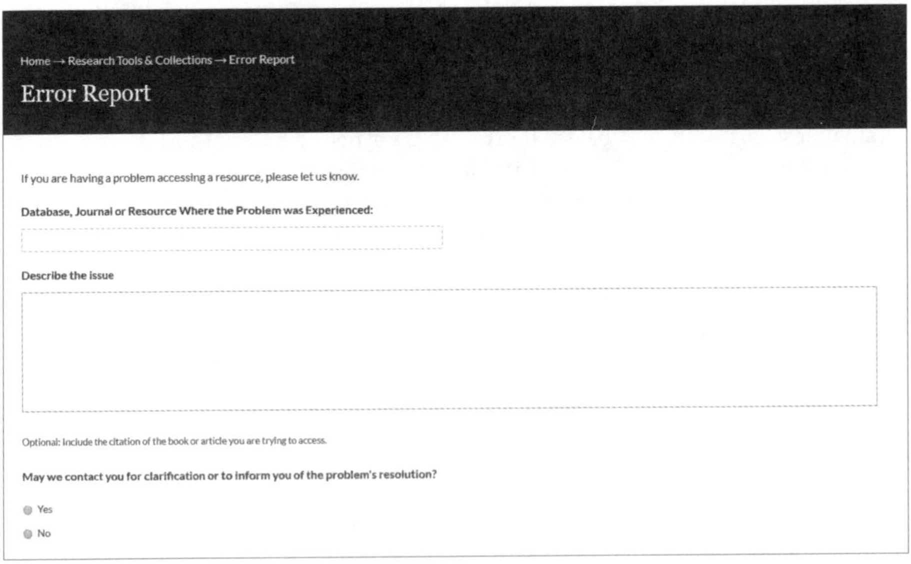

Home → Research Tools & Collections → Error Report

Error Report

If you are having a problem accessing a resource, please let us know.

Database, Journal or Resource Where the Problem was Experienced:

Describe the Issue

Optional: Include the citation of the book or article you are trying to access.

May we contact you for clarification or to inform you of the problem's resolution?

○ Yes

○ No

FIGURE 5.1
Sample Web Form for Error Reporting #1

to troubleshooting keep an eye on the inbox. However, as the number of resources increases or at a larger institution with far more users there are drawbacks to this approach. It can become easy for items to slip through the cracks unless there are email exchanges stating who is working on what problem. Those with less expertise may spend a lot of time trying to solve something that another individual can easily address. Recipients must use "reply all" to let others know that one person has claimed an issue so that work is not duplicated. For example, one person's solution often will not be available to others if they are not copied in, experience and insight may not be effectively shared, and there will be little standardization.

To resolve this, templates for responses should be instituted. For example, having a web form or structure for reporting problems is helpful. Fields can be established to indicate more clearly at what point access to content failed. If using a form, being able to set up a process to capture the point at which failure occurred by auto-populating this information into the report makes the work easier on both the person reporting the problem and the person trying to resolve the issue (see figure 5.2).

When addressing the question of where the problem is occurring, there are then five supplemental questions to ask:

1. Is the problem occurring on a single computer or on many?
   a. Is the problem on a computer at all? Does it happen on mobile devices but not on computers, for example?
2. Is this problem mirrored on campus and off campus?
3. Are only certain browsers affected, or does it affect all browsers on and off campus?
4. Is the problem limited to resources accessed from the library catalog or from the library website, or both?
5. Is access coming directly from internet search engines?

In most cases, developing a decision grid to work through can help lead those new to troubleshooting through a framework of diagnosing a problem (table 5.1).

TABLE 5.1

Decision Grid to Support Problem Reporting

LOCATION OF PROBLEM				
Computer in Library Site	Computer Off-Site from Library	Browser Used	Library Catalog Link	Link from Elsewhere

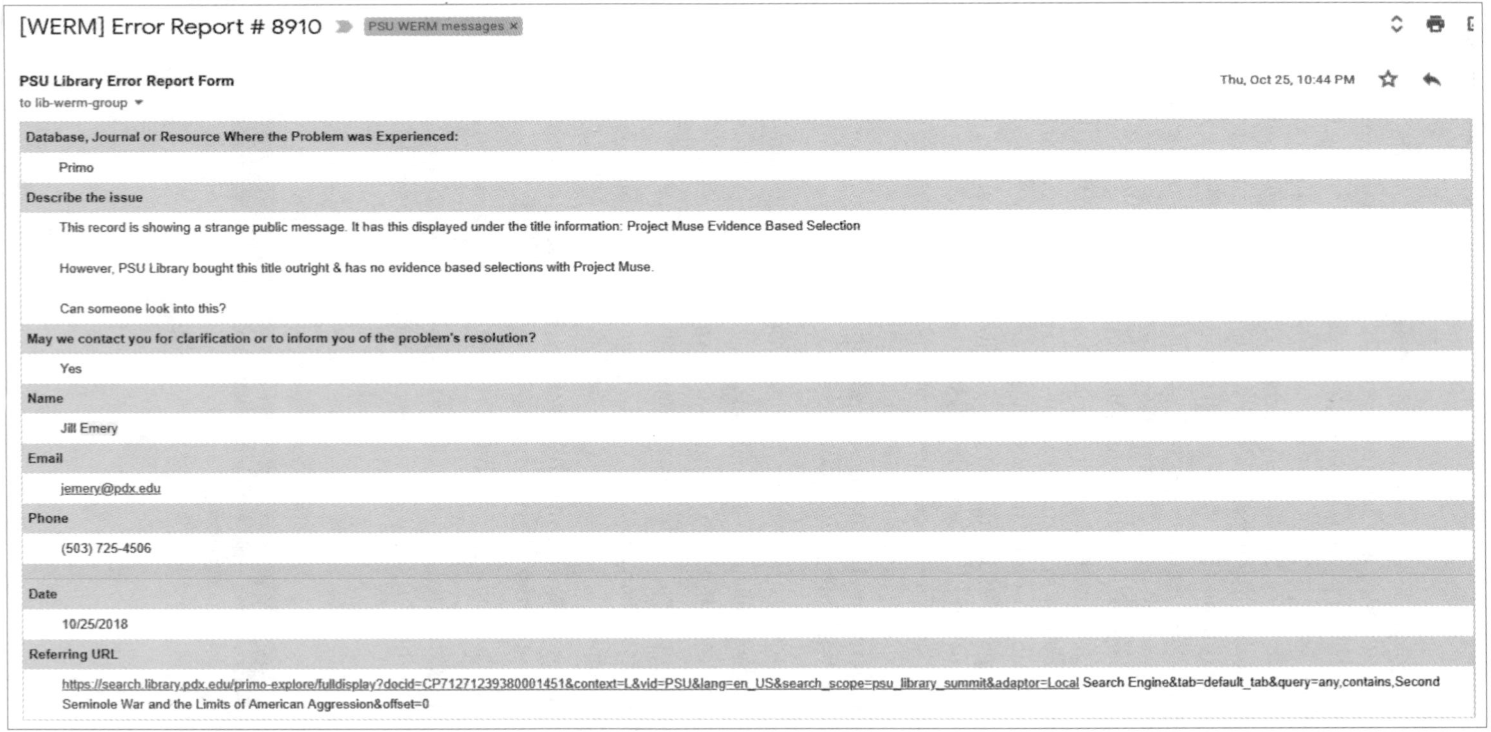

[WERM] Error Report # 8910 › PSU WERM messages ✕

Thu, Oct 25, 10:44 PM ☆ ↰

PSU Library Error Report Form
to lib-werm-group ▾

Database, Journal or Resource Where the Problem was Experienced:

Primo

Describe the issue

This record is showing a strange public message. It has this displayed under the title information: Project Muse Evidence Based Selection

However, PSU Library bought this title outright & has no evidence based selections with Project Muse.

Can someone look into this?

May we contact you for clarification or to inform you of the problem's resolution?

Yes

Name

Jill Emery

Email

jemery@pdx.edu

Phone

(503) 725-4506

Date

10/25/2018

Referring URL

https://search.library.pdx.edu/primo-explore/fulldisplay?docid=CP71271239380001451&context=L&vid=PSU&lang=en_US&search_scope=psu_library_summit&adaptor=Local Search Engine&tab=default_tab&query=any,contains,Second Seminole War and the Limits of American Aggression&offset=0

FIGURE 5.2
Sample Web Form for Error Reporting #2

Once it has been determined where a problem has occurred, the next question is to ask *why* a problem has occurred. By using more complex systems for reporting problems, locating where a problem is occurring can be built into the reporting structure.

Complex Ways to Troubleshoot

Using a CRM system or ticketing system allows you to develop more granular ways to identify where problems are occurring and why they may be happening. In these systems, there are usually more fields to be populated by the person reporting the issue. Given that support for fixing electronic resources problems is a vital part of electronic resources management, institutions will benefit from implementing a tool designed to manage these responses. Such tools can offer end users the ability to find an existing solution without having to submit a problem ticket. It is therefore vitally important to train users of the system about why they need to report a problem fully and systematically.

Many libraries have gone a step further and implemented LibAnswers as a tool for managing problems. At Cornell, the University Library's e-resources group has implemented this specifically for public services library workers.[6] In this case, use of LibAnswers takes place only within technical services, and is limited to addressing problems associated with electronic resources. At Cornell, the LibAnswers-hosted website is where public services staff can submit information about problems they have encountered.[7] Although users can choose from a range of questions about the problem experienced, the only required field is an email address. The benefits of this implementation have been significant. Tickets are easily assigned to experienced individuals who are able to incorporate internal notes as they work on implementing a solution. Tickets that have not been resolved are easily identified and individuals can search completed tickets and use available solutions. Solutions for common problems can be shared with public service library workers, obviating the need to even submit a ticket. An advantage of using a CRM system is the ability to better track and report on an ongoing issue with specific providers or platforms. CRM systems also allow for better overall statistical gathering, one example of which would be the number of times the system was used in a given time period.[8]

Although it is impractical to check all of the following variables, and especially to check all variables against all other variables, having a system that records more data is helpful in diagnosing the problems being encountered. When reviewing reports delivered through the CRM, it should be fairly easy to pinpoint where the problem is occurring and then spend more time figuring out the cause of the issue. In addition, this type of information helps in the overall evaluation of products, as noted in chapter 6, as well as contributing to decision-making regarding retention of resources discussed in chapter 7.

Open Access Troubleshooting

The biggest issue with troubleshooting is getting the end user to report problems encountered. If the end user is trying to access an OA resource through library web pages or the library catalog, then it is easy to have links to the troubleshooting mechanism. However, if end users are going to resources directly, there may not be an easy way to embed a link back to the library to report problems.

This section has focused on ways to develop troubleshooting mechanisms locally and how to approach troubleshooting in a broad sense. The next section delves into more detail about some of the more common problems that arise and discusses the tips and tools to use when troubleshooting or even ways to avoid some of them.

2. Common Problems

As noted at the beginning of this chapter, the majority of problems end users encounter when trying to access resources are readily diagnosed and fairly quickly resolved. More complex problems can take days or weeks to unravel and require quite a bit of follow-up and communication among providers and the end user experiencing the problem. Open access problems may be more routine, such as link checking and through a systematic review of both the descriptive and administrative metadata.

Basic Problems

In this section, we list some of the more basic problems.

Unpaid Invoices

Sometimes the problem is simple. The most basic cause of an access problem is non-payment. For one reason or another, an item has not been renewed as anticipated. This may be because the provider did not invoice within the usual schedule of renewal or the product moved from one provider to another. The first thing to check is whether the resource is still available on the platform where the problem is being reported. If it is, and access is not available, then the next step is to make sure the resource was not cancelled for some reason. If it appears that a renewal should have been processed and wasn't, then the next step would be to renew the subscription. It can be surprising how often an electronic resources provider will shut off access because a library has not paid an invoice that the provider's accounts management team forgot to send. But it happens.

This problem is easily mitigated by using renewal alerts within the acquisitions system to let the acquisitions team anticipate renewal periods and check on the non-receipt of invoices. To resolve, it may simply mean contacting a provider to indicate that the problem exists, then asking for access to be restored until payment is processed.

Site Unavailable

If a site is not available at all, it is easy enough to confirm that the problem is with the site host and not with your own connection to the internet, but it is important to check that the problem is not limited to a particular browser. In most cases, it is worth the time to check if a resource works in at least three different browsers, such as Google Chrome, Firefox, Microsoft Edge, or Safari. There has been an increase with malware attacks on scholarly publishing sites in recent years. When these attacks occur, a company may lose access to many communication channels in-house depending on the malware used. For this reason, it may be worthwhile to check Twitter and library discussion lists to see if others are reporting a large-scale problem with a provider. If there is no set time frame given for when access may be restored, it may be helpful to add a banner note to the library website or within the A–Z listing stating that there is a problem and that library workers are working with the content provider to resolve the problem as quickly as possible.

Site Migrations

Times change, and so do publisher platforms. In some cases, publishers abandon their created platforms for commercial content management platforms. Other times, the migration happens the opposite way with a move from a third-party hosting system to one developed by the content provider. When publishers move their content from one platform to another, access problems arise. Although it is the producers' responsibility to ensure that access continues, the failure to do so is a problem for end users and therefore for electronic resources library workers.

The most common problem with migrations is keeping track of appropriate resource access. That is, understanding what titles and resources the library should have access to on which platforms. For example, when many titles moved away from Ingenta Connect in the early part of the twenty-first century, some publisher content access remained on the Ingenta platform, whereas for other titles all content moved from this platform to the one hosted by the given society or publisher. Title entitlements for a given library are often lost in the conversion process. Once a transition has occurred, library workers should consider doing a test of a small percentage of local holdings to ensure the provisions appear to be correct. If any of the tests find a problem, testing should go forward with more titles to identify where the disconnect occurs.

Changes in paths to content are a frustrating part of these migrations but are almost certainly guaranteed to occur. In some cases, a redirecting URL is used for a length of time. However, this often means that a migration is not discovered as readily as it should be because the old links still appear to work. Link resolver knowledge bases are often delayed in updating to new platform access. This may mean that library workers need to create temporary access targets to use until the link resolver knowledge base catches up with a content shift or change.

Fixing these problems entails work because the vendors are experiencing new and unexpected glitches on their new platforms.

Transfer of Titles

Scholarly societies and content producers choose to move their content from one provider to the next on a five- to ten-year cycle in order to leverage higher returns on the scholarship produced. This results in access loss if this information is not widely communicated at the time of the content move. Library workers experience many problems associated with site and content migrations and should be prepared to address these problems quickly.

One of the best tools to use to identify content shifts from platforms or providers is the Transfer Alerting Service.[9] This tool is hosted by the International Standard Serial Number (ISSN) Organization and allows anyone to search by title, provider, or year to see what journal titles have moved from a given provider or platform and where they may have moved. It is also an invaluable tool to use both at the renewal period and when there is a question about where content now resides. This free service allows individuals to receive notifications when journals change publishers, and includes RSS feeds, an API for automated querying, and a database that can be searched directly.

Aggregated Content Migration

When it comes to aggregated content collections, there are continual content migrations. For this reason, instead of trying to catalog all the content within an aggregated collection, it may be best to just turn on as a target in the local discovery system. Usually publishers and societies have signed agreements to allow access through an aggregated platform for a five- or ten-year period to avoid content shifting around too often. Aggregated e-book providers now try to remove content no more than twice yearly and notify librarians/libraries of these content changes 30-60 days in advance. Streaming media providers are slow to develop a schedule for content moves/shifts and tend to have the most instability. Content is removed and added on a monthly basis with some streaming media providers, making entitlements hard to track and maintain especially in an evidence based or patron driven acquisitions model. Within many aggregated serial collections, most content is embargoed by varying periods, which makes keeping up with holdings problematic. An embargo period can be as short as a single month or as long as two years. Although library workers are comfortable with the fact that content continually comes and goes from large standard aggregated serial collections, end users will not be. A very commonly reported problem is the unavailability of embargoed content, regardless of whether there is a note posted to say that the most recent content is embargoed. This is an example of a standard template reply to the user stating the rules of engagement and access for that resource.

Excessive Downloading

A continual problem for library workers is dealing with excessive downloading issues. Oftentimes, this is a legitimate complaint from a resource provider. This is especially true in research institutions where text and data mining (TDM) is common. There is a growing desire for researchers to mine content or crawl a large set of resources or data looking for specific information. The tools used for these processes often result in an excessive-use case if this is done without the library employees or content provider being alerted beforehand. In addition, some end users do not understand that setting up protocols such as bots or spiders to download a large number of articles or data is an illegal activity in some countries. Although there is a copyright exception in the United Kingdom to cover this (see chapter 3), if an end user does this through the proxy system, then it is likely that the proxy IP will be blocked or shut off from access until the complaint is addressed. Library workers work with their centralized information technology units to identify an end user based on IP or single sign-on account. The end user will need to be sent a cease and desist letter and also be told that this should not occur again. However, it is helpful to also mention that if users have a legitimate reason for crawling a content provider or platform, they should alert the appropriate library workers in advance, so permission can be granted for short periods of time. In some cases, content providers will have a text-mining protocol or API that users employ for this form of research.

Paul Butler of Ball State University has created an EZProxy blacklist hosted on Github that lists specific IP addresses and ranges that have been identified as being regularly used to allow illegitimate access to EZProxy servers.[10] The list contains about 14,250 IP addresses or ranges. By incorporating this list into the local EZProxy admin file, EZProxy administrators can block known bad actors. Of course, there are chances that valid IP addresses or ranges can sneak on to the list, and Butler updates the list as needed, but this free crowd-sourced solution does provide additional levels of protection from blockages related to excessive downloading.

As an example, on a single day at Cornell University, two instances of alleged excessive downloading were discovered. A publisher noted that a particular IP address had downloaded more resources than the publisher felt were legitimate and provided the offending IP address. Because the publisher provided a specific IP address (which was not affiliated with the campus WiFi network), campus IT was able to identify the individual username most commonly associated with that IP address (in this case, the IP address referred to a desktop in an on-campus office). When the individual behind the username was contacted, it turned out that a doctoral student had been performing "sentiment analysis" of recent newspaper articles about a specific environmental topic that had been published in a specific geographic region and specific timeframe. The vendor offered to create a customized space where the individual could work on this data without bumping up against download limits, but the costs made that prohibitive. However, once it was clear that this was the legitimate work of an advanced student, the content provider was willing to work toward a solution.

In another case on the same day, a journal publisher blocked access to its resource after 150 articles were downloaded in fairly quick succession. Because the only IP address that was available in this case was the university's WiFi network, there was not much that could be done, until a student reported being blocked from downloading articles from the very same journal. A follow-up discussion determined that a faculty committee member had told the student, another doctoral candidate, to read every article published in the last two years in that journal to prepare for exams.

Complex Problems

More complex problems are those where the problem cannot be replicated by library workers, the problem requires working through a series of tests in order to resolve, or the problem is the result of a complex series of events. The resolution of the problem will take a longer period of time to diagnose and solve to everyone's satisfaction. If the problems uncover a significant issue, it is worthwhile to share the findings on library discussion lists to inform others about the problems encountered.

Browser Issues and Problems

There are a number of browsers that end users employ depending on the computing or tablet environment they use regularly. Resource providers intend for their products to work in the majority of popular browser environments. There are situations where functionality is optimized for some browsers over others. Testing access in multiple browsers when problems are reported help to diagnose this situation. If the site fails to work correctly in one browser but does work in others, use the failing browser's incognito mode to test without being impacted by browser extensions or existing cookies. If it works in incognito mode, clear the cache and delete cookies from that browser's standard mode, and test again. If it then works, the problem was likely local, but it is important to check on several other machines to confirm the problem has been identified correctly.

If the site fails to work in multiple browsers, test it on different machines. The top browsers represent over 90 percent of desktop browsers in use.[11] Many resources work extremely well in Google Chrome but not all are optimized to fully function in Safari, the browser built into Apple operating systems. When troubleshooting problems, a key question to ask end users is which browser they are using to try to access the content. This single question can help to diagnose and solve a problem more quickly as it allows the person working on the issue to best mirror the search or access point at which access is denied. A helpful diagnostic tool is a browser rubric to work through in order to test access (see table 5.2).

Another problem that occurs is when end users use certain setups with their browsers. If end users or library workers use high security settings on their browsers, especially those that block pop-ups or where cookies are not enabled, these settings can result in problems accessing content from some resource providers and platforms. Asking end users to check their browser settings or try to access the content through a browser they normally do not use regularly will often provide the access that may otherwise be blocked.

For example, library workers in one area found that searches within a major aggregator database website returned no results at all. Somewhat to their surprise, they did not hear other library workers complaining about the problem, but the expectation was that this would be a massive problem

TABLE 5.2

Browser Rubric

	CHROME	FIREFOX	SAFARI	EDGE
PC, on-campus	Success; waited a moment then saw "Welcome to Library/ University" note	Success; same as Chrome		Couldn't download Edge
PC, off-campus	Success; same as On-campus Chrome experience			
Mac, on-campus	Failed	Success; same as On-campus Chrome experience	Success; same as On-campus Chrome experience	
Mac, off-campus	Failed	Success; same as On-campus Chrome experience	Success; same as On-campus Chrome experience	

experienced by many. A day later, the problem remained for the workers in the same area, so they contacted the vendor. The vendor representative could see no issues that might be causing the problem. To investigate further, the library workers went to a public terminal to confirm the problem there. To their amazement, the problem was not replicated on the public terminals and searching worked fine. Going back to their desks and searching in an alternate browser, they discovered the resource worked there as well. Eventually, the cause of the problem was found to be a browser extension on the employees' work machines. This also serves as a reminder to attempt at least some initial investigations before submitting problem tickets to vendors and publishers.

Working through Problems with the Content Provider's Technicians

Complex problems often require contact with the technical support team of the provider or producer of the content. The first thing is to know who to contact. This can be your sales representative, who can usually handle known issues or concerns, or it may be a technical support team. It is helpful if this contact information is recorded within the administrative metadata captured in the acquisitions record for the resource or at the collection level record as was noted in chapter 3. For resources from scholarly content providers, the technical support team may be located in a different locale than the content producer or provider. This is helpful if it allows for technical support to occur in an ongoing way or it may be a hindrance if the support team is in a time zone different from yours. When contacting technical support by email, best practice is to outline the problem first in the body of the email and then write the subject line for the problem after you have defined the situation. The process of describing the problem—as accurately and as dispassionately as possible—leads to a better understanding of that problem. Writing the subject line, or summary, is in fact very important. Whereas a subject line along the lines of "JSTOR Web site won't open!! Help!" is fairly useless, one that reads "Citation links from Journal of Foo won't open when using Firefox" can lead to much quicker resolution without confusion about what is meant. It is extremely useful to the technical support team if a series of screen captures can be provided to illustrate the problem. Most end users have not taken the time to provide screen shots when problems occur, so this may mean replicating the issues occurring. If the problem is intermittent, sometimes you can start to doubt the problem even exists because you cannot always reproduce it.

An example of the time-consuming nature of troubleshooting certain problems is a specific problem encountered at the Cornell University Library. Library workers were unable to access a subscribed resource. Initially, the thought was that it might be because the vendor had failed to invoice for the content and, as a result, payment had not been made, which led to access suspension. That was not the reason in this case. However, establishing the actual cause was quite difficult. Despite impressive work on the part of the sales representative, the problem stumped everyone. Library workers checked the IP addresses multiple times over the course of a week and checked access on multiple machines and through multiple browsers. All of the solutions implemented failed. Finally, through an online conference call that included library workers in upstate New York, a sales representative in London, and a technical services representative in India, screens were shared while trying to access the resource so that the technical team could see the error logs. This information allowed the technical team to eventually resolve this surprisingly challenging problem. Luckily, problems of this magnitude are rare, but they do happen. They may be tricky to troubleshoot and can sometimes require a significant commitment from all sides to resolve the problem.

Unreproducible Problems

Sometimes, a reported problem cannot be replicated. In these cases, the best response to the end user reporting the problem is that it is not possible to reproduce the problem experienced. Temporary issues occur because of internet connection interruptions, latency with page loading due to slow internet connection, or slight glitches that self-correct within minutes. Asking the end user to take screen shots and report back again if they encounter the same problem may result in finding a browser issue or problem.

OA Problems

For research published with funding from federal granting agencies and some private funders, access to the content in the United States can be embargoed before being made freely available. Immediate access may not be available but within six months to a year, the content is released for access. In local repository systems, tracking when access can be made available is critical. In other cases, a scholarly publisher or provider may have made a journal title freely available but then decided that revenue could be generated from subscription and decides to move the content behind a paywall. Another case where OA content becomes inaccessible is if a journal title ceases publication or is discontinued. In these cases, the publisher may opt to move the content into a preservation platform where access is only available by paying the participation fee for that preservation platform.

3. Metadata

Some of the simplest problems encountered with online resources are the descriptive metadata being incorrect or an end user becoming confused about which journal issues and years are available. Indeed, incorrect metadata is such a common problem that it deserves a section of its own. Problems with journal issues are often due to human error. All it takes is one bad entry for the incorrect information to travel across multiple platforms and catalogs. Fortunately, these problems are almost always readily identifiable and easy to correct quickly.

Basic Problems

Incorrect metadata and missing content cause serious problems for all online content. If resources are described incorrectly or have the wrong holdings information given it will seem like resources are available when they are not or unavailable when they are. The source of these problems may stem from incorrect bibliographic record sets, inaccurate KBART files, flawed holdings update information, or rolling walls of content addition or subtraction from a provider. Unfortunately, the result is a poor experience for end users, which leads to reduced usage of some providers' content as well as a reduction in the perceived value by library workers and libraries. It is the e-resource equivalent of mis-shelving a book.

In some cases, a publisher will represent a journal that has changed its name, but under only the subsequent name and throughout the full publication period. This is bad practice because the journal was published under the prior name in its early years. To suggest that it had a different name at that time ensures that links to content under the earlier name will not be found using standard indexes, which will reference the current title. This might seem like a minor problem that affects only a few publishers and will be easy to fix. The latter point is true, but not the former. It is a significant enough problem that the National Information Standards Organization (NISO) spent time and resources to establish a working group of librarians and publishers to write Recommended Practices for the Presentation and Identification of E-Journals (PIE-J), which specifically details the problem and its solutions for journal publishers.[12]

When vendors misrepresent their content through inaccurate metadata, they reduce the functionality of their products. Although searches within the publisher's resource are not negatively impacted by inaccurate metadata because end users search the content directly and do not rely on information about the content, searches that must make use of metadata about the resource's contents, such as through link resolvers and journal A–Z lists, cause failures when they are not correct. Some knowledge base vendors spend time to create tools and systems to correct this data as it is imported into their knowledge base. This work minimizes linking problems and corrects the errors that the publishers failed to fix themselves. In addition, many library workers establish a yearly calendar or schedule to review various packages and resources to ensure that the holdings represented for the collection of content are correct.

Complex Problems

Problems with aggregated monograph and streaming video content are far more complex. Bibliographic descriptions of e-monograph and streaming video collections describe each individual title in a collection but do not always reference the collection back. If library workers choose to catalog individual titles within aggregated e-book collections and e-video collections as opposed to just turning on the collection as a target in a discovery tool, it will be necessary to update the bibliographic collection records on a regular basis. This is also true with e-book collections where content may be added throughout the year or with various end user driven acquisitions models and evidence-based models of purchasing. The access to content in these packages works best when there is a set schedule to update records on a monthly or quarterly basis.

Open Access

The majority of open access content problems are due to errors with descriptive metadata. As discussed above, if embargoed content does not have the correct metadata attached, users will not have access because that content is not retrievable.

Another problem with open access content is that many libraries use their institutional repositories as current research information systems (CRIS) or have completely replaced their repositories with a CRIS. This leads to problems where many records in the repository contain metadata data only with links to subscribed content via a DOI. If end users are using a tool such as OA Button, this results in them thinking an OA article has been deposited into a repository when in fact all that is available is a citation.[13] This can cause quite a confusing circular path on which an end user can get stuck.

4. Tools for Troubleshooting

As noted at the beginning of this chapter, there are various tools and CRM systems that help with creating a ticketing or tracking system for problems. However, there are also tools and practices to utilize with routine functions to help proactively work through known situations that occur regularly. When working through common problems, tools such as Transfer and the EZProxy Blacklist are helpful. However, there are other tools, some open source and some free services that are also useful.

It should be noted that all of the tools described in this section are equally relevant to open access content.

Basic Support Tools

Link Checking

The most common problem all libraries face is the loss of access due to bad URL links. Content is just not available in the format it was published in originally. This condition is known as "link rot."[14] It occurs with subscription-based resources as well as open access content. Ensuring long-term access to these resources, or proactively noting when they fail, is difficult. Georgia Southern University Library workers have begun a process that they refer to as "essential audits" as a way to check on links periodically to try to get ahead of problems occurring for end users.[15] An open source tool that has been created to perform linking checking comes from the University of Georgia Libraries. The tool, known as SEESAU (Serial Experimental Electronic Subscription Access Utilities), is designed to check links through the OpenURL resolver to insure access is still available to the content on a quarterly basis. Given that this process was designed over ten years ago, it is likely an updated version of this tool could be created now.[16]

Another free product to use for link checking is Callisto from Sharp Moon.[17] To use Callisto, a small program is installed on one or more computers within the library's network. This program regularly checks all e-resources that have been included in the institution's Callisto profile to see if that site is active. When sites are not accessible, Callisto sends an email notifying library workers. Another email is sent when access is restored. For a collection with many resources, the end result can be an occasional deluge of emails—sometimes too many to be particularly helpful, but in some cases, this can be useful for indicating when or if a particular site has become inaccessible. For most libraries, Callisto can be implemented as a free service. In addition, LibGuides has a built-in link checking utility. This service can be run periodically to check links in both the A–Z listing as well as links being used on specific guide pages. Furthermore, this tool can be an invaluable for identifying multiple links that may need updating and instituting the changes on a large scale across the platform instead of having to change links one by one.

EZProxy Maintenance

Another way to discover problems proactively is to perform a quarterly or semiannual maintenance or cleanup of EZProxy targets. Going through the list of entries added to EZProxy may uncover platforms that are no longer in use but may be still made available on out-of-date web pages and LibGuides. This is generally a manual process, which can be tedious, but it is useful in helping to keep resource activation up-to-date. It is also a way to discover resources and content that may now be available openly and no longer need to be proxied.

Complex Support Tools

These tools are more complex in part because they require a greater time investment and more coordination. In addition, specific user communities may require more in-depth analysis of platforms and content provider sites. However, investing in more complex processes often does pay off in greater use of resources overall.

User Testing

Developing mechanisms to both directly and indirectly observe how end users navigate and use resources will yield invaluable information. As information professionals, our paths to using content resources are rife with bias. What seems easy and straightforward to use may in fact seem quite complicated and difficult to an end user encountering a specific resource environment for the first time. For this reason, there have been multiple studies performed on the usability design of database A–Z listings to see how readily an end user can get to a specific known resource.[18,19] In the first study, a review of A–Z database listing sites was reviewed and tested to help design the local presentation of resources. A second study undertaken by East Carolina University helped develop staffing for universal design as well as study the use of the A–Z listing of resources. User testing is a way to see where end users may be having issues utilizing the resources. It is a time-consuming effort but can be part of a scheduled review of resources.

Accessibility with Adaptive Technology

A growing concern in all libraries is ensuring all web platforms in use and all resources available are accessible for every user. This requires testing and checking for possible accessibility issues. The web content accessibility guidelines (WCAG) help to define the base level of access needed for web platforms and content to work with assistive technologies.[20] One freely available tool that can help with testing for accessibility is the web accessibility evaluation tool (WAVE).[21] This tool helps identify problems that could occur for users trying to access web platforms and contents while using assistive software and devices. It cannot identify the exact problems occurring but can highlight where problems may occur. The tool can be used through browser extensions or by using the web form to load pages for reviews. Another recommendation is to work with your local disability resource center to have end users with disabilities test the usability of access points as well as specific resources. This will help alert everyone to known problems with specific platforms and content providers and help with the future selection of content based on usability and accessibility.

5. Communication in Troubleshooting

Poor communication within library settings creates problems. For instance, if your information technology office changes IPs for any buildings and does not tell library workers, access to resources will be lost until the new IP range is added to administrative portals.

The main rule with communication in troubleshooting is the KISS principle: (Keep It Simple Stupid).[22] There is an unfortunate tendency among those who work with electronic resources on a regular basis to talk in acronyms and to over-utilize technical language. Part of the training of library workers involved in troubleshooting should always be about how to communicate effectively. In addition, there is also the tendency to make correlations between problems too quickly. Although it is true that problems with specific providers are likely to be interrelated or very similar, this is not always the case. This emphasizes the importance of keeping an open mind when receiving an initial report and considering how to address it. Hiatt has noted that with the increase of electronic access to information, technical services work has become a public service at most libraries.[23] For this reason, all training about interactions with end users should include everyone within the organization.

Basic Communication Efforts

There are many ways to handle the communications needed for troubleshooting, but the best efforts include developing template replies. For example,

> *Thank you for your problem report. We are looking into this matter and will get back to you shortly.* (You may have a standard response time in place where you have to send a human response.)

> *We have discovered that the coverage date of this resource is incorrect, and we do not have access to the (journal/article you have requested. Here is a link to order the needed content from Interlibrary Loan).* (Some libraries will waive any charges if the mistake is theirs.)

> *We have discovered there is a problem with our access to this resource and are working with the provider to resolve the access issue as quickly as possible.*

> *We are unable to replicate the problem you have reported. It appears to have been a temporary glitch. The article/chapter you were trying to access is attached to this email.*

Another basic approach to use when there is a serious problem with a popular resource or title is to add notes where appropriate (e.g., the main library web page as a banner or in the A–Z listing) stating that this is a known problem and the library is working with the provider to resolve it as quickly as possible. Furthermore, many libraries have blogs where they can make this information available.[24] It is also possible to drop these updates into other pages, which ensures a consistent message. The University of Strathclyde in Scotland has created a LibGuide to post regular and ongoing resource problems and provide updates to users regarding specific interfaces and known problems (see figure 5.3).

Poor communication issues between a provider and library can exacerbate a problem. Knowing the right person to contact at a provider is just as important as making the contact with the provider. Oftentimes, the salesperson does not have enough experience with the product and cannot help to solve problems. It is likely that the sales person will need to direct the question to others in their organization, which may not happen immediately. It is important to have a set contact list for each provider and know who to contact with problems, usually through a technical support line or email address. The

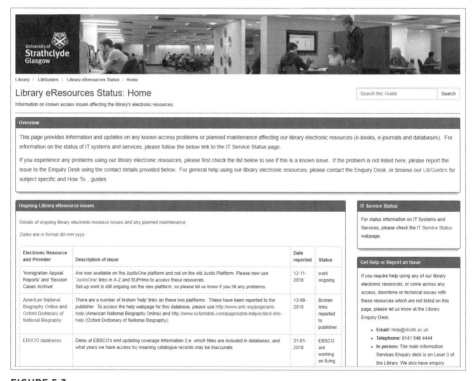

FIGURE 5.3
University of Strathclyde, Library eResources Status Web Page[25]

maintenance of this list is best done by one or two people in an organization and then shared broadly with everyone who needs this information. When problems arise, communication with designated contacts should be succinct and direct in order to convey problems that a library needs help solving. As discussed above, writing out the problem and then developing the subject line of the email can go a long way in helping to resolve problems sooner as opposed to later.

More Complex Communication Efforts

Troubleshooting access problems occurs at many access and reference points within a library. Problems may be mentioned to library workers at circulation or access desks, at a reference desk, or through chat sessions. Given that problems come into a library from multiple access points, it is wise to hold quarterly meetings or open forums between the troubleshooting team and the service point library workers to talk through known problems and issues that arise. Having both the problem reporters and the problem solvers in the room together can lead to finding unexpected solutions and responses. In this way, issues and concerns that may seem minor can be discussed and investigated.

In a study at Georgetown University, Kimbrough outlines a methodology used to mine chat transcripts to identify known problems and issues occurring with electronic resources.[26] The research revealed that just over a quarter of the transcript studies were about electronic resource problems and of those problems, over 85 percent were known item issues where an end user was attempting to access a specific book, article, or resource. The study concluded that more collaboration between library workers answering chat problems and the workers handling electronic resources would be beneficial.

When working with vendors and content providers directly, there will be times where email exchanges cannot resolve a problem or issue. There will need to be phone calls made between the technicians working at a content provider and the local library workers to resolve the problem. No provider wants there to be access issues with their content because this ultimately means loss of business or revenue. Content provider technicians are often in a similar situation to that of library workers in having to deal with concerns and problems and generally understand how to help resolve issues quickly. During a call with a content provider, it is important to be able to state the following basic pieces of information:

- Your institutional identifier, either the standard one or the account number used by the content providing access to content
- Your name and contact information for follow-up as needed
- Your institution's IP addresses and specifically your proxy IP address

- The browser environment most commonly used by your institution and its end users
- Any specific information relevant to your institution or your level of access to the content, for instance, whether your library's subscription is for simultaneous users or if it is a site license, if everyone must use a VPN to access your resources, and so forth.

Politeness when working toward a solution together helps the process to go more smoothly as well as reach a successful conclusion more easily.

Finally, designating someone to monitor relevant discussions lists and activity on platforms like Twitter can be helpful in recognizing major issues and problems. If you belong to a consortia, oftentimes known problems and issues are raised on discussion lists, which can be helpful in informing others in the library about known issues and problems. The key national lists where problems are often discussed are:

ERiL (Electronic Resources in Libraries)[27]

LIS-E-RESOURCES[28]

SERIALST[29]

Monitoring these lists will often provide information about significant downtimes to be expected from resources as well as with large-scale issues that many libraries experience.

Communication Efforts with Open Access

Communication about the availability of open access resources and open scholarly publication tools should be consistently provided throughout the year. Many libraries and library workers focus their efforts around Open Access Week in October and Research Week in May. However, developing a quarterly series of presentations focused on research communication is a worthwhile investment that helps to keep open scholarly practices consistently in mind (see figure 5.4).

6. Negative Impact of End Users Giving Up

You cannot know if there is a problem if no one reports it. This is true for all resources whether they are electronic or in print. Running routine maintenance processes will help to find some problems that may not be reported but many go unreported and unresolved.

In the following chapter we look at the assessment of resources including that of usage data. Very low usage can indicate that there is an unreported problem with the resource and that users have given up. Unless investigated,

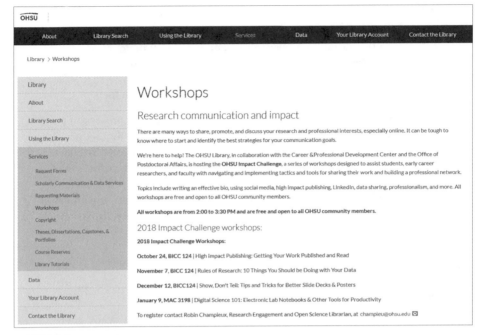

FIGURE 5.4
Oregon Health & Science University, Workshops: Research Communication and Impact[30]

low usage will likely result in cancellation or reduction in the content provided at some future point.

Engaging library workers who ask questions about resources and resource access on a regular basis is really the best way to uncover and find problems that may be going unreported.

NOTES

1. Wikipedia. (2018). Pareto principle. https://en.wikipedia.org/wiki/Pareto _principle.

2. Heaton, Robert. (2018). Tools for troubleshooting: Which ones and what for. *Journal of Electronic Resources Librarianship 30*(1): 9–26. https://doi.org/10.1080/ 1941126X.2018.1443903.

3. Talbott, Holly, & Zmau, Ashley. (2018). *Electronic resources librarianship: A practical guide for librarians* (Lanham, MD: Rowman & Littlefield).

4. Carter, Sunshine, & Traill, Stacie A. (2018). Developing staff skills in e-resource troubleshooting: Training, assessment, and continuous progress. In *Reengineering the library: Issues in electronic resources management* (Chicago: ALA).

5. Graham, Tess, & Hosburgh, Nate. (2014). A user-centered approach to addressing issues of discoverability and access, *Serials Librarian 67*(1): 48–51. https://doi.org/10.1080/0361526X.2014.899290.

6. springshare. (2018). LibAnswers. https://www.springshare.com/libanswers/.

7. Cornell University. (2018). e-resources troubleshooting. http://cornell.libanswers.com/.

8. Borchert, Carol Ann. (2006). Untangling the jungle of e-journal access issues using CRM software, *Library Collections, Acquisitions, and Technical Services 30*(3/4): 224–237. https://doi.org/10.1080/14649055.2006.10766130.

9. NISO. (2018). Welcome to the Transfer Alerting Service. https://journaltransfer.issn.org/.

10. P. R. Butler. (2018). EZProxy_IP Blacklist. https://github.com/prbutler/EZProxy_IP_Blacklist.

11. Statistica. (2018). Market share held by leading desktop internet browsers in the United States from January 2015 to October 2018. https://www.statista.com/statistics/272697/market-share-desktop-internet-browser-usa/.

12. NISO. (2018). Recommended practices for the presentation and identification of e-journals (PIE-J). https://groups.niso.org/workrooms/piej.

13. Emery, Jill. (2018). How green is our valley? Five-year study of selected LIS journals from Taylor & Francis for green deposit of articles. *Insights 31*(23). http://doi.org/10.1629/uksg.406.

14. Wikipedia. (2018). Link rot. https://en.wikipedia.org/wiki/Link_rot.

15. Mortimore, Jeffrey M., & Minihan, Jessica M. (2018). Essential audits for proactive electronic resources troubleshooting and support. *Library Hi Tech News 35*(1) :6–0. https://doi.org/10.1108/LHTN-11-2017-0085.

16. Collins, Maria, & Murray, William. T. (2009). SEESAU: University of Georgia's electronic journal verification system. *Serials Librarian 35*(2): 80–87.

17. Sharp Moon. (2017). Callisto. http://sharpmoon.com/callisto/.

18. Fry, Amy, & Lesher, Marcella. (2011). Beyond lists and guides: Using usability to help students get the most out of e-resources. *Serials Librarian 60*(1–4): 206–212. https://doi.org/10.1080/0361526X.2011.556036.

19. Kavanagh Webb, Katy, Rhodes, Tamara, Cook, Eleanor, Andresen, Christine, & Russell, Roger. (2016). Our experience with user experience: Exploring staffing configurations to conduct UX in an academic library. *Journal of Library Administration 56*(7): 757–776. https://doi.org/10.1080/01930826.2015.1109892.

20. Johnson, Rick. (2018). Ensuring the accessibility of all learning content: The accessibility of learning content is undergoing a dramatic change. *Research Information 94:* 16–17. https://www.researchinformation.info/news/analysis-opinion/ ensuring-accessibility-all-learning-content.

21. WAVE. (n.d.). WAVE help. https://wave.webaim.org/help.

22. Wikipedia. (2018). KISS principle. https://en.wikipedia.org/wiki/KISS_principle.

23. Hiatt, C. Derrik. (2015). Technical services is public services. *Technicalities 35*(5): 8–10. http://hdl.handle.net/10339/57380.

24. University of Huddersfield library. (2018). Electronic resources blog. https://library.hud.ac.uk/blogs/er/.

25. University of Strathclyde. (2018). Library eresources status. http://guides.lib.strath.ac.uk/c.php?g=658906.

26. Kimbrough, John. (2018). Technical Services and the virtual reference desk: Mining chat transcripts for improved e-resource management. *Serials Librarian* 74(1–4): 212–216. https://doi.org/10.1080/0361526X.2018.1428482.

27. Electronic Resources in Libraries LISTSERV. (n.d.). https://www.eril-l.org/.

28. JiscMail. (2018). LIS-E-RESOURCES. https://www.jiscmail.ac.uk/lists/LIS-E-RESOURCES.html.

29. NASIG. (2018). SERIALST. www.nasig.org/site_page.cfm?pk_association_webpage_menu=308&pk_association_webpage=4955.

30. Oregon Health & Science University. (2018). Workshops: Research communication and impact. https://www.ohsu.edu/library/workshops.

6

Assessment

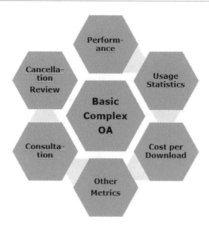

Introduction

This section looks at the assessment of e-resources. It develops the formerly separate evaluation and ongoing access and annual review sections in the original version of TERMs as a more complete section. Assessment is an ongoing process for many resources. However, the actual assessment of a resource may not commence until an annual review is required. For this reason, it is important to understand precisely what is going to be assessed at the acquisition stage, as some assessment criteria may need to be built into the contract itself, for example COUNTER compliance and requirements for the publisher or vendor to provide specific data on titles.[1]

In addition to contractual requirements, the focus is on what is to be assessed and why. These evaluation criteria differ from resource to resource. An aggregated resource needs a simple cost per download calculation to understand value for money. A more complex resource will assess a number of different criteria, such as, the evaluation of the user experience as well as simple downloads. An example of a poor user experience is one in which an end user has trouble accessing content due to heavy digital rights of an e-book being in place. In addition, it is necessary to understand who the actual users are. For example, researchers, undergraduates, or a mix within a given organization. Poor usage does not mean automatic cancellation. If the resource under evaluation is a very specialist resource that is only used by a small research center or faculty then usage will never be "high" but may be entirely "appropriate" for that group. That research center can be responsible for a great deal of research income or may be a particular specialization of the local organization and thus deserve to retain needed content. Evaluation works best when it encompasses a broad spectrum of considerations as opposed to a single designation such as cost per use.

Assessment of an open access (OA) resource is completely different. The assessment could focus on the external use of the institutional repository rather than the internal use by faculty and students. This can be achieved by analyzing citation data and then linking this use to research income.

In addition to learning who the users are, there is also the need to understand the performance of a resource over the reporting period. Therefore, troubleshooting is an important part of assessment (see chapter 5). Was the resource unavailable for any length of time, did this affect the user experience, and is this reflected in usage and or usage comment?

Not only is it necessary to consider the assessment of a resource from the very start of a contract, ideally the assessment will continue over an extended reporting period of at least two years to understand any underlying trends in the usage data or use experience. Most resources, or new business models, take time to embed. In the first year, there will likely be little meaningful data generated (e.g., usage). However, user surveys and troubleshooting reports provide a better picture of use during this time.

The assessment of complex resources will also need improved cooperation between different teams, such as the e-resources and OA teams, as well as subject liaison. Assessment reports must often go to different management levels within the library. Senior management do not want the same level of granularity as the electronic resources or OA team may require. Furthermore, not everyone has the inclination or the time to spend hours poring over a spreadsheet. Visualizations offer a more efficient way to get the information across. A picture paints a thousand words.

On the subject of data and visualizations—there are risks. A visualization needs to be put in context. It can often show more than a spreadsheet— patterns emerge that were not obvious in the underlying data. However, because there is also a risk of misinterpreting the visualization, notes are always required. Furthermore, the data source should always be given to prevent challenges about the accuracy of the information, particularly by senior management or by publishers during the renewal or negotiation process. It is important to back visualizations up with cold hard facts. This works the other way around, of course. During negotiations publishers and providers often present visualizations of their assessments. If the data looks too good to be true, it probably is. Challenge the sources and ask to see the underlying datasets during vendor presentations.

1. Performance of the Resource against the Selection Criteria and Troubleshooting Feedback

To fully understand the performance of a resource, go back over previous processes. For example, how did the resource perform against the negotiation criteria? Check the list of common deal breakers (see chapter 3), to see if your criteria were met. Perhaps more importantly, were they adhered to by the vendor or publisher?

For a new resource, how did the implementation go? If there were issues, did they get resolved? Did access start at the right time?

For any resource, monitor troubleshooting issues. In extreme cases, the attention required could lead to cancellation, or potentially to compensation or a reduced fee in the oncoming subscription period. If an institution entered into a Service Level Agreement (SLA) with the vendor, this should be monitored over the year of service to ensure the SLA has been met. If the agreement was through a consortium, it may have done this for you. It is vital to report any issues so that the consortia can act on your behalf. Just as users report issues, consortia need to hear from the institutions they serve.

Basic Resources

As noted above, before looking at the perceived value of a resource (e.g., cost per download or impact), it is essential to check whether the resource in question satisfied the selection criteria. At its most basic level, this is simply a question of assessing the relevance of the resource. For a single title, it may be that the researcher or even the research institute is no longer part of the university. For an e-book, it may mean that a new edition has been published and the older edition can be removed from the collection. It should be a relatively easy check-box procedure to see if the common deal breakers have been achieved throughout the review period (see table 6.1).

If a supplier fails to supply or work toward a particular deal breaker required by an institution, this should be fed back into the assessment process to inform the decision as to whether to renew, cancel, or seek a revised contract, possibly with a discount if certain terms were not met. For example, if the resource was unavailable for X number of days, a discount should be sought the next year. It is also good to report full compliance to the supplier, as this builds on the goodwill that often occurs in a long-term relationship

TABLE 6.1

Negotiation Deal Breakers

	DEAL BREAKERS		
Negotiation Point	**Extremely Important**	**Somewhat Important**	**Not Important**
Cost	X		
Technical Access	X		
Site Definition	X		
User Definition	X		
Accessibility Requirements	X		
Usage Measurement		X	
Interaction with Discovery System			X
Indemnification Clauses	X		
Privacy Clauses	X		
Exigency Clauses	X		
Venue of Agreement	X		
Perpetual Access Rights/Preservation	X		
Text and Data Mining			X

between an institution and a supplier. This feedback loop can often smooth the way to better agreements.

For new resources (and new interfaces), check to make sure implementation processes were utilized, and that protocols on access will have been put in place (see chapter 4). Did the process run smoothly? If not, then compensation may be due, and this information needs to be fed into the cancellation review. For resources that have multiple access points via different providers, you may have the choice to move from one to another.

Troubleshooting is the third basic criteria to check (the preceding chapter goes into more detail regarding troubleshooting processes). Many resources run fairly effectively with only a few problems during the year, and some of the issues are often out of the control of the publisher, provider, or the e-resource manager. However, if a resource appears to be failing, it might be a deciding factor in assessment. Examples include connectivity issues, unscheduled downtime, or problems with access and authentication. The resource can be so unintuitive to users that it has failed to become embedded at the institution, despite best efforts. These factors should be included in the assessment process at the time of the renewal, which is why it is so important to record data about a resource during the evaluation period.

When these factors occur, record them on a spreadsheet or within the e-resources management system or library management system. Issues with user experience build evidence during the year. Surveys to end users or subject liaisons may reveal further information, these tools could take the form of fairly basic surveys to more complex user consultations, which will be examined below.

Complex Resources

For larger resources such as big deals or large aggregated databases, the continued relevance of content is a key assessment. Of particular interest is the movement of titles in and out of the agreement. Ideally, for journal big deals, the lack of use of the Transfer Code of Practice will be one of the deal breakers.[2] This helps publishers ensure that journal content remains easily accessible by users when there is a transfer between publishers, and to ensure that the transfer process occurs with minimum disruption. The Code contains best practice guidelines for both the Transferring Publisher and the Receiving Publisher. However, even if a big deal publisher has signed up for the code, the publisher that is taking on a particular title may not have. There is also the question of checking whether the transfer of a title is of interest or not.

It is best practice to establish a checking process for titles leaving a big deal. For example,

1. Set up a regular schedule to check transferred titles for a particular publisher's big deal; this usually occurs annually in late summer or early fall when many transfer notices are distributed by publishers/providers.

2. For a list of titles, establish which are actually part of the big deal undertaken, because the agreement may not have access to every title. Ignore the titles that move if they are not included in the agreement.

3. Is the title leaving the deal one of the core subscriptions? For example, was the title a previous subscription prior to the big deal? If yes, then check where the title has gone. A new subscription to the title may be required—this may be at an additional unplanned cost that is not in the current budget cycle. Check usage to review the relevance of the title transferring. If the usage is low, forgo picking up a subscription.

4. If the subscribed title moves to another big deal to which there is a subscription, the associated costs will likely move with it. Transfer into another big deal may prevent the review of the title. The title may remain within an overall subscription portfolio even if demand has declined.

5. If the transferred title is not a core title, check whether it was a highly accessed title. If download statistics are high, investigate a new subscription at an additional cost. If the title moves into another big deal, there will likely be a chance to maintain access at no additional cost—a plus point for the big deal! However, make sure the title does not enter the next big deal as part of a set of additional titles in a separate bundle that is not part of the current contract.

6. Finally, if the title is not part of the core subscriptions and not well used, there is no need to take any further action, other than checking what the access rights are to this title going forward.

A significant number of titles leaving a particular agreement may trigger a clause in the contract that allows for immediate cancellation as we note in chapter 3.

Large full-text aggregated database agreements (e.g., journals, e-books, or streaming media) will not be subject to the Transfer Code of Conduct. Furthermore, transfer of titles in and out of an aggregated database are expected to be far more than for a journal big deal. This means that there is a fair amount of risk in subscribing to a database agreement in order to access a specific title as things tend to be in a constant state of flux. Keeping track of this churn manually is virtually impossible. Fortunately, web-scale discovery systems now automate this process. The easiest way to assess a database agreement may be to look at cost per download (as discussed below). However, if the local institution subscribes to a number of similar database agreements, it is also important to run an overlap analysis as part of any assessment. This could either be done as a manual process by comparing spreadsheets or as part of an automated overlap analysis in a web-scale discovery system (see chapter 2).

For longer agreements, for example, three to five years for big deals, a longitudinal analysis of compliance may be required in order to check on the previous year's compliance.

Contractual compliance may also be carried out at the consortia level for big deals. However, monitoring of all contracts is a good idea to make sure that compliance takes place.

For e-book packages, similar criteria apply; like journals, much of this will have been negotiated at the beginning of the agreement. However, an important question should be asked: Does the agreed business model work and are there new models on offer? Many current e-book deals evolve into a purchase of a front list of titles and then aggregation of backfile titles. This means a library or library consortia purchase the content for a given year but then selectively buy back content as needed. Part of the evaluation should center around the purchase model as opposed to the overall current use of the content.

Consortia often request subscribing institutions to complete surveys in order to assess the success of a particular agreement. Additionally, an institution may wish to consult its users about their user experience, particularly for e-books.

Open Access

Assessment of open access content depends on the reason for use. The dependency focuses on what the requirements are for the assessment. Broadly speaking, this will fall into two distinct categories: assessment for research funders and assessment for libraries and research offices.

Assessment for funders refers to two areas. First, there is funder compliance. For example, funders in the United Kingdom require an annual report from all universities that receive research funding in order to assess open access compliance and to monitor the effectiveness of the Research Councils U.K. (RCUK) open access policy.[3] Both RCUK (now UKRI) and COAF (including the Wellcome Trust) have come together with Jisc to produce a single excel template.[4] A guide from the former RCUK is also available for information.[5]

It might not seem relevant to all e-resource managers to collect this information; indeed, it may be the responsibility of a completely different team. However, use of this template has allowed data in the United Kingdom to be tracked in order to inform the transition to open access. Furthermore, it can be used to monitor the average APC costs for both hybrid and gold APCs. In the United Kingdom, this data is used to produce a report on the annual costs in terms of publisher and type of journal.[6] One of the outcomes of the 2016 Jisc report is to confirm that fully open access journals are becoming a larger part of the landscape—an important trend to note. Therefore, this information proves vital in the negotiation of agreements with fully open access publishers in order to keep the cost of fully OA APCs down.

At an international level, this data feeds into the OpenAPC project at Bielefeld University in Germany, which "releases datasets on fees paid for Open Access journal articles by universities and research institutions under an Open Database License."[7] Currently over 190 universities from Germany, the United Kingdom, Sweden, Norway, Canada, Austria, France, and other countries submit data as part of this project. One of the outcomes of the OpenAPC data is a series of tree maps by country, publisher, and journal for either pure OA titles, offset titles or the combined dataset. The data is used to draw conclusions on the transition to OA and to analyze offsetting deals.[8] The main APC file can be downloaded with an open database license data on GitHub.[9] This data can then be used for other comparisons, such as citation data.

Next, there is OA compliance for publishers themselves. Jisc in the United Kingdom (in conjunction with funders, publishers, and European institutions) produced an OA Publisher Compliance document, which listed, "13 recommended standards for publishers to adopt that will help authors and institutions globally with implementation of open access more effectively and reduce their cognitive and administrative burden."[10] Although this has now been superseded, the principles in this document live on in negotiation criteria. This document was also used as a foundation of work around the assessment of offsetting led by the Max Planck Digital Library in Munich, Germany, as part of the ESAC (Efficiency and Standards for Article Charges) initiative, which will be considered below.[11]

The first offsetting agreement was launched by the Institute of Physics Publishing in Austria in 2014. The 2016–2018 Springer Compact pilot agreement is what could be described as the first of the new offset agreements and was taken up by four library consortia in the Netherlands, Austria, United Kingdom and Sweden plus the Max Planck Digital Library in Germany.

There is now a growing number of offset deals in existence (approximately eighteen in 2018), predominantly in Europe, although in 2018 MIT signed an agreement with the Royal Society of Chemistry that is described as "the first 'Read & Publish' license agreement among North American institution." It includes the following statement:

> Publisher represents that the Read & Publish model, with its foundation in "hybrid" open access—where some articles are paywalled and others published open access—is a temporary and transitional business model whose aim is to provide a mechanism to shift over time to full open access. The Publisher commits to informing Customer of progress towards this longer-term aim on an annual basis, and to adjusting Read & Publish terms based on its progress towards full open access.[12]

It is important to note that offsetting as a concept is far from proven.[13] Schimmer, Geschuhn, and Vogler regard offsetting as representing the early days of the evolution of the hybrid model, where money can be repurposed in the transition to open access.[14] In an assessment of offsetting itself, Earney argues offsetting agreements "have far too easily come to be regarded as 'business as usual' and even contradictory to the objective of open access."[15]

However, as noted above, regardless of the relative immaturity of offsetting as a model, the first of the new agreements are up for negotiation. This means introducing a number of completely new concepts to e-resource assessment.

One of the first elements is to assess whether a particular offset agreement has met the ESAC Customer Recommendations for Article Workflows and Services for Offsetting/Open Access Transformation Agreements.[16] In summary, the following criteria should be assessed to see if an offset deal has conformed to agreed principles:

1. Author and article identification and verification
2. Funding acknowledgement and metadata
3. Invoicing and reporting

An offset agreement must be assessed to determine whether it truly constrained the costs of hybrid open access publishing—the principle that the combined cost to individual institutions remains affordable by linking what an institution pays a publisher for the combination of APCs and subscriptions. This is particularly difficult to assess in agreements where the library pays the subscription, but researchers pay the APC, which is common practice in the United States. This can allow APC costs to run completely unchecked while subscription costs are maintained at a reasonable increase. The argument here is that subscriptions should be being reduced.

In addition to the ESAC recommendations, Jisc's requirements for offsetting agreements can also be used to assess on offset agreement:[17]

1. Journal Agreements must be transitional
2. Agreements must constrain costs
3. Agreements must aid compliance with funder mandates
4. Agreements must be transparent
5. Agreements must support improvements in service and workflow for authors and administrators

As well as an overall assessment of the principles around an offset deal, the overall value of the deal requires assessment. Traditionally a big deal is assessed on cost per download; while this applies to the "read" element of a read and publish agreement, it does not apply to the open access "publish" element. This will be discussed in detail below in the subsection on cost per download.

As this subsection shows, evaluating an offsetting or read and publish deal is very complex. This is encapsulated well by the Vienna University Library.

> The negotiations preceding OA publishing agreements are very rarely straightforward. Several factors may feed into the final outcome, such as previous subscription and APC spend, historic research output by the participants' researchers, and the general terms and conditions of the licence agreement. As if these were not challenging enough, the negotiations often take place in a politically charged environment, and against the backdrop of the often ostensibly opposing goals of the publisher and the University.[18]

2. Usage Statistics

Usage statistics for journals, databases, and e-books have been around in some form since the development of these resources in the 1990s. This enables librarians to understand usage patterns and to work out the value for money of these resources in a far more effective way than they ever could for print journals, and to some extent print book loans. However, until the creation of

Project COUNTER in 2002, the quality and accuracy of usage statistics was often called into question. In short, COUNTER provided a semi-automated and audited solution to a growing problem, "where the same, or at least similar, things are being measured by different publishers, and theoretically they could be combined within a single table by library staff, the different methods of presentation make combination such a time-consuming task that, in practice, it is not undertaken."[19]

Although not all publishers have signed up to COUNTER, most major scholarly content providers and aggregators provide COUNTER reports in one form or another. For a definitive list of COUNTER-approved suppliers, visit the register of COUNTER-compliant publishers and vendors.[20] However, as a rule of thumb, if a supplier is not listed in the register, it is not compliant with the current COUNTER release.

Before looking at how COUNTER statistics can be used in basic, complex, and OA resource assessment, it is important to understand what each report can offer.

COUNTER developed the latest release of the code of practice, Release 5, in July 2017. The expectation is that this release will be in place by compliant providers and publishers from January 2019 with content providers fully compliant by January 2020.[21] This iteration of COUNTER differs from past releases in that instead of separate reports being developed, a single data repository is available with specific reporting queries. This will allow for more continual and incremental updating of COUNTER data with less need to completely change and develop new releases of specific standard reports. With Release 5 of COUNTER, new reports are available to distinguish between full-text databases and databases that are just abstracting and indexing resources. Furthermore, there are unique title reports to help get at the discrete elements made available from a platform or provider. These are the title level reports and provide usage information on how titles are used for both e-books and ejournals.

COUNTER currently providers a gold OA report but in the new release there will also be a more expansive OA report available at the item level (article/chapter). As with previous COUNTER reports, there are access denial reports (known previously as "turnaway" reports) to see what content users may try to access but not have access to. One other area of development is an attempt to provide consortia statistics.

One report that is not available in either Release 4 or 5 is the zero-use report. This is of particular use for assessment in order to understand the "long tail" of titles in a journal big deal that are never used. However, there will be a way of running a comparison between a title master report for journals against a library's KBART files. This should reveal titles where there is no usage. As with any new release of COUNTER, a number of guides and tools will be developed to support libraries and publishers as the release is rolled out.[22-24]

This section of TERMS has concentrated on COUNTER usage statistics. A quick glance at the compliant publishers and vendors reveals that there are many who are not COUNTER compliant. This will be considered under complex resources below.

Basic Resources

At the most basic level, such as a single journal or database subscription, in order to understand the "value" of a resource, usage of the resource needs to be counted.

For an aggregated database this will often be via the database report (DR) indicating total item investigations and requests as well as searches. Item investigations, in this case, replace the historic record view information. For full-text resources, to see total titles usage the better report will be the Total_Item_Requests as this will show how much usage occurred solely on the full text in an aggregated collection.

For individual journals, the Unique_Item_Requests report will give basic usage information. To take this a step further, usage of a big deal in its most basic form also uses this report to show the overall title usage with the exception of zero-usage.

Complex Resources

Understanding usage becomes more complex in a big deal. For starters, a COUNTER report will give you usage data for all journals published by a particular publisher regardless of whether these titles are included in the big deal. For example, for a sample big deal, a title report TR_ J1 report may provide data on over 3,000 titles. However, only around 2,100 may actually feature in the agreed big deal. The first step is to strip out the titles that are not part of the big deal so as not to overcount. As explained above, this can be done by comparing the usage report against your KBART file from the same provider. In addition, in Release 5 you are able to run a report that looks at specific year ranges to indicate usage on a given year as opposed to across all years accessible. This report is the TR_J4.

Then, there is the issue of hybrid journals. Virtually every publisher now publishes hybrid titles. Many of the articles within these titles may have been published by faculty. If you simply want to report on the overall usage of your big deal, then a "frontfile" report will suffice using the TR_JR1. In this case, frontfile includes usage of the subscribed titles in the deal, but includes the gold open access hybrid articles, which are free to access. To understand the "subscribed" usage—the content that has actually been paid for as part of the big deal—gold open access usage should be removed. With Release 5, it is much easier to exclude the gold open access than in previous iterations of

COUNTER. In these instances, simply choose the reporting option to exclude gold open access to avoid counting the usage from the hybrid published articles. This will also result in a downturn of usage in comparison to Release 4 statistics unless these were being adjusted to account for hybrid journals in previous years.

If a library is part of a consortia, some of this data may be collected at a consortia level. In the United Kingdom (Jisc), Sweden (Bibsam), Australia and New Zealand (CAVAL), this data is collected by JUSP (Jisc Usage Statistics Portal).[25] In the United States, the Association for Research Libraries (ARL) and the Association of College and Research Libraries (ACRL) both gather annual collections reports from the majority of institutions of higher education. The make-up and basis of these reports change fairly frequently in regard to what is required to be reported.[26,27]

This section has described the manual process for collecting usage statistics and, as stated, it is important to understand the principles behind the collection of usage data. However, the collection of usage data can also be automated.

The COUNTER website states that

> The advent of the SUSHI (Standardized Usage Statistics Harvesting Initiative) protocol (www.niso.org/workrooms/sushi/) has greatly facilitated the handling of large volumes of usage data, and its implementation by vendors allows the automated retrieval of the COUNTER usage reports into local systems, making this process much less time consuming for the librarian or library consortium administrator.[28]

This data still needs to be understood and analyzed either via the use of spreadsheets or the library system. An additional list of publishers is held on the JUSP web pages; this lists the publishers sending files to JUSP via SUSHI plus the COUNTER reports available—this is not an exhaustive list of all COUNTER compliant publishers.[29]

Some publishers that provide COUNTER statistics do not provide SUSHI and many more besides do not provide any useful usage data at all. This is particularly the case with specialist resources that are not primarily sold to the academic sector, such as business and law resources and also other media. In this case, the collection of usage data may only include the number of user sessions, which, although a fairly meaningless number, is still important to count. Sometimes the value of the resource to faculty outweighs the wish to collect useful data about that resource; this is a decision that needs to be taken at the procurement stage (see chapter 3).

Assessment of e-book collections is less common. However, a growing concern is the weeding or deselection of e-books due to low usage or relevancy. Waugh, Donlin, and Braunstein suggest that currency is perhaps the most important of the two factors.[30] The need for further development of collection, management, and development policies to address e-book assessment and selection will be considered in chapter 8.

However, it should be noted that although important, usage can be a poor proxy for value in both journal and e-book assessment; a low use title may be essential for key researchers.[31] Relying solely on usage can be problematic. A number of studies have shown that usage can also be discipline specific and can be skewed by undergraduate use.[32-34] Therefore, usage should be considered to be one of a number of tools available.

Open Access

The potential use for OA usage statistics differs from the use of statistics to measure subscribed material. COUNTER gold open access usage statistics can be used to measure overall frontfile usage of a resource. However, if memberships or annual support payments have been used to gain access to open access material (see chapter 3), a Gold OA report could be used to measure the internal use of the resource. However, this may not be relevant if membership is used to support the principles of open access, rather than directly supporting article publication. As noted above, COUNTER is working on developing reporting and is likely to have options available in the future to get at usage of OA material at a given institution.

COUNTER has also created the Item_Master_Report. This report would show activity for single items such as articles or videos and can be used to assess usage of content within an institutional repository if the current repository in use does not have an internal statistical package to show discrete items are being used.

An issue for many open access publishers, particularly pure OA publishers (of either books or journals), is that they do not have the resources, infrastructure, or technological expertise to contribute to COUNTER. It is possible to get some usage data. For example, if universities register their IP range with the OAPEN library, then they can obtain COUNTER level usage stats for open access e-books usage for their IP ranges.[35] This is not foolproof; for example, anyone using the system from outside the IP range will not be counted. However, it does give an indication of the possible value of a resource available via OAPEN, for example Knowledge Unlatched e-books.

The lack of sufficient usage data for OA publishers also hinders the second use for open access material. If an institution has paid for an APC, it may want to understand the reach of that output. For example, global downloads per region. Some major publishers have the capacity to do this and it is worth asking about. This would reveal the open access usage of articles from leading authors from an institution as a percentage of that country's leading authors or a country's usage for leading authors verses global usage. However, where this data is available, it sometimes lacks robustness and the raw data is very rarely supplied. For this reason, it may be more reliable to use other metrics, such as citation data (see below).

Finally, open access usage data can be used alongside subscription usage to measure the success of read and publish offset agreements, such as Springer Compact.

3. Cost per Download

To assess the value for money of a subscription, financial data needs to be used alongside usage data to calculate a cost per download figure. This figure can then be used to decide on the value for money of a particular resource. It is important to note that cost per download is only one way to measure value—just because a resource has low usage or a high cost per download does not make it worthy of cancellation. Indeed, unless there is a scenario of drastic budget cuts, where one resource has to go to balance the budget, a high cost per download should be a trigger point to initiate discussions within an institution. Even in the situation of severe budget cuts, high cost per download should never be the sole reason for cancellation, although if all other factors are equal, it may be the deciding factor.

This section will look at the basics of cost per download calculation before considering the added complexities of cost per download in a read and publish or offset agreement. The section will also look at return on investment calculations, which can be used to assess the value of archive collections.

Basic Resources

For a single e-journal subscription the cost per download calculation could not be simpler. Divide the title report (TR) for a given year by the cost of the resource to give the cost per download. For aggregated resources, the same calculation applies, either using the DR to calculate the cost per investigation or the TR to give cost per article download if the resource is full text—these databases traditionally have very low costs, so this should not be a surprise.

Big deals that only include subscribed content follow the same principle where the TR-J1 is divided by the full cost of the big deal. Be careful at this point to include all costs. If the big deal includes print or e-journal subscriptions and an access fee, then this should all be included in the calculation.

A similar calculation can be done for individual e-books. However, it might also be advantageous to compare this cost per download figure with cost per loan data, which can be calculated for the same title in print.

Complex Resources

Where a big deal includes hybrid open access titles, the calculation still follows the same pattern. This time divide the "subscribed" usage (TR_J1-KBART) by the total cost of the subscription. Make sure to exclude the Gold OA when pulling this report. These calculations also allow you to look at trends across years and to benchmark against other publishers.

To understand the value of a title or big deal it is also useful to compare the cost per download figure with the cost of an interlibrary loan (ILL). ALA estimates the average cost of an ILL to be $15.[36] This figure appears to include staff costs. However, if staff costs are factored in at this point, you also need to know the staff cost for the serials team to process a title. Rathmel et al.[37] used an estimated ILL staff cost per article of $7, which would suggest it was appropriate to use $8 as a base cost of an ILL (without staffing costs) in the United States. Clearly costs will vary from country to country or even region to region based on local circumstances. Indeed, Arch, Champieux et al. note that "there is a lack of standardization in how these costs are calculated and what expenditures are included."[38]

However, for the purposes of explanation, if cost per download of a resource in this example is above $8, an ILL may be more appropriate than a subscription.

For journal archive collections that have been purchased outright, return on investment is a more appropriate way of calculating cost per download. This method actually begins with the ILL costs, which are used to create a forecast. Cumulative cost per download calculations are then used to assess the return on investment of an archive over a given period of time.

When deciding on the purchase of an archive from a particular publisher, first retrieve the titles and date ranges of an archive. ILL data then needs to be interrogated in order to see how many articles available within the journal archive were requested in a given year—or averaged over a number of years. This will give a cost per year of ILL requests, which can be used as a predictor of COUNTER usage.

ILL requests do not exactly match usage statistics. When looking at it from the other side, usage drops significantly after cancellation, because ILL creates a significant barrier to many users as it requires more effort (and often personal cost) to retrieve the desired article. Returning to calculating a value for return on investment, it follows that this can also be used the other way to calculate the return on investment for a journal archive based on ILL costs. TERMs suggests that it is not unreasonable to suggest a ratio of 10:1, that is, for every ILL recorded there will be an equivalent of ten COUNTER downloads (for an explanation of this figure, see chapter 7). This then enables forecasting to understand the potential of an archive. If there were fifty ILLs per year at a cost of $8 each, an archive costing $20,000 would require 2,500 cumulative downloads over a five-year period in order to return on its investment. Every download over this amount, either within the return on investment period or after the total had been reached, would be a saving.

This estimate then needs to be assessed itself every year based on actual data to see if the forecasts were accurate.

Open Access

At the most basic level, cost per download calculations are irrelevant for OA journals; the cost per download should always be zero as there is no cost to the subscribing library. However, offsetting agreements are an exception to this.

Where agreements include other criteria, such as APC offsetting, further data analysis is required to calculate value. Current offsetting agreements "are more akin to a 'Read and Publish' agreement such as those used by Springer Compact and the Royal Society of Chemistry, which basically converts former subscription charges of institutions into a publishing fee, often also supplemented by a reading fee."[39]

Therefore, in such a case, two separate calculations of cost are needed. For the read element of the costs, a simple cost per download figure obtained from the subscribed usage is required. If the offset agreement is really transitioning to open access, then this figure should trend toward zero over time. If it does not, then the very nature of the offset deal needs to be called into question (See Earney's concerns).[40]

In order to assess value of the publish part of the agreement, two calculations can be made to assess the APC savings and also the combined fee savings, where the combined fee is the read and publish costs combined.

1. The calculation on APC savings can be calculated by subtracting the total value of APCs for articles published in a given year from the value of the publish fee (usually based on a previous year's hybrid OA costs). If the value of the APCs published is higher than the publish fee, then it can be shown that there are overall savings. This is found by calculating the average APC cost, which, if savings were made, will be less than the listed APC.

   For example, for Springer Compact this is €2,200 in 2018. A new average APC cost can be calculated by dividing the number of APCs published in a year by the publish fee. For example, the release of the Netherlands 2018 Springer Compact agreement shows that by dividing the publishing fee by the total number of eligible articles (2,080), the APC amounts to about €1,350.[41,42]

   This example takes the cost of an APC at the discounted or offset rate well under the average cost of an APC, according to Pinfield et al., of €2,248.47 and closer to the average APC of a pure gold title at around €1,700 in 2016. [43,44]

2. A saving in the publish element leads to a recalculation of the cost per download in the read part of the offset agreement. Therefore, this second calculation assesses if an institution has achieved overall savings on combined fees based on the number of articles published.

If the value of APCs published are greater than the publish fee, then the surplus can be subtracted from the read fee—this naturally results in a lower cost per download figure. If the entire read and publish fee has been offset, then the cost per download for an institution will equal zero *and* the average APC cost would be less than the listed APC indicating that for that institution the offset agreement is transitioning toward full open access.

The one caveat here is that this must then be the case for all subscribers for the whole big deal and has to be consistent throughout the life of the agreement to indicate transition to open access. This is something that still appears to be a long way off.

4. Non-Traditional Bibliometrics

To this point in the chapter, we have looked at traditional forms of assessment such as usage and cost per download and also variations based on return on investment for archive collections and the complexities of offsetting agreements.

It is important to look at other forms of assessment that do not rely on usage. One alternative is what is often referred to as "non-traditional bibliometrics." Figure 6.1 shows commonly used bibliometrics tools.[45]

One of the best places to get started with these new metrics is the independent report from the Higher Education Council Funding Council for England (which was dissolved in 2018). Although published in 2015, it gives a good background to metrics and notes the pros and cons of using them.

Some of the best advice from the report is that metrics are open to misunderstanding and misrepresentation. However, used properly, they can complement traditional metrics, such as usage and citation data.

The report called for a more responsible approach to metrics, built on five principles:

Robustness: basing metrics on the best possible data in terms of accuracy and scope;

Humility: recognizing that quantitative evaluation should support—but not supplant—qualitative, expert assessment;

Transparency: keeping data collection and analytical processes open and transparent, so that those being evaluated can test and verify the results;

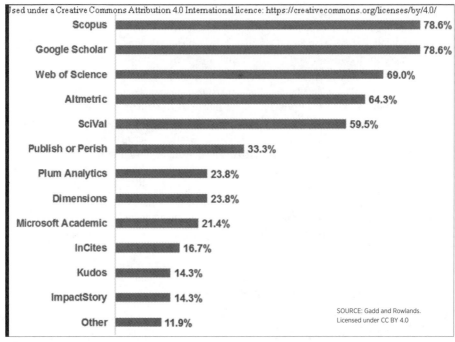

FIGURE 6.1
Tools Regularly Used by Respondents

Diversity: accounting for variation by field, and using a range of indicators to reflect and support a plurality of research and researcher career paths across the system;

Reflexivity: recognizing and anticipating the systemic and potential effects of indicators and updating them in response.[46]

In a response to this, Universities U.K. (UUK) has set up the U.K. Forum for Responsible Research Metrics (FFRRM), which is chaired by the Pro-Vice Chancellor at the University of Surrey. It consists of "research funders, sector bodies, and infrastructure experts . . . working in partnership to promote the responsible use of research metrics."[47]

A July 2018 article in *The Guardian* by James Wilsdon, one of the authors of the 2015 report, suggests that the tide may already be turning against metrics.[48] The article refers to a new metrics report published in the United Kingdom in July 2018 that takes stock of the work of the FFRRM.[49]

Therefore, due to ongoing debate, non-traditional metrics should always be treated with caution. However, this does not mean that they are of no use. For example, the Metrics Toolkit is a good resource that helps researchers and evaluators find the right metric to use.[50] The toolkit "provides evidence-based information about research metrics across disciplines, including how each metric is calculated, where you can find it, and how each should (and should not) be applied." The toolkit also provides examples of how to use the metrics (see figure 6.2).

FIGURE 6.2
Metrics Toolkit Logo

There is a listserv and blog, both of which can offer support to the beginner. Finally, metrics are also used in research assessment.[51,52] How these metrics are used can vary enormously from country to country and from funder to funder. Dr. Muriel E Swijghuisen Reigersberg, who has worked in both the United Kingdom and Australia, has written a useful blog to explain the different approaches in those countries.[53]

Basic Resources

Unlike the other methods of assessment discussed in this section of TERMs, to a large extent non-traditional metrics can be used by researchers to assess the value, or to put a value on their own research rather than providing value of the content outside of the researcher/author through mechanisms like journal impact factors.

Probably the most recognizable non-traditional metric is the altmetric donut. Altmetric describes its resources as

> metrics and qualitative data that are complementary to traditional, citation-based metrics. They can include (but are not limited to) peer reviews on Faculty of 1000, citations on Wikipedia and in public policy documents, discussions on research blogs, mainstream media coverage, bookmarks on reference managers like Mendeley, and mentions on social networks such as Twitter.
>
> Sourced from the Web, altmetrics can tell you a lot about how often journal articles and other scholarly outputs like datasets are discussed and used around the world. For that reason, altmetrics have been incorporated into researchers' websites, institutional repositories, journal websites, and more.[54]

To a certain extent, resources such as altmetrics rely on self-marketing by the researcher in order to make sure that their article is read by their peers or the wiser scholarly community. A resource that enables this is Kudos.[55] Kudos was created in 2013 by three publishing and technology professionals and is a completely free resource for academics. It allows researchers to explain their recent research articles in plain English, to share the research via social media channels such as Twitter, Facebook, and LinkedIn, and then to measure the impact by aggregating the most relevant metrics about that work in one place. A case study on Kudos showed that the process takes an average of around ten minutes per article and led to a 23.1 percent higher growth in full-text downloads than the control group used.[56]

Complex Resources

There is little distinction between basic and complex resources, as bibliometrics can get complicated very quickly. It is worth making the distinction between the free version of Kudos used by researchers from the institutional fee-based version. The for-fee version offers an institutional dashboard that allows the tracking and support of researchers' use of Kudos in order to "maximise the discoverability and impact of their research."[57]

Gadd and Rowlands revealed a further complexity: the unintended consequences of expanded subject coverage of bibliometrics to the arts, humanities, and social sciences (AHSS). For example, citation benchmarking covers a small set of science, technical, and medical journals (STM).[58] There are concerns that using this for AHSS disciplines would change the way research is published to the detriment of these subjects.

This leads to the area of bibliometrics for books. Launched in 2015, Bookmetrix from Springer Nature is "an innovative, new platform bringing together citations, downloads and altmetrics for books and chapters."[59] However, there is little independent research in this area and like COUNTER for books, bibliometrics for books need further development.

Open Access

All of the non-traditional bibliometrics apply equally to open access. Indeed, there is an argument from some quarters of the bibliometric community that ownership of bibliometric data should rest with the scholarly community rather than the suppliers and that "citation data should be opened up for the community to access, reuse and interpret."[60] Indeed, the Initiative for Open Citations (I4OC), launched in April 2017, is a project aimed at doing exactly that; it describes itself as "a collaboration between scholarly publishers, researchers, and other interested parties to promote the unrestricted availability of scholarly citation data."[61]

Additional work is also being carried out around the assessment of pure OA and hybrid journals. For example, research yet to be formally published at Bielefeld University in Germany has investigated whether APCs mirror the impact factor of the legacy subscription model. The research uses the total OpenAPC data set as well as a sub-sample of U.K. data from 2014 to 2016.

Multivariate linear regression was used as a method to analyze APCs actually paid with 1) "source normalized impact per paper" (SNIP) data, 2) whether a journal was open access or hybrid, 3) the publisher and 4) the year.[62] Findings appear to indicate that the "journal's impact is crucial for the level of APCs in pure open-access journals, whereas it little alters APCs for publications in hybrid-journals."[63]

5. Consultation

Consultation can include a variety of approaches in contacting research staff and other stakeholders. In terms of assessment of resources, this could include user surveys, user groups, feedback from customer engagement teams, and anecdotal evidence via subject liaison. Much of this is informal consultation that may give valuable insight into the success of a resource. For example, whether a provider has met any service-level requirements or responsibilities in the agreement or if there any customer service issues with the agreement, such as user experience problems. If an institution runs customer relationship management (CRM) software, this may be recorded automatically. If so, it is essential that time has been taken to define the metadata; otherwise it will be very difficult to pull any meaningful information from the CRM. For example, Pennington et al. show how anecdotal evidence can be used to develop strategies to improve the user experience.[64]

There will also be more formal mechanisms to consult. For example, meetings of the collection management and development group or faculty or research board liaison meetings. Informal consultation may also lead to a more formal method of consultation, such as a survey of the academic community.

If an institution is part of a library consortium, then it may be consulted by the consortia body to provide feedback and review of usage. This information will then be used in the assessment and renegotiation of agreements at consortia level. If an institution does not respond to the consultation, then its views may not be adequately represented in consortia negotiation. Therefore, it is important to respond in order for your voice to be heard.

In addition, other organizations collect data on big deal usage. Data in these reports are treated with strict confidentiality and will usually be anonymized and aggregated so that individual institutions and consortia cannot be recognized. For example, in 2018, the European Universities Association (EUA) released the EUA big deals survey report.[65] This was described as the first mapping of major scientific publishing contracts in Europe. Reports such as this provide important background information and can be used to benchmark local agreements against a national or international landscape. The EUA report details annual price increases, associated rights under big deal contracts (post-cancellation access, archival rights, perpetual access, etc.), big deal e-books contract information, and annual expenditure.

Finally, a number of organizations collect data on behalf of members. This can be used for benchmarking. In the United Kingdom, the Society of College, National and University Libraries (SCONUL) collects library data in an annual statistical survey.[66] In the United States a similar survey is conducted by the Association of College and Research Libraries.[67] Both surveys can be used to measure usage trends.

Basic Resources

For basic resources such as individual subscriptions or subject-based databases and agreements, simple communication, possibly between the collection management and development group or with the faculty or head of department may be all that is required (see chapter 3). The larger or more complex the resource, the wider the consultation may need to be. A multidisciplinary big deal may require university-wide consultation as it will be used by a number of discipline faculty and students across the institution. The consultation could be relatively straightforward, such as, the distribution of an evaluation report and the collation of feedback. This feedback may include title reductions as opposed to cancelling a deal outright.

Consultation includes communication within the library itself. As noted in the introduction to TERMS, electronic resources management may involve several different teams within a library. In order to consult successfully, these teams must be kept in the loop. This may occur as part of a regular meeting, or through an ad hoc meeting so that individual teams understand each other's work and roles in the process of assessment.

Complex Resources

One potentially complex area is the user survey. In relation to resource evaluation, surveying will most likely fall into three broad areas:

- Consultation as part of the assessment itself
- Consultation as part of any planned renegotiation, which may include sections on assessment and will feed into any new negotiations
- Consultation on cancellation after a resource is assessed and the decision is made to cancel it

As stated above, this could be an institutional survey, or it may be part of a wider consortia survey. It might be both, as when a consortium has requested that individual members' faculty are consulted, or an institution might want to re-run a consortia survey at the local level to gain greater insight.

Either way, there are a number of key factors that must be considered as part of the survey process:

Length and complexity of surveys. Surveys should be short and to the point. It is very easy to create a very long and complex survey that asks for every view possible. As a simple rule, look at the finished survey and ask yourself whether you would fill it in if it was sent to you. Chances are that a long and complex survey would wallow at the bottom of your inbox. Always state the time required to complete the survey in the (short) introduction and make sure that a great deal of preparation is not required before completing the survey.

Survey fatigue. Surveys are incredibly useful but beware of survey fatigue. Try not to send a survey every time you need to consult, but only when absolutely necessary. Avoid times of the year when other institutional of external surveys are being sent. Some universities even have a moratorium on internal surveys at certain times of the year.

Introduce the survey. Give a succinct introduction around why you are conducting the survey, what is the purpose, why should people respond? You may also wish to add a confidentiality statement that explains how the data and results will be used and to confirm that any personal data (including IP addresses) will be destroyed.

Ask open questions. It is important to remain neutral in any survey questions in order to get the best response. Therefore, try not to ask leading questions such as "why did you dislike the current agreement?" For example,

> **Q3.** *From the perspective of your institution, what are the positive aspects of the current agreement?*
>
> (Please type in your answers)

and

> **Q4.** *From the perspective of your institution, what are the negative aspects of the current agreement?*
>
> (Please type in your answers)

Mix qualitative and quantitative questions.

Quantitative. Some questions require a yes/no or ranked response using a Likert scale.[68] For example, "on a scale of 1–5, where 1 is strongly agree and 5 is strongly disagree, what are your feelings toward the following statement." On other occasions you may wish to have a series of options either checked/unchecked or ranked by preference. This will allow you to grade the responses as appropriate and even compare across longitudinal and resource surveys.

Qualitative. On other occasions you may wish to know more details. Space for response is usually in the form of a free text box. This could either be a supplemental question to a quantitative question, such as, "if yes, why?" It could also be a separate question.

Data quality. Know what you want to achieve. When deciding on the structure of the survey, think about the responses you require and how you will do the analysis. If you want respondents to indicate a price, for example, give them a range of costs so that they can choose an option. Do not provide a free text box, as the quality of the data will suffer. The cost data will not be consistent—is the currency dollars, Sterling, or Euros, does it include tax?

Thematic analysis. For free text answers, think about using thematic analysis to establish the key themes in order to make reporting back easier. Thematic analysis is described as:

> a process for encoding qualitative information. The encoding requires an explicit "code." This may be a list of themes . . . A theme is a pattern found in the information that at minimum describes and organizes the possible observations and at maximum interprets aspects of the phenomenon.[69]

This will allow you to be surprised but also "guided and influenced by some initial hunches and frames of reference."[70]

When designing your survey, check out a variety of open survey tools, unless your institution has a preferred survey tool.

Consider designing your survey so that the first section asks a number of general questions and the second part delves deeper into the resource you wish to assess. The general questions will allow community feedback to be compared across resources, for example, general satisfaction levels across journal or e-book agreements. If you are conducting the survey over a number of years, such as an annual survey across a three-year agreement, it is wise to change as little as possible from year to year. This will allow you to analyze trends over the life of the agreement.

Once you have designed, conducted, and analyzed your survey, you will need to disseminate it to the community and to senior staff within the organization. Although rows and rows of data can be very appealing to some, many others switch off on receipt of an Excel spreadsheet. This is where visualization comes into its own. A good visualization can vastly reduce the word count and may even bring out areas of the data that had not been spotted in the initial raw data. Visualizations should be thoroughly explained. Do not forgot how easy it is to draw the wrong conclusion without adequate commentary. Gadd and Rowlands draw an analogy from the food industry:

> At a bare minimum, consumers want a list of ingredients (sources), but ideally they want a sense of how healthy those ingredients are, i.e. what percentage of our Recommended Daily Intake do they consist of (how sensible is it to consume these metrics, at what level of granularity, and what risk?); just as with food labelling, this could be colour-coded (and with error bars) if necessary."[71]

There are a number of free to use visualization software options, such as Google Charts and Plotly, as well as commercially available solutions such as Tableau. Library systems may also have limited capability to provide visualizations.[72]

Finally, when presenting findings to the community, always cite the data you are using—you may be challenged regarding the validity of your data, particularly during a cancellation (see below) or by a publisher in a negotiation meeting.

Open Access

Some of the difficulty with open access evaluation occurs because there are many different definitions of what openness means to different constituents in a given library community. The first step in understanding should be to come together on an agreed definition of open access.[73]

It is also helpful to survey the local community authors about which open publishing platforms or publishers they prefer. This can also help surface any issues they might be having with APC payment, especially if this is devolved to the authors. The library may have the publisher agreement, the publisher may send reports, but without consultation and temperature checking, it may have no idea of bad experiences or missing data.

Performing bibliometrics for your campus for a five-year time period allows you to understand which open access publishers local authors are publishing with and to prioritize those publishers over hybrid publishing models or lesser used publishers.

6. Cancellation Review

Previous subsections have discussed the various ways to assess resources. This subsection looks at one outcome of assessment, cancellation review. This will take place for resources judged to have minimal value for money, either because of cost per download, currency exchange issues, transfer of titles in and out of the agreement, pricing models, change in discipline concerns at your institution, or other factors discussed above. It may be the case that there are not enough finances to cover continued access to a given resource.

No matter what the reasons for cancellation, this information should be conveyed to faculty and alternative access needs to be provided where possible.

Basic Resources

It is important to advise all library workers that access to a certain resource is about to be switched off. For basic resources, this requires simply editing the holdings record on the library catalog and/or the discovery system to close the subscription dates. It may also be appropriate to inform everyone of alternative measures such as ILL, where users can gain access to material. For a database of full-text material, there may be alternative access to much of the content, in which case staff need to be directed to the new resources (although the discovery system may take care of this seamlessly).

For an e-book, it may be that a new edition is available, and resources need to be updated accordingly. Examples include required reading lists and teaching material.

Complex Resources

For more complex resources such as a big deal or resources over a certain price threshold, the cancellation review requires further consultation and discussion before an exit strategy is reached (see the subsection on exit strategies in chapter 7). Leaving the big deal can be an emotive subject, and there will be winners and losers in every context. For example, cancellation of big deals based entirely on the maxim that 80 percent of all usage is from just 20 percent of the content does not always take into account the long tail. Replacing the big deal with subscriptions to the most-used content prejudices humanities scholars who require journals that often see far less usage than science titles—STM titles tend to dominate the highest used journals in comprehensive subscription plans.

If a decision is made to leave an agreement, it will likely include a number of steps. First, it is advisable to compile a final analysis report. This report should take the following criteria into account as relevant:

- For consortia, a list of subscribers, including the package taken if appropriate, such as subject clusters
- The complete title list included in the current agreement (including all variant packages, if appropriate)
- Core titles and their subscription costs using relevant data ("core" refers to the titles that were journal subscriptions at the adoption of the big deal)
- Usage data
- Post-cancellation rights (PCA), which includes the big deal content that you have access to as part of the big deal agreement you have with a given publisher. It is very important to understand what this access is and to check that access to this content is maintained after the deal is cancelled (see chapter 7)
- APC data (if appropriate). Total number of vouchers, total number used, and DOIs
- Proportion of OA content published in journals and number of articles published per journal using data from Crossref

- Data regarding green OA, for example, availability in institutional repositories
- Consultation with other libraries and purchasing consortia

This data can be incorporated to complete an initial assessment of the impact of a cancellation on the community. This final consultation reveals reasons to keep the agreement if the risk to research or teaching is considered too great. The continuation of a deal can come about with alternative funding being made available by faculty. It could potentially be used as a negotiation gambit, although this tactic is high risk and should not be used in all negotiations—the perception that a library is crying wolf about finances could result in this tactic backfiring.

As part of the assessment, alternative resources should be considered, such as cancelling a big deal in favor of a core selection of titles based on usage. Note that individual subscriptions or abbreviated title lists cost are likely to be different than what was included in the big deal. Indeed, Nabe and Fowler report that upon leaving their big deals they were presented with a content fee and an immediate large price increase on subscriptions, and that "the stance taken by publishers is to make leaving so painful as to discourage an institution from taking that step."[74]

Another strategy is to source the same or similar content from another supplier. This could include cancellation of the big deal in favor of aggregated full-text journals from a vendor.

Whatever the outcome of the cancellation review, a document highlighting lessons learned from the agreement is essential. Not only does this keep a record of the successes and failures of an agreement, it will inform any decision to re-approach a publisher at a later stage in order to renegotiate. It also provides a set of lessons learned for other negotiations. As stated above, it is important to list the sources of any data cited in this document.

A number of criteria listed in the bullet points above refer directly to big deals that feature hybrid open access journals. This will be discussed further in the section below and expanded upon in chapter 7, which looks at alternative options.

Open Access

There are two roles for open access as part of cancellation review. First, there is the actual review of open access membership agreements, such as those offered by SpringerOpen, where membership offers a discount on APCs. To a certain extent, this is a fairly simple calculation to determine if the savings on the APC expenditure equal or exceed the membership fee. If not, there are grounds for cancellation of the agreement. It is preferable to have at least three years of data in order to access any trends. Like usage, publishing output should not be judged on a single year's worth of data because the research lifecycle moves at a different pace than the electronic resource management lifecycle.

For hybrid open access titles, data on the availability of open access articles, both green and gold, can contribute to the decision to leave the big deal. For example, the higher the percentage of titles available from an institutional or subject repository, the better coverage for institutions leaving the deal. This forms an important part of the exit strategy and will be discussed in full in chapter 7.

NOTES

1. Project COUNTER. (2018). https://www.projectcounter.org/.

2. NISO. (2018). Transfer. https://www.niso.org/standards-committees/transfer.

3. U.K. Research and Innovation. (n.d.). Open access policy. https://www.ukri.org/funding/information-for-award-holders/open-access/open-access-policy/.

4. Jisc Collections. (n.d.). APC data collection. https://www.jisc-collections.ac.uk/Jisc-Monitor/APC-data-collection/.

5. U.K. Research and Innovation. (n.d.). Guidance on Research Council open access compliance and financial reporting 2017–2018. https://www.ukri.org/files/funding/oa/oa-reporting-guidance-pdf/.

6. Shamash, Katie. (2017). Article processing charges in 2016. https://scholarlycommunications.jiscinvolve.org/wp/2017/08/23/article-processing-charges-in-2016/.

7. INTACT. Open APC. https://www.intact-project.org/openapc/.

8. Pieper, Dirk, & Broschinski, Christoph. (2018). OpenAPC: A contribution to a transparent and reproducible monitoring of fee-based open access publishing across institutions and nations. *Insights 31*(39). http://doi.org/10.1629/uksg.439.

9. OpenAPC. (2018). openapc-de. https://github.com/OpenAPC/openapc-de.

10. Jacobs, Neil. (2016). OA publisher compliance document. https://scholarlycommunications.jiscinvolve.org/wp/2016/04/26/oa-publisher-compliance-document/.

11. ESAC. (2018). http://esac-initiative.org/.

12. Finnie, Ellen. (2018). Offsetting as a path to full open access: MIT and the Royal Society of Chemistry sign first North American "read and publish" agreement. http://intheopen.net/2018/06/mit-rsc-read-and-publish-agreementn-access-mit-and-the-royal-society-of-chemistry-sign-first-north-american-read-and-publish-agreement/.

13. Earney, Liam. (2017). Offsetting and its discontents: Challenges and opportunities of open access offsetting agreements. *Insights 30*(1): 11–24 https://doi.org/10.1629/uksg.345.

14. Schimmer, Ralph, Geschuhn, Kai, & Vogler, Andreas. (2015). *Disrupting the subscription journals' business model for the necessary large-scale transformation to open access* (München: MPDL). https://doi.org/10.17617/1.3.

15. Earney, Liam. (2017). Offsetting and its discontents: Challenges and opportunities of open access offsetting agreements. *Insights 30*(1): 11–24 https://doi.org/10.1629/uksg.345.

16. ESAC. (2017). Customer recommendations for article workflows and services for offsetting/open access transformation agreements [first draft]. http://esac-initiative.org/wp-content/uploads/2017/04/ESAC_workflow_recommendations_1st_draft20march2017.pdf.

17. Jisc. (2018). Requirements for transformative open access agreements: Accelerating the transition to immediate and worldwide open access. https://www.jisc-collections.ac.uk/Transformative-OA-Reqs/.

18. Pinhasi, Rita, Blechl, Guido, Kromp, Brigitte, & Schubert, Bernhard. (2018). The weakest link—workflows in open access agreements: The experience of the Vienna University Library and recommendations for future negotiations. *Insights 31*(27). http://doi.org/10.1629/uksg.419.

19. Kidd, Tony. (2002). Electronic journal usage statistics: Present practice and future progress. *Statistics in Practice: Measuring & Managing 15*(1): 67–72. www.lboro.ac.uk/microsites/infosci/lisu/downloads/statsinpractice-pdfs/kidd.pdf.

20. COUNTER. (2018). Register of COUNTER compliant publishers and vendors. https://www.projectcounter.org/about/register/.

21. COUNTER. (2018). The COUNTER Code of Practice for Release 5. https://www.projectcounter.org/code-of-practice-five-sections/abstract/.

22. COUNTER. (2018). Friendly guide to COUNTER Release 5 for librarians. https://www.projectcounter.org/guides/.

23. COUNTER. (2018). YouTube video. https://www.youtube.com/channel/UCptZRuV5XbtP-jWkTckDpIA.

24. USUS. (2018). A community website on usage. www.usus.org.uk/.

25. Jisc. (n.d.). JUSP participants. (n.d.). Institutions. https://jusp.jisc.ac.uk/participants/#link3.

26. Association of Research Libraries. (2012). statistics and assessment. http://old.arl.org/stats/annualsurveys/arlstats/.

27. ACRL. (2018). Statistics, white papers, and more. www.ala.org/acrl/publications/statistics.

28. COUNTER. (2018). The COUNTER Code of Practice for Release 4. SUSHI. https://www.projectcounter.org/code-of-practice-sections/sushi/.

29. Jisc. (n.d.). JUSP participants. http://jusp.jisc.ac.uk/participants/.

30. Waugh, Mike, Donlin, Michelle, & Braunstein, Stephanie. (2015). Next-generation collection management: A case study of quality control and weeding e-books in an academic library. *Collection Management 40*(1): 17–26. http://dx.doi.org/10.1080/01462679.2014.965864.

31. Jurczyk, Eva, & Jacobs, Pamela. (2014). What's the big deal? Collection evaluation at the national level. *portal: Libraries and the Academy 14*(4): 617–631. https://doi.org/10.1353/pla.2014.0029.

32. Blecic, Deborah. D, Wiberley Jr., Stephen E., Fiscella, Joan B., Bahnmaier-Blaszczak, Sara, & Lowery, Rebecca. (2013). Deal or no deal? Evaluating big deals and their journals. *College & Research Libraries* 74(2): 178–193. https://doi.org/10.5860/crl-300.

33. Nicholas, David, Huntington, Paul, & Jamali, Hamid R. (2007). Diversity in the information seeking behaviour of the virtual scholar: Institutional comparisons. *Journal of Academic Librarianship* 33(6): 629–638. https://doi.org/10.1016/j.acalib.2007.09.001.

34. Scigliano, Marisa. (2010). Measuring the use of networked electronic journals in an academic library consortium: Moving beyond MINES for libraries in Ontario Scholars Portal. *Serials Review* 36(2): 72–78. https://doi.org/10.1016/j.serrev.2010.03.003.

35. OAPEN services. www.oapen.org/content/oapen-services.

36. Shrauger, Kristine, & Scharf, Meg. (n.d.). Exploring the value of Interlibrary Loan. ACRL (2017) conference proceedings. At the helm: Leading transformation. March 22–25, 2017, Baltimore, Maryland, Edited by Dawn M. Mueller (Chicago: ALA), 230–235. www.ala.org/acrl/sites/ala.org.acrl/files/content/conferences/confsandpreconfs/2017/ExploringValueofInterlibraryLoan.pdf.

37. Rathmel, Angie, Currie, Lea, & Enoch, Todd. (2015). Big deals and squeaky wheels: Taking stock of your stats. *Serials Librarian* 68(1–4): 26–37. https://doi.org/10.1080/0361526X.2015.1013754.

38. Arch, Xan, Champieux, Robin, Emery, Jill, & Gilman, Isaac. (2018). The Easy Button: Integrating OA buttons into ILL workflows, NWILL. http://works.bepress.com/jill_emery/102/.

39. Geschuhn, Kai, & Stone, Graham. (2017). It's the workflows, stupid! What is required to make "offsetting" work for the open access transition. *Insights* 30(3): 103–114. http://doi.org/10.1629/uksg.391.

40. Earney, Liam. (2017). Offsetting and its discontents: Challenges and opportunities of open access offsetting agreements. *Insights* 30(1): 11–24. https://doi.org/10.1629/uksg.345

41. Netherlands 2018 Springer Compact agreement. (2018). http://openaccess.nl/sites/www.openaccess.nl/files/documenten/springer2018-2021_signed2.pdf.

42. open.access.nl. (2019). New agreement with Springer. www.openaccess.nl/en/events/new-agreement-with-springer.

43. Pinfield, Stephen, Salter, Jennifer, & Bath, Peter A. (2016). The "total cost of publication" in a hybrid open-access environment: Institutional approaches to funding journal article-processing charges in combination with subscriptions. *Journal of the Association of Information Science and Technology* 67(7): 1751–1766. https://dx.doi.org/10.1002/asi.23446.

44. Shamash, Katie. (2017). Article processing charges in 2016. https://scholarly com munications.jiscinvolve.org/wp/2017/08/23/article-processing-charges -in-2016/.

45. Gadd, Elizabeth, & Rowlands, Ian. (2018). How can bibliometric and altmetric suppliers improve? Messages from the end-user community. *Insights 31*(38). http://doi.org/10.1629/uksg.437.

46. Wilsdon, James, et al. (2015). *The metric tide: Report of the independent review of the role of metrics in research assessment and management* (London: Higher Education Council Funding Council for England). DOI:10.13140/RG.2.1.4929.1363. Archived at http://webarchive.nationalarchives.gov.uk/20180322111254/www.hefce.ac.uk/ pubs/rereports/year/2015/metrictide/.

47. UUK. (2018). U.K. Forum for responsible research metrics. https://www .universitiesuk.ac.uk/policy-and-analysis/research-policy/open-science/Pages/ forum-for-responsible-research-metrics.aspx.

48. Wilsdon, James. (2018). Has the tide turned towards responsible metrics in research? *The Guardian,* July 10. https://www.theguardian.com/science/political -science/2018/jul/10/has-the-tide-turned-towards-responsible-metrics-in -research.

49. U.K. Forum for responsible research metrics. (2018). U.K. progress towards the use of metrics responsibly: Three years on from The Metric Tide report. https:// www.universitiesuk.ac.uk/policy-and-analysis/research-policy/open-science/ The%20Forum%20for%20Responsible%20Research%20Metrics/UK%20 progress%20towards%20the%20use%20of%20metrics%20responsibly%20 10072018.pdf.

50. Metrics toolkit. (n.d.). www.metrics-toolkit.org/.

51. Jisc. (2018). LIS-BIBLIOMETRICS home page. https://www.jiscmail.ac.uk/ lis-bibliometrics.

52. The bibliomagician. (2018). https://thebibliomagician.wordpress.com/.

53. Swijghuisen Reigersberg, Muriel E. (2018). Metrics, research assessment and league tables: An Australian perspective. November. https://thebibliomagician. wordpress.com/2018/11/21/metrics-research-assessment-and-league-tables-an -australian-perspective-guest-post-by-muriel-swijghuisen-reigersberg/.

54. Altmetric. What are altmetrics? (n.d.). https://www.altmetric.com/about -altmetrics/what-are-altmetrics/.

55. Kudos. (n.d.). https://www.growkudos.com/.

56. Erdt, Mojisola, Aung Htet Htet, Aw, Ashley, Sara, Rapple, Charlie, & Theng Yin-Leng. (2017). Analysing researchers' outreach efforts and the association with publication metrics: A case study of Kudos. *PLoS ONE 12*(8): e0183217. https:// doi.org/10.1371/journal.pone.0183217.

57. Rapple, Charlie. (2016). Introducing: Kudos for Institutions: 4 ways you can benefit. https://blog.growkudos.com/2016/09/08/introducing-kudos-for -institutions-4-ways-you-can-benefit/.

58. Gadd, Elizabeth, & Rowlands, Ian. (2018). How can bibliometric and altmetric suppliers improve? Messages from the end-user community. *Insights 31*(38). http://doi.org/10.1629/uksg.437.

59. Springer Nature. (2018). Bookmetrix: The Story So Far. https://www.springer nature.com/gp/librarians/news-events/webinars/bookmetrix-the-story-so-far/ 15804200.

60. Gadd, Elizabeth, & Rowlands, Ian. (2018). How can bibliometric and altmetric suppliers improve? Messages from the end-user community. *Insights 31*(38). http://doi.org/10.1629/uksg.437.

61. Initiative for Open Citations (I4OC). (n.d.). https://i4oc.org/.

62. Elsevier. (2016). Journal metrics in Scopus: Source Normalized Impact per Paper (SNIP). https://blog.scopus.com/posts/journal-metrics-in-scopus-source -normalized-impact-per-paper-snip.

63. Schönfelder, Nina. (2018). APCs: Mirroring the impact factor or legacy of the subscription-based model? http://esac-initiative.org/wp-content/ uploads/2018/08/Schoenfelder-2018-APCs.pdf.

64. Pennington, Buddy, Chapman, Suzanne, Fry, Amy, Deschenes, Amy, & Greene McDonald, Courtney. (2016). Strategies to improve the user experience. *Serials Review 42*(1): 47–58. http://dx.doi.org/10.1080/00987913.2016.1140614.

65. Morais, Rita, Bauer, Julian, & Borrell-Damián, Lidia. (2018). EUA big deals survey report. http://eua.be/Libraries/publications-homepage-list/eua-big-deals-survey -report---the-first-mapping-of-major-scientific-publishing-contracts-in-europe .pdf?sfvrsn=4.

66. SCONUL. (2018). sconul statistics. https://www.sconul.ac.uk/tags/sconul -statistics.

67. ACRL. (2018). Academic Library Statistics. www.ala.org/acrl/publications/trends.

68. Wikipedia. (2019). Likert scale. https://en.wikipedia.org/wiki/Likert_scale.

69. Boyatzis, Richard E. (1998). *Transforming qualitative information: Thematic analysis and code development* (Thousand Oaks, CA: SAGE).

70. Siggelkow, Nicolaj. (2007). Persuasion with case studies. *The Academy of Management Journal 50*(1): 20-24. https://doi.org/10.5465/amj.2007.24160882.

71. Gadd, Elizabeth, & Rowlands, Ian. (2018). How can bibliometric and altmetric suppliers improve? Messages from the end-user community. *Insights 31*(38). http://doi.org/10.1629/uksg.437.

72. Hackerearth. (2018). 20 free and open source data visualization tools. https:// www.hackerearth.com/blog/community/20-free-and-open-source-data -visualization-tools/.

73. Rigling, Lillian, Carlisle, Emily, & Waugh, Courtney. (2018). In pursuit of equity: Applying design thinking to develop a values-based open access statement, In the library with the lead pipe (July 25). www.inthelibrarywiththeleadpipe.org/2018/oa-statement/.

74. Nabe, Jonathan, & Fowler, David C. (2012). Leaving the big deal: Consequences and next steps. *Serials Librarian* 62(1–4): 59–72. https://doi.org/10.1080/036152 6X.2012.652524.

7
Preservation and Sustainability

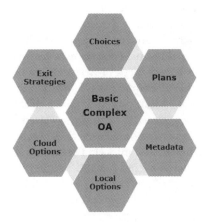

Introduction

With the initial iteration of TERMs, there was quite a bit of feedback regarding the fact that we did not address preservation, perpetual access, and sustainability of content. The problem we all face in regard to preservation and sustainability is that no one has really defined what this may mean.[1] Although there are probably some aspects of digital curation already in place, this is just part of what should be addressed here. Digital curation is a sub-discipline that has a very specific meaning within library and information science.[2] While some of the practices employed in digital curation may be applicable, there is a likelihood these practices would not apply to the majority of electronic resources where the purchase model is based solely on access and not on ownership of the content. Morse made a very astute observation at the Library Publishing Forum in 2018: "it's not just a technology issue but a commitment of resources over time and ultimately, preservation is a series of decisions."[3]

The perception of access to electronic resources is that it is temporal. For resources such as JSTOR, access has been consistently available for over twenty years.[4] Although many of the emergent platforms used in the late

1990s and early 2000s are no longer with us, much of the indexing and content served by those platforms still lives on. That said, link rot is a persistent problem, and when looking at references that use URLs, it is not surprising to find there are some that no longer link to the content referenced.[5] Indeed, the issue of digital preservation is no longer new. Back in 2007, Holdsworth contributed a chapter to the Digital Curation Manual, and its key takeaways are still relevant today.[6]

Part of the problem with preservation and sustainability revolves around the temporality of many resources and determining what will be advantageous to keep in the future. The other issue with electronic material is what Hoeve refers to as "the preoccupation with immediate access of information, which has subsequently resulted in the neglect of sustainable preservation practices."[7] The focus is on what is requested and needed today, rather than what may be needed in the future. In this regard, selection decisions are readily made for content that does not have the viability for long term access and use.

For the purpose of this chapter, preservation and sustainability requires the determination of the selection criteria for resources to be maintained perpetually, development of a local strategy in which to make that sustainability and preservation happen, investigation of the metadata needed, the choice of what local practices and cloud-based practices are most viable for a library, and finally the development and initiation of exit strategies for leaving content and purchasing models successfully. Although this does not bring us to a distinct definition of what preservation and sustainability is, it will allow the reader to determine local frameworks and practices to allow for the local determination of how to best try to sustain and preserve the necessary content. In the end, there is not an easy answer to these concerns.

1. Choosing What to Preserve and Sustain

The first choice is determining what needs to be preserved and maintained. This circles back to the collection development plans and priorities mentioned in chapter 2. When determining what resources to buy, part of that decision-making process should include a consideration of the longevity needed with the content. Most electronic resources are purchased with the idea that the content will be preserved and sustained for a significant period of time. In the cases of subscription material, best practice is to resolve the provision of perpetual access rights upon selection and determine how the title will be made available if it were to cease or if cancellation occurs. Historically, however, this has not been a question that has been asked at the point of selection, but given unstable and increasingly diminishing budgets, the determination of longevity of a content stream must now be discussed. The good news is there are model retention plans for digital collections that serve as starting points for determining the local retention of commercial produced online content. Framing these decisions in this manner will support better alignment between purchased resources and locally created resources.

When purchasing online archives, it is important to understand the reasons why the content is being acquired and how the user community will use it not just in current programming, but in the future. Ongoing access fees and content updates can become a burden on any library budget quickly. Ascertaining upfront the long-term use of content is critical. Knowing what the post-cancellation rights and perpetual rights are with archival purchases is essential in the case of potential cancellation. Archival purchases are significant expenditures and as such, need to be treated with more comprehensive planning and understanding as to their long-term viability. Table 7.1 depicts a chart showing what this could look like:

TABLE 7.1

Resource Retention Chart Example

RESOURCE RETENTION CHART				
Resource Type	Short Term	Perpetual Access/PCA	Purchase Archive	Support Archive Service
Ebook Subscription	X			
Ebook Collection		X		X
Journals		X	X	X
Aggregated Collections	X			
Local Collections	X	X		X

Right now, libraries tend to develop retention plans that primarily focus on digital assets or OA collections. Preservation or retention plans normally spell out why you are choosing to keep or preserve the material and how you are going to accomplish the preservation practice.[8] In these cases, the retention plan is part of the set-up process engaged in with local institutional repositories. Determining which content to retain and for what time frame is usually part of the metadata used for ingesting locally created material as well as for reaching agreement with authors to deposit material. Although some multi-institution networking has begun to create redundant access models, these networks are nascent and still rely on grant funding for development. Developing mechanisms for dark archiving of open content either upon immediate deposit or in the future are often necessary for some disciplines and individuals within your organization. Providing exit strategy clauses for your community to withdraw content or to move it to dark archives is vital as well.

Basic Resources

If the purchased material is needed for a short period of use, temporary access is adequate. This is often the case with streaming media content, for example. Streaming media that is widely used and important to a faculty member today may not be as popular or of much interest in the future. Other short-term content may be purchased for course reserves and reading lists. This content ages very quickly and new editions may be issued annually. Maintaining older versions may not be helpful as assignments tend to be made from the most current versions of the material. Indeed, in some disciplines, such as law, maintaining older editions is strongly discouraged. Electronic material used for specific grants may no longer be of vital interest once the grant period has ended and the research is completed. Finally, most libraries do not provide a commitment to maintain aggregator platforms or content. The full text provided through these services is often seen as supplemental to library holdings as opposed to being essential library holdings. In cases where these are the basis for library holdings, the expectation should be that the content will flip to subscription at the title level for high-use items that drop out of the aggregator package in order to insure longevity of access. However, the opposite may occur in a big deal cancellation.

In the case of journals, some databases, and key abstracting and indexing (A&I) resources, the preservation strategy involves investing in perpetual and accessible archives either directly from the provider or publisher or from a third party such as JSTOR. Once the journal backfiles are purchased, there is a likelihood that the same content is held in print. In the case of most A&I resources, the use of discovery tools in libraries, along with the development of tools like Lean Library, make the retention of some A&I services less important. The other main choice is to use third-party preservation strategies such as LOCKSS or Portico to insure long-term access to journals and e-books.[9-11] We define these tools in detail in the sections below on local and cloud-based services.

Although many librarians consider e-books to be permanent or perpetual additions to their library collections, it is worthwhile to review e-book holdings to determine the value of the content previously purchased. Louisiana State University (LSU) librarians did this with their historic purchases of what were originally NetLibrary titles.[12] They used the weeding criteria established for their print collection and applied it to e-books. However, deselecting e-books can be problematic. In many cases, e-books are bought as collections (this is especially true for historic NetLibrary titles). The LSU librarians needed to find a way to exclude or deselect these titles from the current administrative portal, which required working closely with the current content provider to enact that functionality. A number of lessons can be learned from this study. First, it is worthwhile for librarians at a given library to develop e-book weeding criteria that may be different than print criteria. For example, content that has a certain amount of link rot will be considered for deselection. This should be noted in the collection, management, and development policy.

Another situation is the deselection of the same title in print. In her article, Francis describes the process of weeding print resources in the reference area at the Dakota State University Library.[13] By utilizing online reference collections and individual title purchases, the reference collection was reduced by more than 20 percent. Print volumes of reference material are likely candidates to be replaced by electronic resources as long as e-reference works can be absorbed by the local collection budget. At the Portland State University Library, one e-book vendor pitched for business by asking for a list of print ISBNs in order to see what could be replaced with its e-book collections. To date, this offer has not been explored but it is an intriguing one that may be explored in the future. Again, the issue comes down to whether a budget allows for this change in format can be undertaken in any significant way.

Understanding what the budgetary costs are for preservation and sustainability of electronic resources is an ongoing consideration. In some cases, the annual access fees to be paid for third-party platforms are very straightforward, whereas maintaining and providing content from local servers or via payment for local cloud services will be more ambiguous and may be tied in with other support or maintenance costs.

Complex Resources

With e-book subscription models, patron driven, and evidence-based purchasing models, the culling of underutilized content, or in some cases over-utilized content, is a choice made by the provider or the participating library. For this reason, this decision point is more complex. In these cases, it is best to have a rubric or practice to handle the semi-annual or annual removal of content from the packages offered. This often means having funding available to purchase some content in perpetuity that is not entirely anticipated.

ProQuest announced in 2018 that it was planning to develop Secure Archives For Ever (SAFE), a dark archive to safeguard its e-book content.[14] This could be a situation where obtaining access to the dark archive may become an additional service cost for purchased content. Nonetheless, ProQuest should be commended for making the effort to establish a preservation mechanism as not all providers are committed beyond using third-party platforms at the moment.

Machovec notes in his column in the *Journal of Library Administration* how some library consortia in North America are committing to locally loading e-books onto local platforms for their participating libraries.[15] Examples include OhioLink's Electronic Book Center and the Ontario Council of University Libraries' Scholar's Portal. In addition to these initiatives, E-books Minnesota is a project by the Minnesota Digital Library to preserve the outputs of

Minnesota publishers and Minnesota authors. In the same column, Machovec notes that some commercial publishers will allow libraries to host their content locally for preservation purposes.

With more complex citation abstracting and indexing tools, buying the archives may bring up the problem of flexibility. Throughout much of the early twenty-first century, many libraries invested in purchasing significant back files of these citation tools. When a new product came onto the market, the same libraries found that if they cancelled their current subscriptions to the tool, they would also lose the access to the back files. This locked many libraries into maintaining tools that they wanted to replace. In this case, choosing to preserve resources ended up being a short-sighted decision.

Streaming media is also another content area that can be complex. In some cases, providers allow for a perpetual purchase of the content but insist on the library hosting the files locally. This will require working with local streaming media platforms and managers to provide access to the content. In other cases, streaming media providers allow for extended year licenses, usually at three-, five-, or ten-year intervals. For content that is heavily used in your library environment, purchasing an extended license agreement will insure continuity of access. Recording this information is critical so that others know when access timeframes will expire; this will be discussed in greater detail in the metadata section below.

Open Access

Within a given organization, the thought is usually that if something is in the institutional repository it will be preserved. This is not the opinion of managers of institutional repositories. Some libraries are choosing to use backup servers to archive their institutional repositories and digital library content; others may be using Archive-It from Internet Archive.[16] Archive-It is a relatively affordable third-party web archiving platform for collecting and preserving library web presences and cultural heritage material. However, it is not necessarily the best tool for archiving pre-prints and post-print material. We are not aware of any librarians or libraries that are insuring redundancy of pre-prints and post-print materials with subject discipline repositories, although for health science institutions there is a high likelihood that content may be available in a local repository and will also be hosted on PubMedCentral.[17] A recent announcement from Portico indicates that authors publishing open access material using the Scholastica scholarship portal can choose to have their content deposited into Portico.[18] However, this means that preservation is becoming a closed, paywalled system because only libraries participating in Portico will then have access to this content.

2. Developing Preservation and Sustainability Plans

After making the choice of what should be maintained or preserved for longevity, the next step is establishing the plan or guide for preservation. First and foremost, establishing the required metadata to track content is essential. These metadata elements will be outlined more specifically in the metadata section below. However, knowing upfront what metadata works for insuring sustained retention helps with recording it during the procurement phase or implementation phase of the resource.

Although there are many training courses and broad overviews available on digital preservation and ways to get started, it is much harder to find the statistics on how many libraries worldwide are fully engaged in significant preservation or sustainability plans.[19] That said, there are some significant preservation plans available to get started. One example is the UNT Libraries Digital Preservation Policy Framework at University of North Texas Libraries.[20] This framework presents a glossary of concepts and terms and then neatly frames the mandate that the UNT Libraries has taken on in order to preserve local digital scholarship. This plan could be adapted by other institutions designing their own policies about how the preservation of commercial produced content is retained or sustained. Preservation and sustainability plans should be contextualized to a given environment or institution and often must be scoped to varying areas of preservation and sustainability. Various other collaborative preservation networks have formed, which have influence and impact, but then end as their grant funding runs out. It is worth mentioning the policy documents coming from these initiatives, but this trend indicates that libraries are not fully committed to funding these initiatives to the levels needed to sustain them.[21]

Basic Resources

At a very basic level, an initial step could be identifying the post-cancellation rights of commercially produced scholarship, such as outlined by Carter.[22] Her presentation indicates that there are first steps to take with administrative metadata and to understand what content should be readily available to a given institution through its post-cancellation access rights or perpetual access rights. Many current library management systems provide a designated field to note post-cancellation or perpetual access rights. Furthermore, this information can serve a dual purpose. Once the access rights are recorded, it makes it easier to identify what content should be available as it moves or transfers from one provider or platform to another. However, until library workers take this initial step, it may be impossible to retrace them to fully discover their access rights to electronic content. Another option would be to use these fields to note what digital resources are being archived somewhere else and which ones are not using the Keepers Registry.[23]

Most recently Edina has announced a beta version of a tool called the Entitlement Registry.[24] This tool works as an intermediary between librarians and publishers to help establish the entitlement rights. In summer 2019, Edina ran an extended beta-test of their service in hopes to fully roll out the service by the start of 2020. If successful and priced reasonably, this service is likely to become quite popular.

Complex Resources

Many library workers are deciding to remove print collections that overlap with online holdings of the same content. This is true for print resources beyond the reference collection scenario discussed above. The biggest concern with the replacement of print with electronic formats is the potential for removing resources critical to the library collection and then losing access to the online content as well.

Payne reviews the difficulty with developing and creating weeding projects of print materials during a project at John Hopkins University Libraries.[25] Although Payne does not specifically outline how electronic access played a part of the criteria leading into the project, her points about effective communication are valuable for any weeding activity undertaken. The main takeaway is that it is critical to make sure that everyone understands the reasons and purposes for the weeding project and that this means representing the project in visualized ways rather than passing around spreadsheets. Sasyk provides a couple of scenarios where electronic resource management tools are utilized to provide overlap comparisons between print and electronic resources for deaccession of print journal titles.[26] Her method involves techniques to secure data integrity between both formats in order to create lists of material to remove from a collection. Sasyk's method of creating weeding lists through the electronic resources management system works well for journals but is likely to have less success for books.

There is not a definite approach to use for replacing print materials with electronic ones. This work will require a local library environment to develop the plans and practice that will succeed in its own environment. The process created for removing print resources in favor of electronic must include widely understood documentation of the preservation strategy for the online content.

Open Access

Preservation and sustainability plans for institutional repositories have been discussed for many years.[27] More recently, this has been extended to cover gray literature, such as master's theses.[28] In the United Kingdom, the question as to whether a repository had a formal preservation function was asked by the Universities U.K. Open Access Coordination Group. Its report noted that "The British Library is in the process of enhancing its digital preservation capacities and looking at how it may expand its services to others, including theses (EThOS) and OA publications. Jisc is piloting a Research Data Shared Services Model (RDSS) with a number of higher education institutions, and digital preservation is in the project scope."[29-31] However, regarding institutional repository content, the report found that "preservation of OA content is recognized as a need, however, the pressure on each higher education institution repository to find its solution is a key concern." The report concluded that institutions are not adequately funded to create a solution and often lack technical expertise. A major recommendation of the report was that "(a) study into the feasibility of a national preservation solution be undertaken, recognizing that the British Library and Jisc are key stakeholders."

Some universities do have existing preservation strategies. For example, Cornell University presents a useful table listing file formats for digital content and the likelihood that each format will support full long-term preservation. However, it adds that "PDF is a good file format choice in terms of preservation, with PDF/A being the best option," but that PDF is not a format that will support long-term preservation.[32] This view is supported by research in Sweden that states that using PDFs "implies major challenges for the longevity of files because there is an inherent dependence on the software used to create each file over the full life-cycle for each file." This study concludes the there is "little focus on and awareness of open file formats," However, PDF/A does seem to be a viable option, but only for traditional formats.[33]

Regarding the acquisition of open access journals, particularly hybrid titles, there is a link between the deal breakers discussed in chapter 3 and the development of a preservation strategy for acquiring open access content, including hybrid open access. For example, the Jisc Collections Content, Management and Development Policy states that for hybrid titles, "content should be part of an archiving and preservation solution such as Portico, LOCKSS or LOCKSS."[34] It is recommended that this policy is adopted in institutional policies too.

When it comes to preservation policies for open access publishing, those fully open access publishers that qualify for the Directory of Open Access Journals (DOAJ) gold seal respond to the question on digital archiving policy by choosing one of the following options:

- CINES
- CLOCKSS
- LOCKSS
- PKP PN
- PMC/Europe PMC/PMC Canada
- Portico
- A national library's requirement
- Other

DOAJ states that "'No policy in place' does not qualify for the Seal."[35] When searching in DOAJ, those publishers that have an archiving policy in place have a green tick next to their names. Although this is part of the DOAJ application, it does not form part of the submission for Directory of Open Access Books.

However, there is a digital preservation policy for open access monograph publishers who upload their content to OAPEN. "OAPEN collaborates with the National Library of the Netherlands e-Depot to secure long-term preservation of all publications in the OAPEN Library."[36] This covers publishing platforms, such as Ubiquity Press, which offer preservation via OAPEN. OAPEN also preserves its content in Portico.[37] This will be covered below in the subsection on cloud services.

3. Metadata Needed for Preservation

Metadata for ongoing preservation is a rapidly evolving landscape. Almost a decade ago, a group began work to pilot a journal preservation registry service (PERS) to outline the metadata needed for this work.[38] Part of its framework explored how to arrive at a common vocabulary to accomplish the post-cancellation rights of content. However, this work stopped short of the development of a specific standard or element to be used to identify post-cancellation access or perpetual access to content. Given the lack of national standards, most libraries must develop metadata that is meaningful within their own environments. It is most helpful if the data is readily retrievable by anyone who needs it. A final consideration is how public to make metadata for any given resource.

One approach library workers can take involves the consistent application of persistent identifiers for the creators and works created and for the provenance of the work by using an institutional and funder identification. Often referred to as PIDs, some of these standards are more widely adopted and utilized than others.[39] Although this tends to be done within institutional repositories, at this time these designators are not commonly found in library management systems. In part because the work with library management systems takes place at the journal and e-book level more than at the discrete levels of chapters or articles. However, these key pieces of information are more and more critical in the information retrieval landscape to aid in the discovery and utility of scholarship throughout the lifecycle. We recommend six PIDs to begin with:

1. Digital Object Identifiers (DOIs).[40] The DOI is the key identifier of discrete elements of scholarship. It was designed initially for use with journal articles but has come to be applied to many single items of scholarship such as blog posts, data sets, data objects like tables and

graphs, and book chapters. Once an output has a DOI, access to the resource can be retrieved more readily through various portals in a more seamless and direct way than URLs allow

2. Journal Article Tag Suite (JATS).[41] The Journal Article Tag Suite envelopes an article or discrete part of a journal such as letters to the editor, or a book review in a set of XML descriptive metadata to help distinguish it from other articles or works within a given digital journal. Multiple descriptive schema can use the JATS structure to help make the descriptive information more portable and extensible within a given digital structure. Being structured as XML instead of a static PDF allows the content to be moved more readily from one networked environment to another and to interplay easily with other services

3. ORCID.[42] Although ORCID research identifiers currently play a minimal role in retrieval, this identifier is key for researchers disambiguating themselves from other researchers with similar names as well as receiving the credit for their research outputs. For closed systems, this process will still need to be done manually. Having researcher ORCIDs captured within library systems allows for academic librarians to easily identify the scholarship produced by their local scholars and to highlight and promote these authors readily

4. Funder RegistryRef.[43] Funder Registry from CrossRef is the key identifier used to indicate the funding body supporting the research. With scientific literature, knowing who funded the research is a key component to understanding how the research was developed as well as an indication of why the research was done in the first place

5. International Standard Name Identifier (ISNI).[44] This identifier provides information about the institution where a researcher worked while the research was undertaken. Again, this provides a contextual reference for the research.

6. Research Organization Registry (RoR).[45] This identifier is still in development but is an attempt to create a fully open and readily available code for research organizations.

Basic Resources

As has been noted, in our discussion of developing preservation plans, one of the most immediate activities to undertake is the recording of post-cancellation access or perpetual access within the library management system framework. Although there is not a standard to use for this, the library management system may make this very easy to do by utilizing a checkbox approach or allowing for more descriptive elements such as date ranges or time periods covered. The more description that can be added the better, because not all resources have the same post-cancellation access rights or time frames. Knowing this information is critical for many other operations or decisions in the library, which is why documenting these rights is important.

Regarding streaming media resources, librarians on national LISTSERVs in the United States are discussing public notation of access rights. This entails adding in a descriptor to the link address that provides the term of access for any given streaming video. For instance, Portland State University Library is adopting the following link text for one of the streaming media collections—"Kanopy (film expires xx/xx/xxxx)"—as a way of indicating to the end user the time period of availability of the content on a given platform if perpetual purchase is not possible.

Complex Resources

In the United States, the majority of government information has moved online throughout the early part of the twenty-first century. Given this trend and the most recent administration's habit of removing government sites (although this is a problem for many countries when a refresh of a website happens, or indeed government focus), there has been growing concern among government document librarians about the need for more robust metadata with these resources.[46] There is work, which is still ongoing, to provide a better framework of the metadata required for preservation of this material. This work has given rise to the Preservation of Electronic Government Information (PEGI) project to help identify and preserve at risk government resources and websites, and potentially crowdsource needed descriptive metadata.[47]

The Library of Congress has a statement on Recommended Formats for preservation to allow for consistency with preservation applications.[48] This framework helps to outline and provide a cohesive framework for the base format description to be used with resources. It is an essential document to utilize when defining the scholarly and creative works being preserved.

Open Access

OA material relies on much the same metadata as other electronic resources. Therefore, the PIDs discussed above apply here too. Of particular note, ORCID has created an application programming interface (API), which allows open repository systems to set up a feed to collect ORCID data directly into the repository.[49]

In addition, there are a number of developments occurring around the following initiatives: the Open Archival Information System (OAIS), PREservation Metadata: Implementation Strategies (PREMIS), and PRONOM online file format registry. This work is instrumental in facilitating access, discovery, and management, as well as with expanding the frameworks for preservation of digital resources.[50]

4. Local Preservation Options
(Servers, Media Drives, LOCKSS/CLOCKSS, MetaArchive)

Preservation and sustainability concerns about online content have given rise to numerous projects underway at many institutions. The main problem with both local and networked initiatives is that these initiatives begin with grant funding or start-up investment and lack budgets to sustain and carry projects forward. That said, there are tangible projects such as LOCKSS/CLOCKSS, which is entering its second decade of existence and expanding the capture of content for preservation needed.[51,52]

More complex projects such as the Scholarly Orphans Project provide examples of unique but necessary projects that capture some of the new emerging forms of scholarship.[53] There is the MetaArchive project, a cooperative digital network for capturing cultural memory institutions.[54] Weintraub and Alagna outline the state of local preservation in their Institute of Museum and Library Studies funded research project from 2017.[55] Their findings indicate that standard backups of local repositories tend not to happen due to the lack of funding available.

Basic Resources

The two most basic methods for local preservation are running a local backup service for all hosted scholarly content and participating in the LOCKSS program. In both instances, there are costs involved.

The second most common preservation strategy is through participation in LOCKSS/CLOCKSS. These services also require a local server environment on which you capture the local scholarly content, but the server is networked to other servers maintaining much of the same content at other institutions. Through the balance load of local availability and networked access, the content is made available during any downtime by a participating hosted provider. CLOCKSS is the open environment side of the system that allows open and ready availability of content that is discontinued or ceased publication. In addition, it was announced in July 2018 that CLOCKSS would also host all backups of Crossref data, which allows for ready linking of content through DOIs.[56] LOCKSS has also made a number of case studies available showing how it is being used.[57]

Complex Resources

Much of the work on metadata that could be described as complex is still in development, such as The Scholarly Orphans project, which is discussed further in the chapter 8. However, the MetaArchive began close to fifteen years ago to keep overhead costs minimal but provide easy mechanisms for collaboration. This work has created the infrastructure needed to preserve its shared local digital collections. One of the backbones of the success of MetaArchive has been the use of the LOCKSS preservation network. Although working to arrange the setup of this work took an initial long-term investment, it was found that the work put into setting policies and the community governance structure is just as valuable as the preservation strategy itself.

Open Access

LOCKSS is also active in support of OA publishing and there is also work being performed to help preserve Open Journal Systems (OJS) and insure that open content will remain open even through preservation.[58]

ArXiv is an interesting case study. This pre-print server began in 1991 as a U.S. government hosted website to provide access to research articles focused mostly on physics and relevant physical literature.[59] In the early part of the twenty-first century, the platform and access moved to be hosted by Cornell University and eventually came to the Cornell University Library for management. Along this path, there were times when the sustainability and future of the platform came into question, but each time the community using this platform found ways to fund and support it. Today, Cornell University continues to provide over one-third of the organization's operating expenses, with the remainder provided by the Simons Foundation and pledges from member institutions throughout the world.[60] In 2019, oversight of arXiv will transfer from the Cornell University Library to the Cornell Computing and Information Science. The site is recognized worldwide as a major research portal for physics and physical disciplines and continues to grow in content.

Many additional pre-print servers have grown from the arXiv model, though it seems unlikely that all will survive. Examples include SocArXiv for social sciences, founded in 2016; PsyArXiv for psychological sciences, also founded in 2016, AgriXiv for agricultural and allied sciences: and many others, using the Open Science Framework Preprints structure.[61]

5. Cloud-Based Options
(Archive-It, Portico, Media Portals, DPLA Hubs, Shared Preservation Structure)

As noted above, the desire within the library community to participate in networked and third-party solutions can be problematic. Many of these initiatives begin with grant funding and are just not able to make the essential elements of content preservation and sustainability key factors in financial support. The most successful platforms are ones that exist within larger nonprofit supported organizations that have multiple funding sources to balance the costs.[62]

Basic Resources

The best-known third-party cloud-based systems are Portico, Internet Archive, and Archive-It.[63–65]

More than a thousand libraries worldwide currently participate in Portico and they provide a solution that works for both publishers and for libraries.[66] Publishers can readily deposit content for archiving and libraries can retrieve content as needed during service failures or when content ceases to be available on publisher websites. In addition, Portico has begun to accept digital collections for preservation as well. Libraries pay annual support fees based on the size of their library expenditures to join and gain access to their preserved content.

The Internet Archive is also a nonprofit company that has compiled what is arguably one of the largest digital library presences. The archive began in 1996 and continues to grow and expand. Its website provides access to openly available books, streaming visual files, static visual files, audio files, software, and websites. Its strength is in providing access to content that is out of copyright in the United States or was preserved from platforms that no longer exist on the web. Although grant funded initially, the Internet Archive has managed to promote and crowdsource funding on a regular basis to continue to add to its collections. Libraries can choose to donate support, however, most of the support comes from funding agencies and individuals.

Archive-It is a subsection of the Internet Archive that is supported by libraries and cultural heritage sites through membership fees. Members participate in the governance of the structural system and help to guide development concepts for new iterations of the software and systems. The members establish schedules where the sites they wish to capture are crawled and preserved on a routine basis. This provides a relatively inexpensive and fundamental capture of a given institution's web presence.

Complex Resources

A nonprofit cloud-based preservation entity, the Digital Public Library of America (DPLA) is relatively new, planning began in 2010 and it was launched in 2013.[67] Libraries and library consortia participate by hosting local service and content hubs in order to capture and then uploaded access to the DPLA main site. In November 2018, the DPLA Board of Directors announced that due to a funding shortage, six staff positions were eliminated, and the remaining staff would be restructured. This change coincides with DPLA transitioning from grant-funded support and trying to become a financially independent nonprofit entity. Much concern has been raised in the U.S. library community about the DPLA and its future role in helping to preserve the cultural heritage of U.S. libraries.[68] In particular, the hubs that were in development no longer have the internal support expected to fully get their workflows and processes in place.

Open Access

As noted above, OA publishers who make their content available via OAPEN benefit from OAPEN's preservation policy, which includes the use of Portico.[69] In addition, OA publishers can also preserve their book and journal content directly with Portico for an annual fee.[70] It is important to double-check the list of publishers on Portico. For example, the University of Huddersfield Press, one of the first new library-led university presses in the United Kingdom, has had its OA journal content preserved in Portico since 2013.[71]

6. Exit Strategy

The previous chapter discusses the possibility of an assessment of an e-resource leading to a cancellation review. If further consultation following this review leads to a decision to cancel, then an exit strategy is urgently required. This will differ depending on the resource. Some exit strategies are simple to achieve. However, because others—especially big deals—will affect the ability of researchers to access content, this process must be managed carefully. An exit strategy always features in a collection management and development policy as it is important to have outline both acquisition and disposal or cancellation of resources.[72]

For an indication of the institutions that have taken the decision to cancel the big deal, see the SPARC big deal cancellation website.[73]

Basic Resources

For the purposes of an exit strategy, basic resources include single journals, e-books, and databases. Single journals are treated in very much the same way as a print journal cancellation. The catalog or knowledge base must be edited to close the entry and relevant faculty need to be informed, perhaps via any collection management group, subject liaison, or other means (see chapter 4). E-book weeding also follows the same model as print book weeding: candidates will be those books that have not been used, are no longer current, or have been superceded by new editions.

Demand driven acquisition (DDA), although more complex than the processes described above, is still fairly straightforward. Indeed, it is far more straightforward than switching the collection on! The exit strategy for DDA is to make sure that when the money runs out the collection is switched off immediately. This avoids users selecting a title that is no longer available. The worst-case scenario is when this happens over a weekend.

Exiting a database agreement is slightly different. However, a database is rarely purchased for one title, but rather to give broad subject coverage at a competitive price. If a number of databases are in a collection, it is very likely that there will be overlap with other content available. Unlike a journal subscription, once a database is switched off, the content is gone—there will be no post-cancellation access (see below).

Complex Resources and Open Access

Exiting the big deal can be an incredibly complex affair, often made more so by the cross-disciplinary nature of many large-scale big deals and the volume of content involved. For example, a big deal may contain thousands of journal titles, which translates into millions of articles across twenty to twenty-five years. Therefore, unpacking the big deal is an incredibly complex process. This subsection will run through a suggested checklist designed to lessen the impact of big deal cancellations. This checklist is partly inspired by the work of McGrath on Plan B, which was first developed by Research Libraries U.K. (RLUK) in 2011 for its Wiley and Elsevier negotiations as a strategy rather than a viable alternative. Like the University of California negotiation toolkit mentioned in chapter 3, this checklist will help set the stage for renegotiations of packages as well as the leaving of package deals. Indeed, McGrath considered that "maintaining Plan B beyond about three years is problematic owing to the ever-increasing amount of material that becomes unavailable to users."[74] However, the Plan B work focuses very much on interlibrary loans (ILL) as an alternative. This subsection suggests that open access is also a viable alternative to be considered as part of the exit strategy.

Post-Cancellation Access (PCA)

Post-cancellation access or post-termination access can be described as entitlements that "specify the conditions that allow ongoing access to the journal volumes a subscriber has paid for."[75] When exiting a big deal, understanding PCA rights is vital. In some cases, this might entitle the library to access everything published during the duration of the agreement, whereas in other cases PCA access may only include core titles. Points to look out for include the introduction of "rolling wall" access to this content, where you may find access is lost to older articles and to archive content, as well as the introduction of a service charge after a given period of time.

During a negotiation, some publishers may offer to reduce the cost of the agreement by a nominal figure that represents the value of PCA. Although this may seem attractive at the start of an agreement, if the big deal is ever cancelled, this could represent a significant amount of content that cannot be accessed. This will become apparent when defining the exit strategy.

Core Titles

Core titles are related to PCA. Essentially, they represent the titles subscribed to individually before the big deal was negotiated and purchased. Big deals usually include a no-cancellation clause for these titles, so after the big deal is terminated, subscriptions to these titles resume unless they have also been cancelled at the same time as the big deal. These core titles form part of PCA in that access should be granted for the years subscribed. However, there are complications. Some publishers allow the swapping of titles during the big deal. This may mean that the coverage of those core titles will not cover the whole duration of the agreement. Unlike PCA, core titles will differ from institution to institution depending on historical subscriptions.

Both PCA and core titles should be available within a discovery system to ensure ongoing access. Depending on a publisher's PCA policy and a library's historical subscription spend, this could represent a substantial percentage of titles. However, it may not!

Gold and Green Open Access

At the article level, gold and green open access titles will also have ongoing access. However, these are harder to lock down, because a big deal might include millions of articles. A percentage of these will be gold or green open access, but coverage through a discovery system is likely to be patchy at best.

Research claims that the overall "free" availability is as high as 54.6 percent, although subject and country coverage may differ.[76] It would be fair to assume that there are more science titles available than arts, humanities, and social science material. However, free does not mean gold and green open access. Free could include gold, green, delayed green (with up to two years embargo), bronze and "other" sources, such as that from ResearchGate.[77] As discussed in chapter 4, sources such as ResearchGate should not be relied upon as they can be unreliable.

Based on Unpaywall data, when looking at gold and green open access for 2017, the percentage of OA articles drop to 31.7 percent.[78] This percentage decreases the older the article, but conversely, the authors of this research add that the percentage does rise year on year, so 2018 data should be higher. It is very important to note that this percentage will also vary between publishers—for many it could be far lower. For a big deal that covers up to twenty years, the older material, which will not be available on open access, will also reduce the percentage significantly.

Chapter 4 notes that tools such as OA Button and Unpaywall are available as browser extensions.[79,80] CORE's mission is "to aggregate all open access research outputs from repositories and journals worldwide and make them available to the public."[81] Although CORE does not cover all gold and green open access material, it is a good place to start and can be linked to discovery systems to allow seamless access.

Bronze Open Access

Bronze open access represented 15.3 percent of content in the Unpaywall data.[82] However, this is not truly open access. Piwowar et al. define bronze as "free to read on the publisher page, but without a clearly identifiable license." This could represent gold and green open access with bad metadata. It is more likely to represent content made free at some point in time by a publisher. For example, many publishers make the first issue of new titles available as a sampler, while others make selected articles free for a short period of time. Therefore, the figure of 15.3 percent for 2017 articles will most likely have changed since the sample was taken. Even if the percentage remains the same, the articles may have changed.

PCA, core titles, and gold and green open access represent content that can be reliably depended upon as an alternative to a big deal. Furthermore, there is a good chance that this content is made available via the discovery layer, which will ensure seamless access to a percentage of content. However, this percentage is very difficult to calculate reliably and will differ from institution to institution and from big deal to big deal. However, this content is the baseline for any exit strategy.

Bronze open access content will increase the amount of content available, but it cannot be linked to reliably. Libraries may prefer to advise their researchers that bronze open access content should be acquired legally by researchers, but that researchers will have to seek it out for themselves.

Analyzing Usage Data

This still leaves a large percentage of content that is effectively closed to researchers. Just as the long tail of little-used titles in a big deal are used as a reason to cancel, this long tail can also be used to bring the percentage of closed access material down.[83] Schöpfel and Leduc cite the Pareto 80:20 distribution to explain this.[84] If 20 percent of the titles in the big deal represent 80 percent of usage, it stands to reason that the long tail representing 20 percent of the usage is very unlikely to be in demand after the big deal is cancelled.[85]

Working this out as an actual percentage of the big deal is probably easier said than done and would require a fair amount of computing power. The clear message here is that the amount of closed content that might be of local interest is likely lower than the raw data might suggest.

Interlibrary Loans

No matter how you work out the number of items left on closed access, the remaining articles from the big deal can be provided via ILL. Potentially this figure could look horrific, particularly for small- to medium-sized libraries, which often benefit the most from the big deal because historically they have fewer core subscriptions to fall back on.

There is some relatively good news. Research shows that ILL requests are always far lower than usage in the big deal. McGrath bases much of the work around Plan B on document delivery, using a 35 percent ratio for conversion of previous usage to ILL, although a lower figure of 10 percent is discussed.[86] Nabe and Fowler find that ILL use for Wiley represented 9 percent of previous COUNTER use in the deal and 3 percent of previous use for Elsevier.[87] Research at the University of Wisconsin-Milwaukee suggests a COUNTER:ILL ration of 17:1, although Scott warns that variations among publishers (and disciplines) may be observed, therefore this ratio should be used as a general estimate.[88]

TERMs suggests that a 10 percent ratio is used to calculate the potential ILLs, so every one hundred downloads in the big deal, would convert to just ten ILLs requested. The drop is because of the barrier to access that the ILL request puts in place. Having to fill out a form or simply clicking through to the ILL request reduces demand. This figure has the potential to be reduced further as open access tools such as OA Button become embedded into the workflow.[89] The destinations of these tools must be checked to prevent the library accidently endorsing access to material that is not truly open access for example bronze OA.

Once the potential ILL requests are estimated, then a cost can be assigned to this part of the exit plan. If this figure looks too unaffordable, check it against current ILL figures. Chances are there is room for small increases. However, if the increase over the existing ILL costs is very large, you may need to consider additional staffing costs too.

In chapter 6 we note the average cost of ILL is around $8. However, this cost is subject to wide variation, as there is often a lack of standardization in how these costs are calculated and what expenditures are included.[90] Therefore, there are always weaknesses in these estimates. A more standard and transparent formula is certainly needed.

In addition, there are further variations in costs. For example, Florida State and Caltech both offer two levels of ILL: expedited delivery costs $30 and guaranteed delivery in twenty-four hours is free. This will increase the costs.

It is also worth noting that Rathmel et al. use an estimated additional staff cost per article of $7 and this should be a factor in any costings.[91] Knowing the staff costs of other areas would be necessary to make a true comparison, for example, repository staffing costs, serials team and e-resource team costs.

If there is a possibility of a large number of ILLs for a particular journal, this implies that an additional subscription should be taken out. Pedersen et al. view the use of ILL costs in cost per download analysis of the big deal as a primary criterion for decision making.[92] In their case study at Iowa State University, only 3 of the 1,598 titles cancelled, which had not been substantiated by this method of cost-per-use assessment, were reinstated due to demand.

At the end of these steps, you will have two figures. The cost of continued subscriptions and the additional costs of ILLs. If these costs are less than the big deal you wish to exit, then the decision is viable.

As discussed in chapter 6, the decision to leave a big deal must be done in full consultation with faculty. Some big deal publishers are well aware of the potential reputational loss to a university library if this is not managed well and will encourage negotiations to continue for as long as possible, thereby leaving not enough time for a careful and organized exit from a large collection. It is all the more critical that libraries plan ahead, potentially having worked out any potential exit plan in advance of an actual decision.

Once that decision is made, in the absence of a completely automated solution to the exit plan, the library must inform its patrons about alternative methods of access. Although, as explained above, some parts of the plan will be automated through the discovery layer, other access points will need explanation. An example of best practice in marketing alternative methods of access is the Bibsam consortium in Sweden. Its well-publicized exit from the Elsevier agreement in June 2018 was followed by a blogpost giving guidance to libraries and researchers.[93]

NOTES

1. Emery, Jill, McCracken, Peter, & Stone Graham. (2018). UKSG presentation & notes from the flipcharts TERMS. http://6terms.tumblr.com/post/17289 2767654/uksg-presentation-notes-from-the-flipcharts.

2. Higgins, Sarah. (2018). Digital curation: The development of a discipline within information science. *Journal of Documentation* 74(6): 1318–1338. https://doi.org/ 10.1108/JD-02-2018-0024.

3. Staines, Heather, Robertson, Wendy, & Morse, Jeremy. (2018). Digital preservation for library publishers: Raising awareness. https://librarypublishing. org/wp -content/uploads/2017/09/LPF18_Preservation.pdf.

4. Schonfeld, Roger. (2003). *JSTOR: A history* (Princeton NJ: Princeton University Press).

5. Wikipedia. (2018). Link rot. https://en.wikipedia.org/wiki/Link_rot.

6. Holdsworth, David. (2007). Preservation Strategies for Digital Libraries. In DCC Digital Curation Manual, S. Ross & M. Day (eds). http://hdl.handle.net/ 1842/3358.

7. Hoeve, Casey D. (2018). Cultural memory in danger: Sustainable information, preservation, and technology in the humanities: A theoretical approach. *Collaborative Librarianship 10*(2). article 6. https://digitalcommons.du.edu/collaborativelibrarianship/vol10/iss2/6.

8. University of North Texas. (2017). UNT Libraries Digital Preservation Policy Framework: IV purpose. www.library.unt.edu/policies/other/unt-libraries-digital-preservation-policy-framework#purpose.

9. Lean Library. (2017). https://www.leanlibrary.com/.

10. LOCKSS. (n.d.). Lots of Copies Keep Stuff Safe. https://www.lockss.org/.

11. Portico. (2018). https://www.portico.org/.

12. Waugh, Mike, Donlin, Michelle, & Braunstein, Stephanie. (2015) Next-generation collection management: A case study of quality control and weeding e-books in an academic library. *Collection Management* 40(1): 17–26. https://doi.org/10.1080/01462679.2014.965864.

13. Francis, Mary. (2012). Weeding the reference collection: A case study of collection management. *Reference Librarian 53*(2): 219–234. https://doi.org/10.1080/02763877.2011.619458.

14. ProQuest. (2018). "Dark Archive" to protect 600 terabytes of ProQuest data. https://www.proquest.com/about/news/2018/Dark-Archive-to-Protect-600-Terabytes-of-ProQuest-Data.html.

15. Machovec, George. (2018). Consortial ebook archiving environmental scan. *Journal of Library Administration 58*(1): 81–90. https://doi.org/10.1080/01930826.2017.1399706.

16. Archive-It. (2014). Welcome to Archive-It! https://archive-it.org/.

17. National Library of Medicine. (n.d.). PubMed Central (PMC). https://www.ncbi.nlm.nih.gov/pmc/.

18. Portico. (2018). Scholastica users can now deposit articles automatically into Portico. https://www.portico.org/news/scholastica-users-can-now-deposit-articles-automatically-into-portico/.

19. Verheyen, Peter D. (2016). Library preservation today! Preserving digital collections: An overview. http://downloads.alcts.ala.org/ce/03162016_Library_Preservation_Part3_Preserving_Digital_Collections_Slides.pdf.

20. University of North Texas. (2017). UNT Libraries Digital Preservation Policy Framework. www.library.unt.edu/policies/other/unt-libraries-digital-preservation-policy-framework.

21. Digital Preservation Declaration of Shared Values v2. (2018). https://docs.google.com/document/d/1cL-g_X42J4p7d8H7O9YiuDD4-KCnRUllTC2syfXSn5s/edit.

22. Carter, Sunshine. (2018). The Perpetual Access Rights "problem." https://docs.google.com/presentation/d/1ZVNm2bQRIKn6wuwmdm_guh2M1DLZIUlc8dqK7FcbkO8/edit#slide=id.p.

23. Jisc. (2018).The keepers registry. https://thekeepers.org/.

24. UKSG E-News (2019). Entitlement Registry beta. https://www.uksg.org/news letter/uksg-enews-444/entitlement-registry-beta.

25. Payne, Susan. (2017). Project feedback loops: Visualizing collection evaluation decisions. *Serials Review 43*(3–4): 251–255. https://doi.org/10.1080/00987913 .2017.1370301.

26. Sasyk, Zorian M. (2018). Invoking the digital to manage the tangible: Print serials weeding through an ERMS. *Journal of Electronic Resources Librarianship 30*(1): 49–50. https://doi.org/10.1080/1941126X.2018.1444341.

27. Lynch, Clifford A. (2003). Institutional repositories: Essential infrastructure for scholarship in the digital age. *Portal: Libraries and the Academy 3*(2): 327–336. https://doi.org/10.1353/pla.2003.0039.

28. Schopfel, Joachim, Vanacker, Sylvain, Kergosien, Eric, & Jacquemin, Bernard. (2018). Master's theses and open scholarship: A case study. *Digital Library Perspectives 34*(4): 276–287. https://doi.org/10.1108/DLP-07-2018-0021.

29. Universities U.K. Open Access Coordination Group. (2018).Open Access repositories: Report and recommendations. https://www.universitiesuk.ac.uk/ policy-and-analysis/reports/Documents/2018/open-access-repositories-report -and-recommendations.pdf.

30. British Library. (2018). EThOS. http://ethos.bl.uk/.

31. Jisc. (2018). Research data shared service: Advancing research data management through collaboration. https://www.jisc.ac.uk/rd/projects/ research-data-shared-service.

32. Cornell University. (2018). Recommended file formats. http://guides.library .cornell.edu/ecommons/formats.

33. Francke, Helena, Gamalielsson, Jonas, & Lundel, Björn. (2017). Institutional repositories as infrastructures for long-term preservation. *Information Research 22*(2). https://files.eric.ed.gov/fulltext/EJ1144764.pdf.

34. Jisc Collections. (2017). Collection management and development policy annexes: 2016–2017. https://www.jisc-collections.ac.uk/Documents/CMD%20Policy%20 annexes%20ver1.2.pdf.

35. DOAJ. (2018). Journal application form. https://doaj.org/application/new.

36. OAPEN. (2018). OAPEN services. http://oapen.org/content/oapen-services #preservation.

37. Ubiquity Press. (n.d.). Publishing with Ubiquity Press. https://www.ubiquitypress .com/site/publish/.

38. Burnhill, Peter, Pelle, Françoise, Godefroy, Pierre, Guy, Fred, Macgregor, Morag, Rees, Christine, & Rusbridge, Adam. (2009). Piloting an e-journals preservation registry service (PEPRS). *Serials 22*(1): 53–59. http://doi.org/ 10.1629/2253.

39. Digital Preservation Coalition. (2018). Persistent identifiers. https://www
.dpconline.org/handbook/technical-solutions-and-tools/persistent-identifiers.

40. DOI. (2018). https://www.doi.org/.

41. U.S. National Library of Medicine. (n.d.). Journal Publishing Tag Set. https://jats
.nlm.nih.gov/publishing/.

42. ORCID. (2018). https://orcid.org/.

43. Crossref. (2017). Funder registry. https://www.crossref.org/services/funder
-registry/.

44. ISNI, International Standard Name Identifier (ISO 27729). www.isni.org.

45. ROR, Research Organization Registry. https://www.ror.community

46. Johnson, Daniel, & Mullins, Jennifer. (2018). Filling in the gaps: Missing
preservation metadata. A report of the ALCTS PARS Preservation Metadata
Interest Group meeting. American Library Association Annual Meeting, Chicago,
June 2017. *Technical Services Quarterly 35*(3). 280–282 https://doi.org/10.1080/07
317131.2018.1456853.

47. Center for Research Libraries. (n.d.). Preservation of Electronic Government
Information (PEGI). https://www.crl.edu/preservation-electronic-government
-information-pegi.

48. Library of Congress. (n.d.). Library of Congress Recommended Formats Statement:
https://www.loc.gov/preservation/resources/rfs/TOC.html.

49. ORCID. (2018). PUBLIC Draft recommendation: Supporting ORCID in repository
systems. https://docs.google.com/document/d/14nKwsdoPWCTbuCasjCrzxxxAee
h0BxdMTsXvw62LgmU/mobilebasic.

50. Rieger, Oya Y. (2018). The state of digital preservation in 2018: A snapshot of
challenges and gaps. https://doi.org/10.18665/sr.310626.

51. LOCKSS, Lots of Copies Keep Stuff Safe. (n.d.). https://www.lockss.org/.

52. CLOCKSS. (2018). https://clockss.org/.

53. Van de Sompel, Nelson, Michael L., & Klein, Martin. (2017). To the rescue
of the orphans of scholarly communication. https://www.slideshare.net/
martinklein0815/to-the-rescue-of-the-orphans-of-scholarly-communication.

54. Educopia Institute. (2018). MetaArchive. https://metaarchive.org/.

55. Weinraub, Evviva, & Alagna, Laura. (2017). Beyond the repository: Integrating
local preservation systems with national distribution services. https://figshare
.com/articles/Beyond_the_repository_Integrating_local_preservation_systems
_with_national_distribution_services/5415136.

56. CLOCKSS. (2018). CLOCKSS announces preservation of Crossref data. https://
clockss.org/2018/06/clockss-announces-preservation-of-crossref-metadata/.

57. LOCKSS. (n.d.). Case Studies. https://www.lockss.org/join-lockss/case-studies.

58. Sprout, Bronwen, & Jordan, Mark. (2018). Distributed digital preservation: Preserving open journal systems content in the PKP PN, Digital library perspectives *34*(4): 246–261. https://doi.org/10.1108/DLP-11-2017-0043.

59. Cornell University. (n.d.). General Information About arXiv. https://arxiv.org/help/general.

60. Cornell University. (2018). arXiv Member Institutions. https://confluence.cornell.edu/pages/viewpage.action?pageId=340900096.

61. Centre for Open Science. (2018). OSF Preprints. https://osf.io/preprints/.

62. Rosenthal, David. (2018). Ithaka's Perspective on Digital Preservation. https://blog.dshr.org/2018/11/ithakas-perspective-on-digital.html?m=1.

63. Portico. (2018). https://www.portico.org/.

64. Internet Archive. (n.d.). https://archive.org/.

65. Archive-It. (2014). Welcome to Archive-It! https://archive-it.org/.

66. Portico. (2018). Libraries. https://www.portico.org/coverage/libraries/.

67. Digital Public Library of America. (n.d.). History. https://pro.dp.la/about-dpla-pro/history.

68. Digital Public Library of America Board of Directors. (2018). Letter of concern. http://dpla.wpengine.com/wp-content/uploads/2018/11/DPLA_Board_of_Directors_Community_Letter_Response.pdf.

69. Portico. (2018). OAPEN. https://www.portico.org/publishers/oapen/.

70. Portico. (2018). How can publishers join. https://www.portico.org/join/how-publishers-can-join/.

71. ITHAKA. (2013). University of Huddersfield Press preserves e-journals with Portico. https://www.ithaka.org/portico_news/2013.

72. Jisc Collections. (2017). Collection management and development policy annexes: 2016–2017. https://www.jisc-collections.ac.uk/Documents/CMD%20Policy%20annexes%20ver1.2.pdf.

73. SPARC. (2018). Big deal cancellation tracking. https://sparcopen.org/our-work/big-deal-cancellation-tracking/.

74. McGrath, Mike. (2012). Fighting back against the Big Deals: A success story from the U.K. *Interlending & Document Supply 40*(4): 178–186. https://doi.org/10.1108/02641611211283831.

75. Jisc Collections. (2016). Post Cancellation Access co-design project. https://www.jisc-collections.ac.uk/KnowledgeBasePlus/Related-Services-and-Projects/jisc-co-design-programme/Post-cancellation-access-co-design-project/.

76. Martín-Martín, Alberto, Costas, Rodrigo, van Leeuwen, Thed, & Delgado López-Cózar, Emilio. (2018). Evidence of open access of scientific publications in Google Scholar: A large-scale analysis. *Journal of Informetrics 12*(3): 819–841. https://doi.org/10.1016/j.joi.2018.06.012.

77. Researchgate. (2018). https://www.researchgate.net/.

78. Piwowar, Heather, Priem, Jason, Larivière, Vincent, Alperin, Juan Pablo, Matthias, Lisa, Norlander, Bree, Farley, Ashley, West Jevin, Haustein, Stefanie. (2018). The state of OA: A large-scale analysis of the prevalence and impact of Open Access articles. *PeerJ* 6: e4375 https://doi.org/10.7717/peerj.4375.

79. Open Access Button. (n.d.). About. https://openaccessbutton.org/about.

80. Unpaywall. (n.d.). https://unpaywall.org/products/extension.

81. Jisc/Open University. (n.d.). About Core. https://core.ac.uk/about.

82. Piwowar, Heather, Priem, Jason, Larivière, Vincent, Alperin, Juan Pablo, Matthias, Lisa, Norlander, Bree, Farley, Ashley, West, Jevin, & Haustein, Stefanie. (2018). The state of OA: A large-scale analysis of the prevalence and impact of Open Access articles. *PeerJ* 6: e4375.

83. Best, Rickey D. (2009). Is the big deal dead? *Serials Librarian* 57(4): 353. https://doi.org/10.1080/03615260903203702.

84. Schöpfel, Joachim, & Leduc, Claire. (2012). Big deal and long tail: E-journal usage and subscriptions. *Library Review* 61(7): 497–510. https://doi.org/10.1108/00242531211288245.

85. Nabe, Jonathan, & Fowler, David C. (2012). Leaving the big deal: Consequences and next steps, *Serials Librarian* 62(1–4): 59–72. https://doi.org/10.1080/0361526X.2012.652524.

86. McGrath, Mike. (2012). Fighting back against the Big Deals: A success story from the U.K., *Interlending & Document Supply* 40(4): 178–186. https://doi.org/10.1108/02641611211283831.

87. Nabe, Jonathan, & Fowler, David C. (2012). Leaving the big deal: Consequences and next steps. *Serials Librarian* 62(1–4): 59–72. https://doi.org/10.1080/0361526X.2012.652524.

88. Scott, Mitchell. (2016). Predicting use: COUNTER usage data found to be predictive of ILL use and ILL use to be predictive of COUNTER use. *Serials Librarian* 71(1): 20–24. https://doi.org/10.1080/0361526X.2016.1165783.

89. Open Access Button. (2016). New tools to put OA into Interlibrary Loan from the Open Access Button. https://blog.openaccessbutton.org/new-tools-to-put-oa-into-interlibrary-loan-from-the-open-access-button-e3b4bb9a8d95.

90. Arch, Xan, Champieux, Robin, & Emery, Jill. (2017). The easy button: Integrating OA buttons into ILL workflow. Northwest ILL resource sharing conference. https://www.google.com/url?q=https://docs.google.com/presentation/d/1Rv AWs9pLKu7B1YnrgOMAUiaa2bmfU0632h7T0qWXObs/edit%23slide%3Did. g409c9a3d97_0_0&sa=D&ust=1542669077640000&usg=AFQjCNFXSsT3PZ tLG8e0WO0E9lbY00tM5Q.

91. Rathmel, Angie, Currie, Lea, & Enoch, Todd. (2015). Big deals and squeaky wheels: Taking stock of your stats. *Serials Librarian* 68(1–4): 26–37. https://doi.org/10.108 0/0361526X.2015.1013754.

92. Pedersen, Wayne A., Arcand, Janet, & Forbis, Mark. (2014). The big deal, interlibrary loan, and building the user-centered journal collection: A case study. *Serials Review* 40 (4): 242–250. https://doi.org/10.1080/00987913.2014.975650.

93. Sjögårde, Peter. (2018). How to get access to Elsevier journals after July 1st. https://kib.ki.se/en/whatsup/blog/how-get-access-elsevier-journals-after -july-1st.

8

Conclusion

A t the start of this book, we mention how electronic resources management has changed over the five years since the last version of TERMs was published. In the conclusion to that version, we suggested topics such as e-book management were growing in importance and other forms of scholarship were developing, such as open access publishing.[1] In this version of TERMs, e-book management models are included along with streaming media and the ready incorporation of open access scholarship models. Other areas highlighted in the Library Technology Report version highlighted the emerging developments of the latest generation of library management systems and the need for workflow versioning. In addition, through our presentations and continued crowdsourcing, we received feedback on the need for us to cover issues such as troubleshooting and preservation. While researching and writing this current work a number of new considerations are emerging, specifically COUNTER Release 5, resource assessment tools, entitlement registries, and Plan S.

We live and work in a world of almost constant churn and this is certainly true for electronic resources management. Indeed, library workers involved with this content must be comfortable with change management and flexibility. There will continue to be shifting roles for library workers and new configurations of work environments due to changes in content collection and provision. Staffing roles are altering in many libraries already and this will continue to be a trend going forward.[2]

Throughout this book we highlight emerging concerns and issues in the life cycle (albeit with brief discussion). In this final chapter, we revisit those areas to examine these items a little further. Of course, these will be only some of the areas in development over the next five years, and with time, our focus on these topics may provide to be wrong-headed. There are many initiatives for electronic resources management and open access publishing that never fully come to fruition or that sputter out in a short time span.

In going back to our initial version and its conclusion, the focus on work-flows remains extremely relevant for codifying the work we all undertake on a daily basis. Having a roadmap or framework of how we accomplish this work now and understanding how to best adapt these processes to new work models and provision of content is the best practice.

The Next Major Collection Topic: Data and Other Scholarly Outputs

The pace of change is accelerating, and it can be hard to fully comprehend how the decisions being made today will affect libraries in the next five to six years. However, one new content area that is already developing is data and data management. This is largely driven by research funders and the requirement to have the data underlying major research efforts readily discoverable. This requires the use of a range of persistent identifiers. The main international nonprofit dedicated to ensuring persistent identifiers for research data is DataCite.[3] Its work is significant because:

- Researchers in their efforts to find, identify, and cite research data and other research objects
- Data centers by providing DOIs for datasets, workflows, and standards
- Journal publishers by enabling research articles to be linked to underlying data and objects
- It supports funding agencies by helping them understand the reach and impact of their funding

As this is an emerging field of work, many libraries are recruiting a single individual, team, or committee to take on the work. The importance of incorporating this work and management into the current organization structure in a meaningful way is critical. The work at hand is shown to be greater than a single person's workload. An option to consider is writing a local data management plan into the collection development plans and priorities as a way of broadening the scope of responsibility so that a single individual does not become overwhelmed by the work.

Another area of rapid development is the emergence of the COUNTER Code of Practice for Research Data in Repositories.[4] This initiative is led by DataCite, the California Digital Library, National Information Standards Organization (NISO), and Project COUNTER, among others. This project, also known as Make Data Count, provides a standard data use metric to be applied by data repositories and platform providers.[5] This project outlines a way to readily understand the use of research data and assists the work underway to develop best practices with data provision and citation.

As librarians and libraries build and populate their institutional repositories, library workers are finding ways to add far more content elements than would be provided by traditional library catalogs. These resources range from recorded interviews or presentations given at a specific institution to visualizations of products made with 3D printers as part of the scholarly process. These resources often require differing metadata and persistent identifiers as noted below in the discussion of future changes in implementation. These types of scholarly outputs are seen as part of the next wave of scholarship from the academy. Thinking about how these items are selected and incorporated into current workflows will be ongoing work.

The Next Major Procurement and Licensing Topic: Significant OA Growth

Two specific developments from late 2018 are having significant impact on the discussions around open access and higher education in the United States. The first is Plan S and the second is California Digital Library's hard stance with Elsevier/RelX in negotiations for a read and publish agreement for the University of California Libraries.[6-8] These discussions have brought open access publishing to the attention of campus administrators in ways that librarians could not before now. Librarians in higher education in North America are prepared for these discussions and able to join the conversations about how campuses can begin to engage in meaningful ways. For example, some librarians/libraries do this by presenting the OA deals and APCs using LibGuides through direct email promotion to faculty in various schools and disciplines, and with in-person meetings with key faculty and committees on campus.[9]

Pushing this information out to local faculty only works so well. A better model is to help faculty understand what is available to them at the point when content is submitted to a publishing platform. This is a proactive way for libraries to indicate the level of support available. Many commercial publishers are developing dashboard mechanisms that work in this way.[10] These services often come at additional costs to libraries. Other publication systems allow libraries easy access to the content published OA on their platform and send alerts when new content is submitted.[11] This service allows library workers to understand where investments should be made to support continued OA publishing on transparent and trusted platforms.

In the United States, there is hesitancy about broad-scale publicity regarding OA provision within the local environment. In other parts of the world, this type of advertising of services is commonplace. A recent press release from the Royal Library KB, Sweden's National Library, outlines all the ways in which it supports open scholarship models.[12] Such endeavors serve as examples of how to approach and present large-scale marketing of open services to a given community.

The Next Major Implementation Topics: Knowledge Bases and Persistent Identifiers

As we move further and further away from a world of monographs and serials, more and more content simply does not appear in the knowledge bases that generate link resolver data or bibliographic data. In some cases, such as streaming films or dissertations, it is reasonable to expect that an electronic resources knowledge base should include this content. However, the producers of knowledge bases used with library management systems tend to support only traditional scholarly outputs. The biggest knowledge base provider who has a handle on other research outputs at this point is Crossref.[13] As the official Digital Object Identifier Registration Agency of the International DOI Foundation, its registry allows for the best representations of scholarship from a myriad of viewpoints.[14] The other knowledge base to keep an eye for development is Unpaywall.[15] Although Crossref refers to its database as one containing articles, due to the nature of its DOI linking, it is uncovering data and other scholarly outputs that reference publications' DOIs. This can be seen as a benefit as well as a bane to the discovery of content. The adaptation of this data setup could be readily mirrored to focus on other scholarly outputs.

Rapid development is also occurring with the recognition and need for standardized persistent identifiers for new forms of scholarly outputs. Presently, DOIs are carrying most of the responsibility for discoverability. Description for these works then becomes defined by their relation to other scholarly works such as articles and book chapters. Although DOIs are extremely useful in discovering resources, there is still quite a bit of work to be done to develop the descriptive metadata for other scholarly outputs. DataCite's work on the development of descriptive metadata schema for data may be a model to use with the development of enhanced descriptive metadata for other scholarly outputs. Work on further and refined persistent identifiers will continue to grow and impact libraries. Library workers should ensure that the systems they employ for management of all resources are agile and open enough to incorporate these changes as they take place. Developing toolkits to outline useful persistent identifiers is a good way to help your research community fund ways to increase the impact of their research outputs.[16]

The Next Major Troubleshooting Topic: Web Browser Plug-ins

Almost all troubleshooting mechanisms currently available for use in libraries exist within a library's website or library management systems. Although these tools are vital, they do not meet end users where end users usually begin their research process: the open World Wide Web. One idea that came up in discussions with library workers is to have a browser extension or plug-in specifically designed for troubleshooting problems with access to content. The development of troubleshooting browser plug-ins are worthwhile explorations for library workers. However, after a review of the current literature on troubleshooting electronic resources, this concept does not appear to be under investigation by anyone. It will be interesting to see if this idea is pursued beyond discussions at library conferences.

The Next Major Assessment Topics: COUNTER Release 5 and Book Data Enhancements

When we began writing this book, COUNTER Release 5 had just been issued as the latest COUNTER Code of Practice.[17] As publishers and providers began implementing the new code, they found numerous issues and concerns that the administrative bodies of Project COUNTER had to address. This led to some fairly substantial revision of the latest of Code of Practice.[18] The new release will allow library workers and content providers to use the data in more extensive ways than in the past. However, it isn't possible to model the potential use cases until the standard is in place. While writing this book, we tried to leave chapter 6's discussion about assessment open enough to cover these changes. In anticipation of potential confusion and concern about the version, COUNTER has published a series of YouTube videos entitled Counter Foundation Classes.[19] One thing that is certain is that the new COUNTER Release 5 will make it easier to assess the usage of hybrid and pure OA titles and COUNTER intends to develop another possible statistical point, "Other_free_to_read," which would help to capture bronze OA material as well. However, this metric will not be issued concurrently with the Release 5 implementations in 2019.

Knowledge Unlatched and Springer/Nature both held webinars in 2018 on expanded e-book metrics that provide usage representation beyond COUNTER download statistics for sections and whole e-books. Because these initiatives are still in the very early stages of development, the webinars may prove useful, but once again, until in use it is hard to fully comment on the potential impacts of this work.[20,21]

The Next Major Preservation Topic: Preservation of Non-Traditional Scholarly Outputs

The Scholarly Orphans Project, a recent initiative funded by the Mellon Foundation is exploring the feasibility of capturing and preserving scholarly works outside of traditional formats.[22] The project explores ways to discover, capture, and archive the scholarly artifacts that researchers deposit in portals across the web. It begins with an institutional perspective and uses web archiving techniques to capture the content to be preserved. Most of the content resides on platforms that record scholarship but are not intended for long-term preservation of scholarly outputs such as GitHub. The intent is to use a distributed network approach such as LOCKSS to capture this output and provide a longer-term preservation strategy for the content. The project leaders find that depending on the harvesting mechanisms used, the level of content preserved varies greatly. At the end of the study, they hope to provide recommendations of the best harvesting mechanisms and the best preservation platform to utilize. At the time of writing, this initiative is funded with grants that will be ending in the near future; it will be interesting to see what the next steps may be in order for this work to continue as well as where the funding to keep it viable will come from.

Open Access as a Real Alternative?

This version of TERMs introduces open access into the mix. We suggest that open access should stand alongside traditional subscription-based models and although the administration of OA is often carried out by a different library team, the e-resources manager needs to understand both sides. This is particularly true for hybrid open access titles and big deals, where offsetting and read and publish agreements require an understanding of both subscriptions and open access worlds.

But what about pure gold titles? Where do these fit in the cycle? One argument is that in a world where there are no subscriptions, negotiation will no longer be required. However, although hybrid APC costs are 25 percent higher than pure gold titles, gold is increasing at a faster rate.[23] Therefore, we suggest that negotiations must move from issues of limiting or negating the above inflationary increases of subscription journal, to negotiations about capping the increase in APC costs. This concern must also be included in collection, management, and development policies in the near future.

Crawford differentiates between "APCLand" and "OAWorld": "APCLand accounts for 14 percent of the fully-analyzed DOAJ journals with articles in 2015 and 29 percent of the 2015 articles in those journals. It also accounts for 74 percent of the maximum potential APC revenues."[24] According to Crawford, only eleven publishers account for this revenue, whereas thousands of publishers in OAWorld account "for 86 percent of the active journals and 71 percent of the articles, but only 26 percent of the revenues." Indeed, 81 percent of these do not charge APCs.

This leads to another potential development. Is it sufficient to automatically switch on resources such as the Directories of Open Access Journals and Books, or does the content need to be assessed like other e-resources in the collection, management, and development policy?[25,26] It would certainly be easy to treat them like full-text databases, where content is not assessed at the individual title level. However, one risk is that the discovery system will be flooded with English-language abstracts that lead to non-English articles. This could prove frustrating for users.

Nobody can predict if and when a full transition to open access will occur. However, it is likely that more libraries will look to OA in order to exit their big deals and will therefore need resources that help to locate alternatives. This is a very fast-paced environment, with new projects being announced frequently from initiatives such as OA Button and Unpaywall.[27,28] For example, in November 2018, OA Button announced Direct2AAM,

> "a set of guides to turn the often unsuccessful hunt for author accepted manuscripts (AAM) into a simple set of instructions that'll always bring results. The guides, available for most major journals, provide easy to follow instructions for authors to obtain an Author Accepted Manuscript from their journal submission system, where the AAM is stored during the publishing process."[29]

Another expanding area is the library as publisher and academic-led publishing. Since 2017, a number of reports and papers have been published including landscape studies, and studies on metadata and visibility and the supply chain.[30-35] Indeed, an entire issue of *Learned Publishing* was devoted to the 2018 University Press Redux conference.[36]

Further output is expected from the United Kingdom, in support of the four U.K. HE funding bodies intent to mandate OA for monographs submitted to the Research Excellence Framework beyond the 2021 assessment and U.K.

Research and Innovation (UKRI), a signatory of Plan S, has launched its own open access policy review, which will include monographs and book chapters, and other European countries in relation to the monograph element of Plan S.[37] Various Mellon funded initiatives are also underway in the United States.[38]

Another OA initiative gaining traction involves OA textbooks, or open educational resources (OERs). This is an area we mention a few times in this book but we do not delve deeply into the topic. The focus has been on the development and promotion of benefits for utilizing OA textbooks up to this point and the future focus will be on the concerns about management and ongoing support.[39] A recent study performed by the University of Georgia indicates that impacts on student learning are positive when faculty use OERs as course material.[40] This is another area where OA content will grow and be incorporated into library collections.

The announcement of Plan S in September 2018 is a potential game changer for the way e-resources (both journals and, at a later stage, monographs) are dealt with.[41] The Wellcome Trust in the United Kingdom became the first funder to publish a Plan S compliant policy and this was followed in 2019 by a set of revised guidelines for Plan S compliance.[42,43]

- Open Access publishing venues (journals or platforms): Authors publish in an Open Access journal or on an Open Access platform

- Subscription venues (repository route): Authors publish in a subscription journal and make either the final published version (Version of Record (VoR)) or the Author's Accepted Manuscript (AAM) openly available in a repository

- Transition of subscription venues (transformative arrangements): Authors publish Open Access in a subscription journal under a transformative arrangement.[44]

Johnson has published a helpful commentary of the discussion that took place during the two months between the announcement and the issue of the draft guidelines.[45] There is still a long way to go, and it will be interesting to see which funders outside of Europe sign up to cOAlition S and how they interpret the guidelines and the actual compliance itself. An early indication from the 14th Berlin Open Access Conference held in December 2018, at which research-funding and research-performing organizations from thirty-seven countries were represented, gives significant influence:

- We are all committed to authors retaining their copyrights.

- We are all committed to complete and immediate open access.

- We are all committed to accelerating the progress of open access through transformative agreements that are temporary and transitional, with a shift to full open access within a very few years. These agreements should, at least initially, be cost-neutral, with the expectation that economic adjustments will follow as the markets transform.

- Publishers are expected to work with all members of the global research community to effect complete and immediate open access according to this statement.

An infographic has also been produced that interprets the guidance.[46]

There have been questions about the effect of what is essentially a European plan on transformations to open access worldwide.[47] However, it looks like China, although not yet signed up to cOAlition S, is sending a strong signal to publishers. China's National Science Library, its National Science and Technology Library, and the Natural Science Foundation of China have expressed support for Plan S.[48]

Plan S is looking likely to dominate discussion around open access for some years to come.[49]

Given everything we have seen occur while writing this book over the past two years, we can foresee a future where we will need to update our work again. This iteration of TERMs begins to explore the ways we are currently incorporating OA material into our collections and workflow. Five to ten years from now, the work to be written will be on how to manage legacy subscription content within an OA scholarly universe.

NOTES

1. Emery, Jill, & Stone, Graham. (2013). Looking forward. *Library Technology Reports 2* (February): 39–43. https://journals.ala.org/index.php/ltr/article/view/4731/5633.

2. Audio/PowerPoint presentation from The ALCTS Technical Services Directors of Large Research Libraries Interest Group (aka Tech Services Big Heads) held at its Midwinter 2018 meeting on Thursday, January 25, 2018, at 11:00-12:30 PST/1:00–2:30 CST/2–3:30 EST. http://downloads.alcts.ala.org/ALCTS_Big_Heads_Meeting_20180125.mp4.

3. DataCite. (n.d.). Our mission. https://www.datacite.org/mission.html.

4. GitHub Make-Data-Count. (n.d.).Implementing the COUNTER Code of Practice for research data in repositories: Getting started. https://github.com/CDLUC3/Make-Data-Count/blob/master/getting-started.md.

5. Fenner, Martin, Lowenberg, Daniella, Jones, Matt, Needham, Paul, Vieglais, Dave, Abrams, Stephen, Cruse, Patricia, & Chodacki, John. (2018). Code of practice for research data usage metrics release 1, *PeerJ Preprints 6*: e26505v1 https://doi.org/10.7287/peerj.preprints.26505v1.

6. Smith, MacKenzie, & Ventry, Jr., Dennis J. (2018). Potential changes to UC's relationship with Elsevier in January 2019. https://www.library.ucdavis.edu/news/potential-changes-to-ucs-relationship-with-elsevier-in-january-2019/.

7. European Commission. (2018). "Plan S" and "cOAlition S'—Accelerating the transition to full and immediate Open Access to scientific publications. https://ec.europa.eu/commission/commissioners/2014-2019/moedas/announcements/plan-s-and-coalition-s-accelerating-transition-full-and-immediate-open-access-scientific_en.

8. University of California. (2019). UC terminates subscriptions with world's largest scientific publisher in push for open access to publicly funded research. https://www.universityofcalifornia.edu/press-room/uc-terminates-subscriptions-worlds-largest-scientific-publisher-push-open-access-publicly.

9. Oregon State University. (2018). Open access at USU. https://guides.library.oregonstate.edu/c.php?g=285945&p=5909778.

10. Taylor and Francis. (2018). Research dashboard. https://librarianresources.taylorandfrancis.com/product-info/open-access/research-dashboard-membership/.

11. MDPI, Institutional Open Access Program (IOAP). (n.d.). https://www.mdpi.com/about/ioap.

12. Kungliga biblioteket. (2018). Fem utredningar om öppen tillgång: Välkommen med synpunkter! https://amp.mynewsdesk.com/se/kungliga_biblioteket/pressreleases/fem-utredningar-om-oeppen-tillgaang-vaelkommen-med-synpunkter-2755119?_twitter_impression=true.

13. Crossref. (n.d.). https://www.crossref.org/.

14. Crossref. (n.d.). Dashboard. https://www.crossref.org/dashboard/.

15. Unpaywall. (n.d.). https://unpaywall.org/.

16. Jisc. (2018). Research Data Management toolkit. https://rdmtoolkit.jisc.ac.uk/share-and-publish/identifiers/.

17. COUNTER. (2018). The COUNTER Code of Practice for Release 5. https://www.projectcounter.org/code-of-practice-five-sections/abstract/.

18. COUNTER. (2018). Amendments and clarifications to the Code of Practice Release 5. https://www.projectcounter.org/amendments-clarifications-code-practice-release-5/.

19. COUNTER. (2019). YouTube videos. https://www.youtube.com/channel/UCptZRuV5XbtP-jWkTckDpIA.

20. Knowledge Unlatched. (2018). KU Webinar DeltaThink OAPEN Latest Thinking. https://www.youtube.com/watch?v=PuS8XMva6E4#action=share.

21. Springer Nature. (2018). Bookmetrix 2.0. https://www.springernature.com/gp/librarians/news-events/webinars/new-content-item/15545396.

22. Van de Sompel, Nelson, Michael L., & Klein, Martin. (2017). To the rescue of the orphans of scholarly communication. https://www.slideshare.net/martinklein0815/to-the-rescue-of-the-orphans-of-scholarly-communication.

23. Jubb, Michael, et al. (2017). *Monitoring the transition to open access: December 2017.* (London: Universities UK). www.universitiesuk.ac.uk/policy-and-analysis/reports/ Documents/2017/monitoring-transition-open-access-2017.pdf.

24. Crawford, Walt. (2016). *Gold open access journals: 2011–2015* (Livermore, CA: Cites and Insights Books). https://waltcrawford.name/goaj1115.pdf.

25. DOAJ. (2018). About DOAJ (Directory of Open Access Journals). https://doaj.org/ about.

26. DOAB. (n.d.). Directory of Open Access Books. https://www.doabooks.org/.

27. Open Access Button. (n.d.). About. https://openaccessbutton.org/about.

28. Unpaywall. https://unpaywall.org/products/extension.

29. OA Button. (2018). Announcing Direct2AAM: helping authors find Author Accepted Manuscripts. https://blog.openaccessbutton.org/announcing -direct2aam-helping-authors-find-author-accepted-manuscripts-f71462a68d1a.

30. Adema, Janeka, & Stone, Graham. (2017). *Changing publishing ecologies: A landscape study of new university presses and academic-led publishing* (Bristol: Jisc). http:// repository.jisc.ac.uk/6666/.

31. Ferwerda, Eelco, Pinter, Frances, & Stern, Niels. (2017). *A landscape study on open access and monographs* (Bristol: Knowledge Exchange). http://repository.jisc .ac.uk/6693/.

32. Stone, Graham, & Marques, Marques. (2018). *Knowledge Exchange survey on open access monographs* (Bristol: Knowledge Exchange). http://repository.jisc.ac .uk/7101/.

33. Neylon, Cameron, Montgomery, Lucy, Ozaygen, Alkim, Saunders, Neil, & Pinter, Frances. 2018. *The visibility of open access monographs in a European context.* (Zenodo). http://doi.org/10.5281/zenodo.1230342.

34. Watkinson, Charles, Welzenbach, Rebecca, Hellman, Eric, Gatti, Rupert, Sonnenberg, Kristyn. (2017). *Mapping the free ebook supply chain: Final report to the Andrew W. Mellon Foundation* (Ann Arbor, MI: University of Michigan). http:// hdl.handle.net/2027.42/137638.

35. Stone, Graham. (2018). OA monographs discovery in the library supply chain: Draft report and recommendations. https://scholarlycommunications.jiscinvolve .org/wp/2018/10/25/oa-monographs-discovery-in-the-library-supply-chain -draft-report-and-recommendations/.

36. Cord, Anthony, & Speicher, Laura. The university press redux II. *Learned Publishing 31* (September): 278–279. https://onlinelibrary.wiley.com/toc/17414 857/2018/31/S1.

37. Snaith, Helen. (2018). Open access and monographs. https://re.ukri.org/blog/ helen-snaith/open-access-and-monographs/.

38. Watkinson, Charles. (2018). The academic eBook ecosystem reinvigorated: A perspective from the USA. *Learned Publishing 31* (September): 280–287. https:// re.ukri.org/blog/helen-snaith/open-access-and-monographs/.

39. Bell, Steven. (2018). "Course Materials Adoption: A Faculty Survey and Outlook for the OER Landscape." ACRL/Choice, publisher. http://choice360.org/librarianship/whitepaper.

40. McKenzie, Lindsay. (2018). Free digital textbooks vs. purchased commercial textbooks. *Inside Higher Ed*. (July 16). https://www.insidehighered.com/digital-learning/article/2018/07/16/measuring-impact-oer-university-georgia#.XBcvhL_QhnE.link.

41. European Commission. (2018). "Plan S" and "cOAlition S"—Accelerating the transition to full and immediate Open Access to scientific publications. https://ec.europa.eu/commission/commissioners/2014-2019/moedas/announcements/plan-s-and-coalition-s-accelerating-transition-full-and-immediate-open-access-scientific_en.

43. Wellcome Trust. (2018). Open access policy 2020. https://wellcome.ac.uk/sites/default/files/wellcome-open-access-policy-2020.pdf.

43. Science Europe. (2018). cOAlition S. https://www.scienceeurope.org/coalition-s/.

44. Science Europe. (2019). Principles and implementation: https://www.coalition-s.org/principles-and-implementation/.

45. Johnson, Rob. (2018). From coalition to commons: Plan S and the future of scholarly communication. Zenodo. http://doi.org/10.5281/zenodo.1478531.

46. Max Planck Digital Library. (2018). 14th Berlin open access conference: Aligning strategies to enable open access. https://oa2020.org/b14-conference/.

47. LIBER. (n.d.). https://libereurope.eu/blog/2018/12/06/liber-statement-plan-s-guidelines/.

48. Schiermeier, Quirin. (2018). China backs bold plan to tear down journal paywalls, *Nature 564:* 171–72. https://doi.org/10.1038/d41586-018-07659-5.

49. S. Bordignon, Frédérique, Noel, Marianne, & Cabanac, Guillaume. (2018). Les mots/maux du Plan https://jnso2018.sciencesconf.org/data/pages/Les_motsmaux_du_Plan_S.pdf.

Glossary

In the first iteration of TERMs, we did not provide a glossary of concepts or terms because we expected most of the people reading the work would already be involved in the management of electronic resources. This time around, we find that a glossary is helpful for those not familiar with some of the more esoteric acronyms and terms.

ACQNet   A discussion list run by the Acquisitions section of ALA that provides information on acquisitions questions and problems and support of acquisitions practices.

ALCTS   The Acquisitions Library Collections and Technical Services division of ALA is made up of the acquisitions section, cataloging and metadata management section, collection management section, continuing and ongoing resources section, and the preservation and reformatting section.

Altmetrics   Ways to account for impact of scholarly content outside of historic practices.

APCs   Article Processing Charges are the amount a publisher charges for the publication of a single article in its journal as open access content. They can be used for both fully open access content journals such as PLoS ONE (Public Library of Science) and hybrid journals that are also part of a subscription package or individual subscription.

BOAI   The Budapest Open Access Initiative, the initial event that helped to define open access to scholarly content as free and unrestricted online availability of content.

Bronze Open Access   Free to read at a publisher's website, which may include open access material without the appropriate licenses or other free content of a temporal nature

CC The Creative Commons licensing scheme used for most open access content. Can be applied to presentations, images, and figures, as well as articles, journals, and books.

CDL The California Digital Library is the consortium of the University of California Libraries, which provides many best practices and models for electronic resource management.

cOAlition S An international consortium of research funders supporting Plan S.

COAR The Confederation of Open Access Repositories, an international association of libraries, universities, research institutions, government funders, and others who are working to develop repository networks in order build capacity, align policies and practices, and act as a global voice.

Cost avoidance A term used when calculating the savings on potential APC charges as part of an offsetting or read and publish agreement. Without the agreement, these costs may not have been saved, rather they were avoided.

COUNTER COUNTER is the nonprofit organization that develops the practice and standards for online usage information so that the reporting of usage information can occur in a consistent way.

Courseware The systems used by instructional designers to provide a structured framework for courses in higher education. Can be used as a braid concept for learning management systems (LMS) and virtual learning environments (VLEs).

CrossRef The organization that makes research outputs easy to find, cite, link, and assess.

DDA/PDA Demand driven acquisitions or patron driven acquisitions is a practice of purchasing (usually with ebooks or streaming media) where an organization commits to a ballpark amount of money which includes short-term access costs and loads a large selection of records into their local discovery or library management system and given the "triggering by patrons clicking on access" or usage of titles, the most used titles are to be retained either on the annual schedule set by the provider or permanently if possible.

DOI The Digital Object Identifier is the recognized standard for metadata control with articles, datasets, figures, slides, and other forms of scholarship.

DRM Digital right management are controls put in place by publishers to limit access to content (user limits of e-books for example).

EBA/EBP Evidence-based acquisitions or evidence-based purchasing is the practice when an organization commits to a specific spend amount and loads a selection of records into its local discovery or library management system and given the usage of titles, then selects titles to be retained permanently either by the amount of use or by a given year of content.

Eigenfactor A research project from the University of Washington intended to provide a more meaningful measure for evaluating the impact of scholarly periodicals, mapping the structure of academic research, and for helping researchers navigate the scholarly literature.

Embargo The time period during which scholarly content must be kept in a closed access system or behind a paywall before being made more readily available.

End User A person who wishes to access and use scholarly content.

Entitlements The titles licensed for access along with years of access provided from any given provider.

ERiL Electronic Resources in Libraries is a discussion list that provides information on electronic resources questions, problems, and support for electronic resource practices.

ESAC Efficiency and Standards for Article Charges is an initiative to keep up the discussion about open access workflows and administrative burdens related to the management of open access article processing charges (APCs).

ESPReSSO Establishing Suggested Practices Regarding Single Sign-On is a NISO an initiative published in 2011 that helps outline best practices for this authentication method in the information chain.

EThOS The Electronic Theses Online Service provides access to most doctoral dissertations and theses published in the United Kingdom.

EZProxy The most-used proxy service for providing remote access to commercial electronic content.

Gold Open Access Scholarly content that is made open access and viewable in the same way as it would be if behind a publication paywall.

Green Open Access A pre-print (prior to peer review) or post-print (after peer review) version of scholarly content that lacks the formatting and final typesetting on the final published version.

Hosting Platform Society publishers, academic content providers, scholarly publishers, and independent publishers use hosting platforms for their content. These can be open-source platforms or commercial platforms. Be Press' digital commons is a content hosting platform. Other well-known hosting platforms include Atypon, Folio, Highwire, Ingenta, Janeway, JSTOR, Open Journal systems, OSF Preprints, Project Euclid, Samvera, SciELO, Sheridan PubFactory, Silverchair, and Ubiquity Press.

Hybrid Journals Subscription journals that are mostly published by commercial scholarly publishers that also allow authors to pay to have their individual articles available open access.

IP Ranges Internet protocol ranges that allow access to electronic resources without entering individual usernames and passwords.

IR Institutional repositories are usually platforms outside of library management systems and discovery tools that provide access to local scholarship and scholarly content. There are also subject-oriented repositories managed by both nonprofit and commercial scholarly entities.

ISBN The International Standard Book Number is a standard used for providing metadata control to books and monographs.

ISNI The International Standard Name Identifier is a standard used for providing metadata about a given institution.

ISO The International Standards Organization develops metadata for information management internationally.

ISSN The International Standard Serial Number is a standard used for providing metadata control to periodicals.

JATS The Journal Article Tag Suite is a group of XML coded data that enhances the description of resources in institutional repositories.

Jisc The digital solutions provider for education and research in the United Kingdom.

JUSP The Jisc Usage Statistics Portal offers a single point of access to journal, e-book, and database usage statistics.

KB Knowledge bases are extensive databases maintained by a given developer that contains information about electronic resources such as title lists, coverage dates, inbound linking syntax, etc.

KBART Knowledge Bases and Related Tools (NISO RP-9-2014) is a NISO recommended practice for the communication of electronic resource title list and coverage data from content providers to knowledge base (KB) developers.

LibLicense A discussion list that provides information on licensing questions, problems, and support for licensing practices.

Licenses/Licensing The contracts signed by libraries to provide access to content online.

Link Resolvers The mechanisms by which end users are associated with the online content they have permission to access.

LIS-E-Resources A discussion list hosted in the United Kingdom to provide information on electronic resources best practices, problems, and questions.

LMS Learning management systems are usually provided by third party producers such as Blackboard, Canvas, Desire2Learn (D2L), Google Sites, Moodle, Sakai, etc.

LOCKSS/CLOCKSS A user-based membership program that is an open source, library-led distributed digital preservation system built on the principle that "lots of copies keep stuff safe." CLOCKSS is a community governed and supported digital preservation archive for scholarly content.

NASIG A professional organization in the United States whose work and conferences explore many issues and concerns with electronic resource management and scholarly communication.

NISO The National Information Standards Organization helps to develop best practices for management of electronic resources and standards for information resource management.

Non-Linear Lending purchasing mechanism used with ebooks primarily from ProQuest that allows for a set limited usage in a given year—325 downloads as opposed to unlimited usage/access.

OA2020 An initiative launched by the Max Planck Digital Library to transition from the payment of subscriptions into support for open access scholarly content.

Offsetting A practice that uses big deal subscription spending by consortia and large libraries to support open access publishing at their institutions. Credits or discounts on APCs are given related to the subscription spending in place.

OpenAIRE A European initiative to shift scholarly communication towards openness and transparency and facilitate innovative ways to communicate and monitor research.

OpenAthens A single sign-on gateway that provides ready access to commercial scholarly content.

OpenDOAR Hosted by Jisc, it is a global directory of open access repositories and their policies.

OpenURL A standard description format used to link content to end users within most libraries.

ORCID A nonprofit initiative to help disambiguate between scholars and associate them with the proper institution through a recognized scholar identification standard.

PDF/A A specialized version of the PDF format, modified specifically for archival and long-term preservation needs. PDF/A implements certain rules and elements for creating PDFs to create documents that are more likely to survive well into the future. Version PDF/A-4 (also to be known as "PDF/A-NEXT") is based on PDF 2.0 and is expected to be published in 2019.

Persistent Identifier (PID) A long-lasting reference to a digital resource.

PIE-J The NISO best practice for the presentation and identification of e-journals.

Plan S An international initiative, which requires that, from 2021, scientific publications that result from research funded by public grants must be published in compliant Open Access journals or platforms.

Portico A subscription preservation approach by the nonprofit ITHAKA for ejournals, e-books, and digital collections.

Pre-Print Servers Subject repositories that provide open access to scholarly content that may or may not be fully published.

Proxy IP The dedicated IP range(s) used for remote proxying of end users to resources.

Read and Publish An approach to open access publishing in which an institution pays a set annual fee to cover all APCs for articles by contributing authors from that institution in all of the specific publisher's open access journals.

RA21 Rights Access for 2021 is a NISO-led initiative to build an authentication method to provide a more secure single sign-on option for access to commercially produced scholarly content.

RLMS Reading List Management Systems can be third party systems or home development management systems for reading lists.

SCONUL The Society of College, National and University Libraries (SCONUL) represents all university libraries in the United Kingdom and Ireland, irrespective of mission, as well as national libraries and many of the United Kingdom's colleges of higher education.

SERU The Shared Electronic Resource Understanding is a NISO best practice outlining an alternative to a commercial contract for access to electronic resources.

Transfer The Transfer Code of Practice is the best practice hosted and managed by NISO indicating how content that moves from one publisher to another or from one platform to another should be communicated to the library community at large.

UKSG A professional organization in the United Kingdom that is dedicated to connecting the knowledge community through publications and events. It supports discussion of the issues facing UKSG members.

UKSG E-News An online newsletter that provides up-to-the-minute news of current issues and developments within the global knowledge community.

UN/P Shorthand for username password, the standard access method in the online environment.

USUS A community website on usage data collection and best practices.

VLE Virtual learning environments are usually provided by third party producers such as Blackboard, Canvas, Desire2Learn (D2L), Google Sites, Moodle, Sakai, etc.

VPN Virtual private networks are frameworks to provide authentication on the open world-wide web in a way that remains private and more secure.

About the Authors

JILL EMERY is the collection development librarian at Portland State University Library and has over twenty years of academic library experience. She has held leadership positions in ALA ALCTS, ER&L, and NASIG. In 2015, she was appointed as the ALA-NISO representative to vote on NISO/ISO standards on behalf of ALA. She also serves on the Project COUNTER Executive Committee. Jill serves as a member of *The Charleston Advisor* editorial board and is the columnist of "Heard on the Net," and is on the editorial board for *Insights: the UKSG Journal*. In 2016, she became a co-editor of the open access journal *Collaborative Librarianship*.

GRAHAM STONE is senior research manager at Jisc in the U.K. He manages a cross team research unit, which monitors and evaluates national consortial agreements as part of the transition to OA in line with funder policy and cOAlition S guidelines. He also supports new forms of OA publishing, such as library- and academic-led publishing. Previously, he has over twenty-three years of library experience where he managed library resources budgets, OA services and a New University Press. He is a Chartered Librarian (MCLIP) and a Fellow of the Higher Education Academy (FHEA). In 2017, he was awarded his professional doctorate for research on New University Press publishing.

PETER MCCRACKEN is electronic resources librarian at Cornell University. His previous work has included roles as a reference librarian at the University of Washington; a co-founder of Serials Solutions, which helps libraries manage electronic resources; and a co-founder of ShipIndex.org, an electronic resource offered to libraries. Together, these experiences in public services, technical services, and multiple sides of electronic resources management, have informed his views of how libraries and vendors can best offer and manage electronic resources.

Index